ABOUT THE FOURTH EDITION

This 2016 edition of *Freedom in the 50 States* presents a completely revised and updated ranking of the American states based on how their policies promote freedom in the fiscal, regulatory, and personal realms.

This edition again improves upon the methodology for weighting and combining state and local policies to create a comprehensive index. Authors William Ruger and Jason Sorens introduce many new policy variables suggested by readers. More than 230 policy variables and their sources are now available to the public on a new website for the study. Scholars, policymakers, and concerned citizens can assign new weights to every policy and create customized indices of freedom, or download the data for their own analyses.

In the 2016 edition, the authors have updated their findings to

- Improve estimates of the "freedom value" of each policy (the estimated dollar value of each freedom affected to those who enjoy it);
- Provide the most up-to-date freedom index yet, including scores as of December 31, 2014;
- Include citizen choice among local governments as an important factor modifying the freedom value of more locally based taxation;
- Significantly expand policies affecting business and personal freedom, including new variables for occupational licensing, tort liability climate, land-use regulation, entry and price regulation, alcohol laws, and civil asset forfeiture;
- Analyze how the policies driving income growth and interstate migration have changed pre– and post–Great Recession.

In addition to providing the latest rankings for year-end 2014, the 2016 edition provides biennial data on economic and personal freedom and their components back to 2006, plus scores for 2000 for long-range comparisons.

Now published by the Cato Institute and accompanied by demographic and economic data on each state, *Freedom in the 50 States* is an essential desk reference for anyone interested in state policy and in advancing a better understanding of a free society.

www.freedominthe50states.org

2016 EDITION

FREEDOM IN THE 50 STATES

AN INDEX OF PERSONAL AND
ECONOMIC FREEDOM

FOURTH EDITION

WILLIAM P. RUGER AND
JASON SORENS

To Jennifer and Mary—
our respective partners in life, mothers of our children, and two
who sacrificed countless nights and weekends for this 4th edition.

Cover illustration by Joanna Andreasson.

Cato Institute
1000 Massachusetts Avenue, N.W.
Washington, D.C. 20001
www.cato.org

Library of Congress Cataloging-in-Publication Data

Names: Ruger, William, author. | Sorens, Jason, 1976- author.
Title: Freedom in the 50 states : an index of personal and economic freedom /
    William P. Ruger and Jason Sorens.
Other titles: Freedom in the fifty states
Description: Fourth edition. | Washington, D.C. : Cato Institute, 2017. |
    Includes bibliographical references.
Identifiers: LCCN 2016029768 (print) | LCCN 2016033050 (ebook) | ISBN
    9781944424336 (print) | ISBN 9781944424343 (ebook)
Subjects: LCSH: Liberty. | State governments--United States. | Fiscal
    policy--United States--States. | Liberty--Indexes. | State
    governments--United States--Indexes. | Fiscal policy--United
    States--States--Indexes.
Classification: LCC JC599.U5 R77 2017 (print) | LCC JC599.U5 (ebook) | DDC
    323.0973--dc23
LC record available at https://lccn.loc.gov/2016029768

First printing: 2016
Printed in the United States of America.

CONTENTS

Introduction   1

Part 1: Dimensions of Freedom   12

     Fiscal Policy   15

     Overall Fiscal Policy Ranking   31

     Regulatory Policy   35

     Overall Regulatory Policy Ranking   56

     Overall Economic Freedom Ranking   58

     Personal Freedom   61

     Overall Personal Freedom Ranking   92

Part 2: Politics of Freedom   110

Part 3: Freedom State by State   150

Appendix A: Dimension, Category, and Variable Weights   256

Appendix B: Alternative Indices   262

Further Reading   282

Acknowledgments   285

About the Authors   287

Where liberty dwells, there is my country.

—Benjamin Franklin

INTRODUCTION

This study ranks the American states according to how their public policies affect individual freedoms in the economic, social, and personal spheres. Updating, expanding, and improving on the three previous editions of *Freedom in the 50 States*, the 2015–16 edition examines state and local government intervention across a wide range of policy categories—from taxation to debt, from eminent domain laws to occupational licensing, and from drug policy to educational choice.

For this new edition, we have added many more policy variables; improved the way we measure fiscal decentralization, civil liability systems, and civil asset forfeiture; and improved the innovative, objective system for weighting individual variables introduced in the last edition. We also provide a much more recent snapshot of state freedom, using provisional state fiscal data to create an index of freedom as of the end of 2014. Our time series now covers six years over the period 2000–2014. Finally, we now investigate the causes and consequences of freedom in much greater detail and with more sophisticated methods.

We began this project to fill a need: *Freedom in the 50 States* was the first index to measure both economic and personal freedom and remains the only index to do so at the state level. We also strive to make it the most comprehensive and definitive source for economic freedom data on the American states.

Measuring freedom is important because freedom is valuable to people. At the very least, it is valuable to those whose choices are restricted by public policy. Although the United States has made great strides toward respecting each individual's rights regardless of race, gender, age, or sexual orientation, some individuals face growing threats to their interests in some jurisdictions. They include smokers, builders and buyers of affordable housing, professionals wanting to ply a trade without paying onerous examination and education costs, and so on.

In the American system, even "benefit to others" cannot justify trampling on certain freedoms. Books may not be banned simply because the ideas and arguments they present offend some readers. Racial segregation would be unjustified even in the unlikely event it were somehow considered efficient. Likewise, state and local governments ought to respect basic rights and liberties, such as the right to practice an honest trade or the right to make lifetime partnership contracts, whether or not respecting these rights "maximizes utility." This index measures the extent to which states respect or disrespect these basic rights and liberties.

Although states that excel in one area of freedom—fiscal policy, regulatory policy, or personal freedom—do not always score well in the other areas of freedom, we recognize important relationships among all these dimensions of freedom. In his 1962 book *Capitalism and Freedom*, Milton Friedman explores the connection between economic and political freedoms, finding that political freedom in the absence of economic freedom is unlikely to last. He writes, "It is a mark of the political freedom of a capitalist society that men can openly advocate and work for socialism."[1] Likewise, at the state level, Americans cannot expect personal freedom to endure without high levels of economic freedom. Although some states currently score well in one dimension of freedom and lag in others, Friedman's work suggests that all three types of freedoms discussed in this index support one another.

Several different audiences will find the information and analysis contained in this book useful:

- State legislators and governors, their staffs, and local policymakers interested in liberty can use the data and rankings to see where their states stand relative to other states and to determine where real improvements can be made. Although policymakers are better situated than we are to make precise judgments about the benefits of specific legislation, this book does offer reform ideas tailored for each state. These ideas are contained in the state profiles located at the end of the study.

- Scholars can use the index to model politics and policy outcomes in areas such as economic growth and migration. These data are also a valuable resource for teachers and students, providing easy

1. Milton Friedman, "The Relation Between Economic Freedom and Political Freedom," chapter 1 in *Capitalism and Freedom* (Chicago: University of Chicago Press, 1962), p. 16.

access to information that can be used for policy analysis or statistical projects. [2]

- Businesses considering new investment opportunities or relocation can use the data to analyze state tax and regulatory regimes and the relative openness and toleration that attract highly productive employees.

- Reporters can use the data to understand their states' policy debates in a national context. They could also use them to hold elected officials accountable for infringements on freedoms and state performance.

- Individual citizens can use the data to better understand what their state governments are doing and thus be better-informed participants in the democratic process. The data are also useful to those seeking to move to a freer state.

This book scores all 50 states on their overall respect for individual freedom, and also on their respect for three dimensions of freedom considered separately: fiscal policy, regulatory policy, and personal freedom. To calculate these scores, we weight public policies according to the estimated costs that individuals suffer when government restricts their freedoms. However, we happily concede that different people value aspects of freedom differently. Hence, our website provides the raw data and weightings so that interested readers can construct their own freedom rankings; this information is available at http://freedominthe50states.org.

DEFINING FREEDOM

"Freedom" is a moral concept. What most people mean by freedom is the ability to pursue one's ends without unjust interference from others. Of course, reasonable people can disagree about what counts as unjust interference, and it is also controversial whether freedom in this sense ought to trump other desiderata such as social welfare. These questions cannot be answered in a value-neutral way, but citizens and policymakers must try to answer them nonetheless. We are forthright about our moral philosophy so that we can be precise about what counts as "freedom" for us, but we recognize that others may define freedom differently. We have made the data and weights available online so that people can alter our index to fit their own conceptions of freedom. We consider it an open, but interesting, question whether freedom

---

2. For examples of how the data have been used in research, see State and Local Public Policies in the United States website, http://www.statepolicyindex.com.

is in any way related to indicators of aggregate social welfare such as income growth and migration. Chapter 5 takes up this question in more detail.

We ground our conception of freedom on an individual rights framework. In our view, individuals should not be prevented from ordering their lives, liberties, and property as they see fit, so long as they do not infringe on the rights of others.[3] This understanding of freedom follows from the natural-rights liberal thought of John Locke, Immanuel Kant, and Robert Nozick, but it is also consistent with the rights-generating rule utilitarianism of Herbert Spencer and others.[4] From the Declaration of Independence, through the struggles for the abolition of slavery, and up to the 20th century, this conception of freedom was the traditional one in the United States. As Justice Louis Brandeis wrote in his 1928 dissent in *Olmstead v. United States*, "The makers of our Constitution ... conferred, as against the government, the right to be let alone—the most comprehensive of rights and the right most valued by civilized men."[5] In the context of the modern state, this philosophy engenders a set of normative policy prescriptions that political theorist Norman Barry characterized as "a belief in the efficiency and morality of unhampered markets, the system of private property, and individual rights—and a deep distrust of taxation, egalitarianism, compulsory welfare, and the power of the state."[6]

In essence, this index attempts to measure the extent to which state and local public policies conform to this ideal regime of maximum, equal freedom.[7] For us, the fundamental problem with state intervention in consensual acts is that it violates people's rights. To paraphrase Nozick, in a free society the government permits and protects both capitalist and noncapitalist acts between consenting adults.[8] Should individuals desire to "tie their own hands" and require themselves to participate in social insurance, redistributive, or paternalist projects, they should form voluntary communities for these purposes.[9]

Those who endorse the "law of equal freedom" at the heart of libertarianism and the political order espoused in this index do not necessarily reject

3. We recognize that children and the mentally incompetent must be treated differently from mentally competent adults, and also that some rights may not be alienated even by consenting adults.

4. See John Locke, *Second Treatise of Civil Government*; Immanuel Kant, *Foundations of the Metaphysics of Morals;* Robert Nozick, *Anarchy, State, and Utopia* (New York: Basic Books, 1974); and Herbert Spencer, *Social Statics, or the Conditions Essential to Happiness Specified, and the First of Them Developed* (London: John Chapman, 1851).

5. *Olmstead v. United States*, 277 U.S. 438 (1928).

6. Norman Barry, "The Concept of 'Nature' in Liberal Political Thought," *Journal of Libertarian Studies 8*, no. 1 (1986): 16n2.

7. The "equal freedom" that persons enjoy in a free society is, for us, equality of rights and equality before the law, not equality of opportunities or "positive freedom." On positive freedom, see Isaiah Berlin, "Two Concepts of Liberty," in *Four Essays on Liberty* (Oxford: Oxford University Press, 1969).

8. Nozick, *Anarchy, State, and Utopia*, p. 163.

9. Almost all real-world governments do not constitute voluntary communities because their constitutions do not enjoy the unanimous consent of the governed. Homeowners' associations, by contrast, do in theory fit into this category.

the notion of "constraints." Neither the liberal order nor the libertarian approach requires that one take an ethically or normatively neutral stance about how people use their freedom. For instance, it is perfectly consistent to reject "libertinism" ("do whatever you want so long as you do not hurt anyone else, whether it be snorting cocaine or engaging in casual sex") and even make strong moral claims about the proper way to live a virtuous, flourishing life without sacrificing one's credentials as a friend of liberty. Libertarianism does not imply libertinism, and the two may even stand in some tension, if Steven Pinker is correct that the "civilizing process" has encouraged the adoption of new moral and mannerly constraints to allow people to interact more peacefully with each other without Leviathan. [10] Supporting the right of consenting adults to use drugs or of bakers to contract with bakeries to employ them for more than 60 hours a week does not require judging those behaviors to be wise or even morally justified. Therefore, the freedom index makes no claim about the wisdom or morality of the behaviors that states should allow adults to pursue freely. It is left to philosophers, theologians, and all of us as moral agents to make arguments about the legitimacy of particular moral constraints. [11]

Although our belief in limited government and a free society is based on the moral dignity of each human being, empirical evidence suggests that the protection of individual rights tends to foster economic growth and the coinciding improvements in people's living standards. Economist Robert Lawson explains the relationship between economic freedom and economic growth:

> Numerous studies have shown that countries with more economic freedom grow more rapidly and achieve higher levels of per-capita income than those that are less free. Similarly, there is a positive relationship between changes in economic freedom and the growth of per-capita income. Given the sources of growth and prosperity, it is not surprising that increases in economic freedom and improvements in quality of life have gone hand in hand during the past quarter of a century. [12]

We also recognize that freedom, properly understood, can be threatened

---

10. Steven Pinker, *The Better Angels of Our Nature: Why Violence Has Declined* (New York: Viking, 2011).

11. We consider ourselves to be "virtue libertarians" (a term we have adopted as the result of many conversations over the years about our particular "conservative libertarian" brand of ethical and political thinking)—espousing strong support for a libertarian political order but also strong convictions about what a flourishing, moral life demands and how we ought to use our freedom (with proper humility, of course, about our ability to know with any certainty what the best life is for any individual or for people in general). We also think that certain behaviors are more consistent than others with the preservation and security of a free society. Our approach owes much to the work of Frank Meyer, Albert J. Nock, and Walter Block.

12. Robert A. Lawson, "Economic Freedom and the Wealth and Well-Being of Nations," in *The Annual Proceedings of the Wealth and Well-Being of Nations*, 2009–2010, vol. 2, ed. Emily Chamlee-Wright and Jennifer Kodl (Beloit, WI: Beloit College Press, 2010), pp. 65–80.

as much by the weakness of the state as by overbearing state intervention. Individuals are less free when they have reason to fear private assaults and depredations, and an appropriate government punishes private aggression vigorously. However, this book focuses on threats to individual liberty originating in the state. Therefore, we do not code the effectiveness of state governments in reducing rights violations. For instance, we do not calculate measures of the efficacy of state police and courts or of violent and property crime rates.[13] Thus, our "freedom index" does not capture all aspects of freedom, and we encourage readers to use our scores in conjunction with other indicators when assessing government effectiveness or quality of life. At the same time, we do attempt to capture the extent of "overcriminalization" by state, as well as the extent to which state civil liability systems put property rights at risk.

Our definition of freedom presents specific challenges on some high-profile issues. Abortion is a critical example. According to one view, a fetus is a rights-bearing person, and abortion is therefore almost always an aggressive violation of individual rights that ought to be punished by law. The opposite view holds that a fetus does not have rights, and abortion is a permissible exercise of an individual liberty, which entails that legal regulation of abortion is an unjust violation of a woman's rights. A third view holds that a fetus gains personhood and rights at some threshold during its development, and at that point legal regulation is *pro tanto* justified. Rather than take a stand on one pole or the other (or anywhere between), we have not included the policy in the official freedom index. We have coded the data on state abortion restrictions and made them available online at http://www.statepolicyindex.com, and for the first time, in this edition of the book, we have added a section that includes alternative indices based on three of many possible state abortion regimes.

Another example is the death penalty. Some argue that murderers forfeit their own right to life, and therefore state execution of a murderer does not violate a basic right to life. Others contend that the right to life can never be forfeited, or that the state should never risk taking away all the rights of innocent individuals by falsely convicting them. State sentencing policies short of the death penalty could also be debated, such as lengthy periods of solitary confinement. We personally have serious reservations about some of these punishments, but we do not include them in the freedom index, although we have coded the death penalty data and made them available

13. Measuring the efficacy and justice of criminal penalties, arrest procedures, and so forth with regard to deterrence, proportionality, retribution, rehabilitation, and the like is an extremely complex endeavor that deserves a lengthy treatment on its own. See Richard A. Posner, *The Economics of Justice* (Cambridge, MA: Harvard University Press, 1981). See, for example, the CIRI Human Rights Dataset, http://ciri.binghamton.edu.

14. See, for example, the Polity IV Project, http://www.systemicpeace.org/polity/polity4.htm.

online at http://www.statepolicyindex.com.

The freedom index stands within the mainstream tradition in social science of measuring normatively desired phenomena, such as democracy,[14] civil liberties, [15] and human rights. [16] Clearly, our index will have intrinsic interest for classical liberals and libertarians. However, nonlibertarian social scientists will also benefit from the index, because it is an open question how individual liberty relates to phenomena such as economic growth, migration, and partisan politics in the American states. In the same way, although political scientists may value democracy for its own sake, they can also research empirically what causes democracy and how democracy affects other phenomena. In fact, a broad range of social scientists and policy analysts have already used this index to investigate a range of interesting questions, including the effects on growth, migration, corruption, entrepreneurship, accident death rates, veterans' earnings, and state bond ratings. [17]

CREATING THE INDEX

We started this project by collecting data on state and local public policies affecting individual freedom as it is defined above. For data other than taxes and debt, we code laws enacted as of December 31, 2014 (even if they come into force later). We also code these variables for at least 2000, 2006, 2008, 2010, and 2012. For taxes and debt, the latest available data covering both state and local governments come from fiscal year 2012, which for most states ran from July 2011 to June 2012. However, we have actual state tax collections for FY 2013 and FY 2014 as well. By assuming constant local debt and taxation levels, we can get an estimated value of state plus local debt and tax burdens for FY 2013. We can also get provisional data for FY 2015 by looking at enacted state budgets. Thus, we can construct a freedom index for 2014 that includes laws enacted as of year-end 2014 and provisional tax and debt numbers for FY 2015. The 2012 freedom index should be more accurate, however. For each even-year freedom index, we use tax and debt data from the subsequent fiscal year, since state budgets are enacted in the year before.

Similarly, other variables in the index do not vary over time, such as one of the land-use regulation variables and several measures of occupational

15. See, for example, the Freedom House indicators, http://www.freedomhouse.org.

16. See, for example, the CIRI Human Rights Dataset, http://www.humanrightsdata.com/p/data-documentation.html.

17. Noel D. Johnson et al., "Corruption, Regulation, and Growth: An Empirical Study of the United States," *Economics of Governance* 15, no. 1 (2014): 51–69; Richard J. Cebula, "The Impact of Economic Freedom and Personal Freedom on Net In-Migration in the US: A State-Level Empirical Analysis, 2000 to 2010," *Journal of Labor Research* 35, no. 1 (2014): 88–103; Nicholas Apergis, Oguzhan C. Dincer, and James E. Payne, "Live Free or Bribe: On the Causal Dynamics between Economic Freedom and Corruption in US States," *European Journal of Political Economy* 28, no. 2 (2012): 215–26; Rick Weber and Benjamin Powell, "Economic Freedom and Entrepreneurship: A Panel Study of the United States," *American Journal of Entrepreneurship* 1 (2013): 67–87; Leland K. Ackerson and S. V. Subramanian, "Negative Freedom and Death in the United States," *American Journal of Public Health* 100, no. 11 (2010): 2163–64; Alberto Dávila and Marie T. Mora, "Terrorism and Patriotism: On the Earnings of US Veterans Following September 11, 2001," *American Economic Review* 102, no. 3 (2012), pp. 261–66.

licensing. We have to carry forward and back the data for these policies in order to include them, and generally reduce their "weight" in the index because of their potential to mask changes occurring at the state level. With a series of 14 years, our extrapolations should not be too problematic as yet, but in future editions we will likely drop variables that are not available for more than one year.

The index also includes variables that do not differ across states for particular years. Usually, they are a result of policies' being nationalized at the federal level. Sometimes, this centralizing process occurs in a pro-freedom direction, as when the Supreme Court struck down Chicago's gun ban and several states' sodomy laws, but more often it occurs in an anti-freedom direction, as when the Patient Protection and Affordable Care Act legislated health insurance community rating, guaranteed issue, prior approval of premiums, and an individual health insurance mandate nationwide.

The top-level data used for creating the index are available in a downloadable spreadsheet at http://freedominthe50states.org, titled "rsi_data_15.xls." However, to obtain details on data sources and the construction of indices (such as the eminent domain reform and renewable portfolio standards indices), interested readers should navigate to http://www.statepolicyindex.com and download the policy category spreadsheets. Each variable in the top-level spreadsheet has a code, such as "adebtpi" (state and local debt divided by personal income). The first letter of that code corresponds to the particular spreadsheet where its details may be found. Thus, "adebtpi" comes from the "a_fiscal_15.xls" spreadsheet for fiscal policies. Quite often, these spreadsheets contain additional policies not included in the freedom index, as well as data for additional years where available. Some state and local tax and spending data are available annually back to FY 1977 and quinquennially back to FY 1957. Some alcohol policies are available from 1937.

Because we want to score states on composite indices of freedom, we need some way of "weighting" and aggregating individual policies. One popular method for aggregating policies is "factor" or "principal component" analysis, which weights variables according to how much they contribute to the common variance—that is, how well they correlate with other variables.

Factor analysis is equivalent to letting politicians weight the variables, because correlations among variables across states will reflect the ways that lawmakers systematically prioritize certain policies. Partisan politics is not always consistent with freedom (e.g., states with more marijuana freedom offer less tobacco freedom). The index resulting from factor analysis would be an index of "policy ideology," not freedom. [18]

Factor analysis is also not justified if important variables do not line up

18. Jason Sorens, Fait Muedini, and William P. Ruger, "U.S. State and Local Public Policies in 2006: A New Database," *State Politics and Policy Quarterly* 8, no. 3 (2008): 309–26.

with a clear ideological position but have a major effect on freedom. That is in fact the case. Occupational licensing is neither more nor less prevalent in conservative versus progressive states. The lawsuit environment is also not related to state ideology. In a factor-analysis approach, these variables would be discounted, but they are important variables in our study because of their economic impact.

Because policy ideology will interest some readers, we include a section on it in this edition of the study. We even try to ascertain whether the data indicate a second, "libertarian-communitarian" dimension of state policy ideology.

Another approach, employed in the Fraser Institute's "Economic Freedom of North America," is to weight each category equally, and then to weight variables within each category equally. [19] This approach assumes that the variance observed within each category and each variable is equally important. In the large data set used for the freedom index, such an assumption would be wildly implausible. We feel confident that, for instance, tax burden should be weighted more heavily than court decisions mandating that private malls or universities allow political speech.

To create the freedom index, we weight variables according to the value of the freedom affected by a particular policy to those people whose freedoms are at stake. Each variable receives a dollar estimate, representing the financial, psychological, and welfare benefits of a standardized shift of the variable in a pro-freedom direction to those people who enjoy more freedom. We base these values on estimates derived from the scholarly literature in economics and public policy that quantifies the effects of policies on behavior.

The "freedom value" of each variable represents the benefits to only those people whose freedoms have been respected. We do not include the benefits to those who wish to take away freedoms. For instance, private companies may benefit from receiving eminent domain transfers, but we count only the costs to those whose property has been taken away.

We do so because we do not want to create a utilitarian calculus. An index of social welfare is not the same as an index of freedom. We leave it an open question whether deprivations of freedom have net social benefits or costs. Of course, the costs of these deprivations to their victims would be part of a utilitarian calculus, but we do not want to foreclose future empirical research on whether government intervention that classical liberals consider unjust might nevertheless have some beneficial social consequences.

Our approach shares something in common with John Rawls's famous criticism of utilitarianism:

---

19. "Economic Freedom of North America," Frasier Institute, 2015, http://www.freetheworld.com/efna.html.

As an interpretation of the basis of the principles of justice, classical utilitarianism is mistaken. It *permits* one to argue, for example, that slavery is unjust on the grounds that the advantages to the slaveholder as slaveholder do not counterbalance the disadvantages to the slave and to society at large burdened by a comparatively inefficient system of labor. Now the conception of justice as fairness, when applied to the practice of slavery with its offices of slaveholder and slave, would not allow one to consider the advantages of the slaveholder in the first place.... The gains accruing to the slaveholder, assuming them to exist, cannot be counted as in any way mitigating the injustice of the practice.[20]

That is precisely our position, not only with regard to the extreme example of slavery, but also to the more mundane but equally systematic deprivations of freedom in contemporary American society. Therefore, we count only the disadvantages to victims of government action.

In addition, we have techniques for including second-order victims in our calculations, who may not lose property or freedom directly, but who can be expected to suffer fear of having their rights violated in the future ("if they can do that to X, they can do that to me"). We discuss some of these techniques in the relevant sections below. Our raw data contain comments describing in detail the justification for each variable's weight and citing relevant sources.

Consistent with the method employed in the previous edition of the index, the value of the freedom affected by a given policy represents the dollar-terms value of the freedom to potential victims if a one-standard-deviation change in that variable were imposed nationwide. That common standard allows us to compare variables with each other and sum their costs. When we discuss below the values of a particular freedom or, equivalently, the victim costs of restrictions on that freedom, we are referring to that metric.

Again, the value of a freedom represents not just financial benefits, but consumer surplus, psychological benefits, and so on. These estimates are based on economic and policy research, but admittedly, that research does not always allow precise, certain estimates. We lack the resources to conduct in-depth statistical analysis on the social and economic consequences of each of the 175 top-level variables in the data set. Absent that capability for precision, our aim in this edition was to construct weights that are accurate

20. John Rawls, "Justice as Fairness," Philosophical Review 67, no. 2 (1958): 187–88 (emphasis in original).

within an order of magnitude. Using dollar values derived from the literature imposes greater discipline on our weighting choices than a rougher, more qualitative assessment of individual policies' significance like that used in the first two editions of this index.

With plausible variable weights, quantifying freedom permits researchers to investigate the relationship between freedom and other desiderata quantitatively and to judge changes in freedom over time objectively, rather than anecdotally. Measurements of freedom will improve as scientific estimates of the relative values of different freedoms improve, but taking the first step toward an objective assessment of different freedoms' values is essential to the social-scientific enterprise.

Thus, our index of freedom should be understood to represent each state's relative respect for freedom, as reflected in the value enjoyed by the "average" person who would otherwise be deprived of the freedoms we measure. However, each individual will value different policies differently, and for that reason, again, we encourage readers to apply their own weights and personalize the freedom index at http://freedominthe50states.org. Readers can download the "rsi_data_15.xls" spreadsheet to create their own weights for each variable. We have used Excel's "comment" function to annotate important information about how variables were coded and weighted and what particular columns and rows mean. To investigate how any particular variable was created or coded, anyone can download the constellation of policy category spreadsheets at http://www.statepolicyindex.com. Variables and the policy category spreadsheets are named with an initial letter so as to make their location clear. For instance, debt as a percentage of income, *adebtpi*, is found in the fiscal policy spreadsheet, "a_fiscal_15.xls." The individual policy category spreadsheets contain a "metadata" worksheet with detailed information on data sources.

PART I
DIMENSIONS OF FREEDOM

For the purposes of the freedom index, this book identifies three overarching "dimensions" of freedom and further divides each dimension into categories composed of one or more of the variables used to generate the state scores and rankings. Following our objective weighting system described in the last chapter, variables in the fiscal policy dimension end up with 29.8 percent of the summed freedom values of all variables for the average state, variables in the regulatory policy dimension with 38.7 percent, and variables in the personal freedom dimension with 29.4 percent.[21] Taken individually, the categories may interest readers on core topics of concern, such as taxation, state debt, health insurance regulations, restrictions on alcohol sales, and so on. The following sections explain how each category was constructed and earned its respective weight within the index. Together, these categories comprise the overall rankings, found in the next chapter.

---

21. Because of the manner in which we weight local taxation, the weights for the fiscal dimension vary by state. They range from 29.5 percent (for the state with the most competing jurisdictions) to 32.0 percent (for the state with the fewest competing jurisdictions). For further explanation see the section titled "Local Taxation."

FISCAL POLICY

The fiscal policy dimension consists of five variables: (a) state tax revenues, (b) local tax revenues, (c) government employment, (d) government subsidies, and (e) government debt, each of which earns a significant weight because of its importance (see Figure 1). The tax and debt variables are measured for each fiscal year, whereas the employment and subsidies variables come from different sources and are available for the calendar year.

In past editions, we have included fiscal decentralization (ratio of local to state taxation) as a separate variable. In this edition, we do something much more sophisticated. We separate state and local taxation and assign different weights to each. See the following section for details.

FIGURE 1 Fiscal Policy Weights

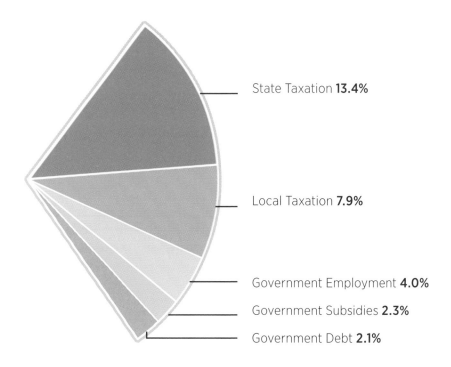

State Taxation **13.4%**

Local Taxation **7.9%**

Government Employment **4.0%**

Government Subsidies **2.3%**

Government Debt **2.1%**

STATE TAXATION

13.4% State and local tax burdens are measured by calculating state and local tax revenues as a percentage of each state's personal income, excluding taxes on motor fuel, mineral severance, alcohol sales, and tobacco sales.[22] Gas taxes are excluded because they approximate user fees (they are paid roughly in proportion to use by the user, unlike other taxes). [23] Mineral severance taxes are excluded because they are paid by energy companies that pass the costs on to consumers worldwide, not just to residents of the state where they operate. Alcohol and tobacco sales taxes are excluded because they are included in the personal freedom dimension. Personal income is the denominator because it represents the size of each state's economy: it statistically correlates better with state and local revenues and expenditures than any other commonly used measure of economic size, such as gross domestic product. [24]

The taxation variables therefore roughly represent the average tax burden that state taxpayers face. Because of interstate investment, commuting, and tourism, tax collections do not always line up exactly with tax burdens on residents. The Tax Foundation adjusts for those effects to derive a purer indicator of average tax burden, but the differences between its indicator and the one used in this book are usually small. The Tax Foundation's calculation of tax burden is much more complex and uses proprietary data. [25]

In the previous edition, the weight for tax burden was simply the standard deviation of state and local taxes collected as a percentage of personal income, multiplied by national personal income. Effectively, we assumed that every dollar of tax was a diminution of taxpayer freedom. The main problem with that assumption, as we then recognized, is that some taxpayers would consent to pay their full tax burden conditional on others' doing the same, and some of what those taxes pay for does not diminish and may even enhance freedom (e.g., protection of rights). Some even advocate a higher tax burden, in order to pay for services they value.

In this edition, we address this problem in the following way. First, we assume that the current tax burden in each state represents the ideal point of the median voter. Positive theories of democracy suggest that this is as good a guess about where public opinion lies as any. [26] Then, half of the vot-

---

22. The Census Bureau taxation measures used here exclude user fees (such as state university tuition) from the tax category, but include business, motor vehicle license, and alcohol license fees, which is appropriate for the freedom index.

23. Some people would argue that gas taxes that merely pay for roads are too low, because a higher gas tax could discourage pollution, a negative externality. Others would argue that some states' existing gas taxes are too high, because state governments often divert them to nonroad uses.

24. When total spending and total taxes are regressed on personal income, gross domestic product, and earnings by place of work, only the first correlates positively with the fiscal variables.

25. Liz Malm and Gerald Prante, "Annual State-Local Tax Burden Ranking FY 2011," Tax Foundation, April 2, 2014, http://taxfoundation.org/article/annual-state-local-tax-burden-ranking-fy-2011.

26. Anthony Downs, *An Economic Theory of Democracy* (New York: Harper, 1957).

ers would prefer a higher tax burden (and the services it would finance), and half would prefer a lower tax burden. Right away, we can slash the tax burden weight in half, because half of the voters nationally would not see the taxes they currently pay as any diminution of their freedom at all.

Now, this move assumes that the median-dollar taxpayer is the same as the median voter. That is unlikely to be the case. In fact, the median-dollar taxpayer is likely to be somewhat wealthier than the median voter and thus more ideologically conservative and more hostile to taxation. Thus, if anything, slashing the tax burden in half on these grounds is slightly too aggressive. We discuss our solution to this problem below.

Before we solve for that issue, we continue with the exposition. Of at least half of the taxpayers who would prefer a lower tax burden, most of them would not see all of the taxes they pay as a diminution of their freedom. That is, conditional on others doing the same (absent the collective action problem), they would be fully willing to pay a lower tax burden that is greater than zero. To illustrate the logic, assume a normal probability density function over possible tax burdens, as seen in Figure 2.

FIGURE 2 Normal Curve with Median at 9.5

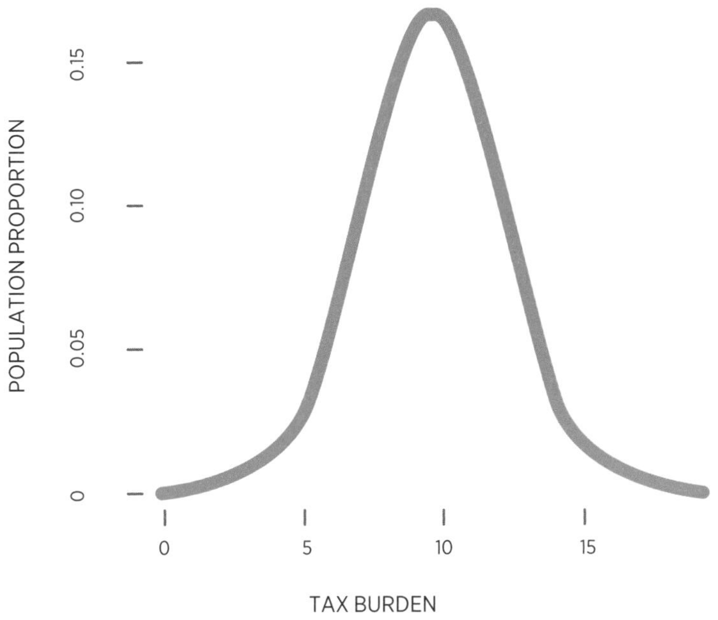

On the x-axis of Figure 2 is tax burden, and on the y-axis is the proportion of the population corresponding to a particular view on tax burden. Fifty percent of the curve lies to the left or right of the mean of the tax burden distribution, which is 9.5, the actual national mean of state plus local tax burden. (We have drawn the curve under the assumption of a standard deviation of 2.375, a fourth of the mean, but nothing that follows hinges on this assumption. Note that the standard deviation of voters' views on taxation should be significantly greater than the standard deviation of actual state tax burdens, because each state tax burden roughly represents a median of a distribution.)

What that means more simply is that, we guess, half of the voters are satisfied with tax burdens of 9.5 percent or higher, while half of the voters prefer tax burdens below 9.5 percent. Taxes take away the freedom of only the second group. Also, the vast majority of the second group does not want to get rid of all taxes. Only part of their tax burden reduces their freedom.

How much of their tax burden is a loss of freedom? We could imagine a "loss curve" that looks like a mirror image of the left side of the normal density function. In other words, those who want zero taxation will see all 9.5 percent of income taxed away as a loss of freedom, those who want taxation of 2.5 percent of income will see 7.0 percent of income taxed away as a loss of freedom, and so on. Half of all the taxes that people who prefer lower taxes pay do not take away their freedom, if we assume a normal distribution of preferences over taxes. (The area under the loss curve is 0.5, like the area under the left side of the normal curve.) So only 4.75 percent of personal income, in total, is a loss to those who prefer lower taxation. We can divide the tax burden's weight by two again, or by four in total. Then, we multiply by 1.1 to take account of the fact that the median taxpayer is richer than, and likely more anti-tax than, the median voter.

The values in Tables 1 and 2 represent the number of standard deviations better (lower tax) than the 2000–2014, 50-state average. Vermont looks abnormally poor on state taxes and good on local taxes (Table 3), because the state classifies all of the property tax as a state tax, even though towns do have some control over the local rate. Since we reward states for fiscal decentralization, the net effect is to depress Vermont's fiscal policy and overall freedom score somewhat.

TABLE I

Rank	State	State Tax Burden Ranking, 2012
1.	Alaska	2.2
2.	New Hampshire	2.0
3.	South Dakota	1.7
4.	Texas	1.5
5.	Florida	1.3
6.	Wyoming	1.2
7.	Louisiana	1.2
8.	Tennessee	1.1
9.	Colorado	1.1
10.	Missouri	1.0
11.	Georgia	0.9
12.	Virginia	0.9
13.	Oklahoma	0.7
14.	Alabama	0.6
15.	South Carolina	0.6
16.	Nebraska	0.5
17.	Arizona	0.4
18.	Washington	0.4
19.	Montana	0.4
20.	Pennsylvania	0.3
21.	Ohio	0.2
22.	Maryland	0.2
23.	Oregon	0.2
24.	Utah	0.1
25.	Kansas	0.1

Rank	State	State Tax Burden Ranking, 2012
26.	Rhode Island	0.1
27.	New Mexico	0.0
28.	North Carolina	0.0
29.	Iowa	0.0
30.	New Jersey	0.0
31.	Idaho	−0.1
32.	Nevada	−0.1
33.	Kentucky	−0.2
34.	Massachusetts	−0.3
35.	Michigan	−0.3
36.	Wisconsin	−0.3
37.	Illinois	−0.3
38.	Indiana	−0.4
39.	West Virginia	−0.7
40.	Maine	−0.7
41.	New York	−0.7
42.	North Dakota	−0.7
43.	Mississippi	−0.8
44.	California	−1.0
45.	Connecticut	−1.0
46.	Arkansas	−1.2
47.	Delaware	−1.5
48.	Minnesota	−1.8
49.	Hawaii	−2.8
50.	Vermont	−2.9

TABLE 2

Rank	State	State Tax Burden Ranking, 2014 Provisional		Rank	State	State Tax Burden Ranking, 2014 Provisional
1.	Alaska	2.7		26.	Iowa	0.1
2.	New Hampshire	2.1		27.	Maryland	0.1
3.	South Dakota	1.6		28.	Idaho	0.0
4.	Texas	1.5		29.	Oregon	0.0
5.	Florida	1.3		30.	New Jersey	0.0
6.	Wyoming	1.2		31.	New Mexico	−0.1
7.	Tennessee	1.2		32.	Michigan	−0.1
8.	Louisiana	1.1		33.	Wisconsin	−0.1
9.	Missouri	1.1		34.	Nevada	−0.2
10.	Colorado	1.1		35.	Kentucky	−0.2
11.	Virginia	0.9		36.	Illinois	−0.3
12.	Georgia	0.9		37.	Indiana	−0.3
13.	Oklahoma	0.7		38.	Massachusetts	−0.4
14.	Alabama	0.7		39.	West Virginia	−0.4
15.	South Carolina	0.7		40.	Maine	−0.5
16.	Arizona	0.6		41.	North Dakota	−0.5
17.	Montana	0.5		42.	New York	−0.8
18.	Kansas	0.4		43.	Mississippi	−0.8
19.	Nebraska	0.4		44.	Connecticut	−0.9
20.	Ohio	0.4		45.	California	−1.0
21.	Pennsylvania	0.4		46.	Delaware	−1.1
22.	Washington	0.4		47.	Arkansas	−1.3
23.	Utah	0.3		48.	Minnesota	−1.9
24.	Rhode Island	0.2		49.	Hawaii	−2.5
25.	North Carolina	0.2		50.	Vermont	−3.0

LOCAL TAXATION

7.9% We separate local taxation to take account of fiscal decentralization. Fiscal decentralization affects freedom in that when more taxes are raised at the local level, residents may have more choice over their tax burden and public services. They can more easily vote with their feet—that is, move to a jurisdiction with their preferred policy mix—at the local level than at the state level.

But that very ability to foot-vote varies not just by the amount of revenue raised at the local level, but by the number of local jurisdictions. If local governments are spatially large, it is difficult for residents to exercise choice. When a city like Houston annexes other independent municipalities, it becomes more difficult for movers to the area to choose a jurisdiction to their liking. Hawaii's single statewide school district prevents parents from moving to an area where they think the schools are better run. Since the relevant decision for a homeowner is typically over local jurisdictions within driving distance to a place of employment, the metric for variety of choice that we use is the effective number of local jurisdictions per square mile of privately owned land (we exclude publicly owned land because it is presumably not developable).

"Effective number of local jurisdictions" counts up the weighted sum of general-purpose local governments in each state, where the weights are the percentage of local tax revenue raised by each local government tier. If a state has 10 counties and 100 municipalities, and counties raise 40 percent of local taxes while municipalities raise 60 percent, then the state's effective number of local jurisdictions is $10*0.4+100*0.6=64$. We then divide that number by the number of square miles of private land in the state.

The variable for the effective number of local jurisdictions per square mile determines the weight on the local taxation variable, which therefore varies by state. It is the only variable in the index with a weight that varies by state. (The weight for local taxation reported in Figure 1 is the average for all 50 states over the 2000–2014 period.) The idea here is that high decentralization (high local taxation relative to state taxation) matters less when there are fewer jurisdictions per square mile and more when there are more. Specifically, we multiply the standard taxation weight (on which more below) by 0.75 for the state with the most jurisdictions per square mile (New Jersey) and give a hypothetical state with no local governments the full taxation weight, then ranging the other states linearly according to their effective number of jurisdictions per square mile. In New Jersey, we are assuming that local taxation is only three-quarters of the restriction on freedom that state taxation is. In Hawaii, the most territorially centralized state, local taxation is almost the same as state taxation—the prospective homeowner has virtually no local exit option—so local taxes are little more likely than state taxes to reflect distinctive local preferences.

Local tax collections come from the most recent fiscal year data released by the Census Bureau (FY 2012). The numbers here represent the combined formula incorporating both the level of local taxation and the weight as determined by the number of competing local jurisdictions. As a result, the numbers in Table 3 are not directly comparable to the figures for state-level taxation already given.

TABLE 3

Rank	State	Local Tax Burden Ranking Incorporating Decentralization, 2011	Rank	State	Local Tax Burden Ranking Incorporating Decentralization, 2011
1.	Vermont	0.23	26.	Virginia	−0.01
2.	Arkansas	0.17	27.	Connecticut	−0.02
3.	Delaware	0.17	28.	Florida	−0.02
4.	North Dakota	0.11	29.	California	−0.02
5.	Idaho	0.10	30.	Missouri	−0.02
6.	West Virginia	0.10	31.	Arizona	−0.02
7.	Mississippi	0.09	32.	Wisconsin	−0.03
8.	Oklahoma	0.09	33.	Oregon	−0.03
9.	Kentucky	0.09	34.	Iowa	−0.04
10.	Alabama	0.08	35.	Kansas	−0.04
11.	Minnesota	0.08	36.	New Jersey	−0.05
12.	Hawaii	0.07	37.	Maryland	−0.05
13.	Montana	0.06	38.	Georgia	−0.05
14.	Tennessee	0.06	39.	New Hampshire	−0.06
15.	North Carolina	0.05	40.	Maine	−0.06
16.	Massachusetts	0.05	41.	Rhode Island	−0.06
17.	Michigan	0.05	42.	Ohio	−0.06
18.	Indiana	0.05	43.	Louisiana	−0.07
19.	New Mexico	0.04	44.	Alaska	−0.07
20.	Pennsylvania	0.03	45.	Wyoming	−0.08
21.	South Dakota	0.02	46.	Nebraska	−0.08
22.	Nevada	0.01	47.	Texas	−0.08
23.	Utah	0.00	48.	Colorado	−0.10
24.	Washington	0.00	49.	Illinois	−0.11
25.	South Carolina	−0.01	50.	New York	−0.29

GOVERNMENT EMPLOYMENT

4.0% We also include government employment, which can crowd out employment in the private sector. To the extent that government-run enterprises are less efficient than private ones, government employment costs the local economy. Economists Jim Malley and Thomas Moutos use a cointegration framework on time-series data from Sweden and find that a 1.0 percent increase in government employment is associated with a 0.43 percent decrease in private employment. Economist Evi Pappa uses U.S. state data and also finds that aggregate employment does not increase at moments when government employment does, implying substantial crowding out in the short run and presumably the long run as well.[27]

According to the Malley-Moutos elasticity estimate applied to state data from 2009, there was an aggregate disemployment effect from an increase in government employment that year. Although that might be true, it seems like an aggressive assumption. After all, government employment is very high in Sweden; thus, its marginal effect there might be more negative than its marginal effect just about anywhere else.

Instead, following Pappa's results, the freedom index assumes a net zero effect on total employment from an increase in state and local employment. The private disemployment effect of a one-standard-deviation increase in the ratio of government to private employment, as of 2013, would be 3.47 million nationwide. Average compensation per job in the United States in 2014 was $47,230. The index assumes that compensation equals marginal productivity and that government jobs are only 90 percent as productive as private jobs. The victim cost of a nationwide, one-standard-deviation increase in the government employment ratio is therefore 3.47 million times $47,230 divided by 10, or $16.4 billion.

Government employment is available on a calendar-year basis from the Bureau of Economic Analysis.

27. Jim Malley and Thomas Moutos, "Does Government Employment 'Crowd Out' Private Employment? Evidence from Sweden," *Scandinavian Journal of Economics* 98, no. 2 (1996): 289–302; Evi Pappa, "The Effects of Fiscal Shocks on Employment and the Real Wage," *International Economic Review* 50, no. 1 (2009): 217–44.

TABLE 4

Rank	State	Government Employment Ranking		Rank	State	Government Employment Ranking
1.	Nevada	1.8		26.	New York	0.3
2.	Florida	1.6		27.	Utah	0.3
3.	Pennsylvania	1.5		28.	Vermont	0.2
4.	Massachusetts	1.5		29.	South Dakota	0.1
5.	Rhode Island	1.4		30.	Hawaii	0.1
6.	New Hampshire	1.0		31.	North Dakota	0.1
7.	California	1.0		32.	Virginia	0.0
8.	Illinois	0.9		33.	Nebraska	0.0
9.	Tennessee	0.9		34.	Montana	−0.1
10.	Michigan	0.9		35.	Idaho	−0.1
11.	Connecticut	0.8		36.	Iowa	−0.1
12.	Ohio	0.8		37.	Louisiana	−0.1
13.	Minnesota	0.8		38.	Kentucky	−0.2
14.	Texas	0.7		39.	Washington	−0.3
15.	Maryland	0.7		40.	North Carolina	−0.4
16.	Indiana	0.7		41.	Arkansas	−0.6
17.	Oregon	0.7		42.	Alabama	−0.6
18.	Arizona	0.6		43.	South Carolina	−0.7
19.	Georgia	0.6		44.	Kansas	−0.7
20.	New Jersey	0.5		45.	Oklahoma	−0.8
21.	Missouri	0.5		46.	West Virginia	−1.4
22.	Maine	0.5		47.	Mississippi	−2.0
23.	Colorado	0.4		48.	Alaska	−2.1
24.	Wisconsin	0.4		49.	New Mexico	−2.4
25.	Delaware	0.3		50.	Wyoming	−2.8

GOVERNMENT SUBSIDIES

2.3%   In this edition, we treat state and local subsidies separately from other forms of government spending. We assume that, unlike taxes paid for public services and social transfers, taxes paid for subsidies to business are a loss of freedom for all taxpayers, because virtually no taxpayers would want to transfer their own wealth to managers and owners of large corporations. At best, subsidies are zero-sum, merely redirecting particular business activities from one place to another. However, once the opportunity costs and distortions of subsidies are considered, they generally reduce the incomes of local taxpayers.[28] This is a rough solution, since economic theory could support subsidies for goods that produce positive externalities. But most subsidies paid by state and local governments do not fit this logic. This variable also ignores nonrefundable tax benefits, which also redistribute the fiscal burden unfairly, but data on tax exemptions are not available for all states. And perhaps most important for a freedom index, subsidies reduce freedom unless they are Pareto improving, since they are coerced, and can be justified only by a utilitarian ethic that can harm some for the benefit of others.

Government subsidies are available on a calendar-year basis from the Bureau of Economic Analysis.

---

28. Ronald Steenblik, "A Subsidy Primer," International Institute for Sustainable Development, n.d., https://www.iisd.org/gsi/subsidy-primer/.

TABLE 5

Rank	State	Government Subsidies Ranking
1.	Wyoming	1.4
2.	Arkansas	1.0
3.	Kansas	0.9
4.	Iowa	0.9
5.	North Dakota	0.8
6.	Nebraska	0.8
7.	Idaho	0.8
8.	Mississippi	0.8
9.	Alabama	0.7
10.	Wisconsin	0.7
11.	South Dakota	0.7
12.	Oklahoma	0.7
13.	West Virginia	0.7
14.	Montana	0.6
15.	Texas	0.6
16.	South Carolina	0.6
17.	Kentucky	0.6
18.	New Hampshire	0.6
19.	Virginia	0.6
20.	Nevada	0.4
21.	Minnesota	0.4
22.	New Mexico	0.4
23.	Tennessee	0.4
24.	Missouri	0.4
25.	Arizona	0.3
26.	North Carolina	0.2
27.	Michigan	0.2
28.	Indiana	0.2
29.	Georgia	0.1
30.	Utah	0.1
31.	Florida	0.1
32.	Vermont	0.0
33.	Colorado	0.0
34.	Ohio	−0.1
35.	Connecticut	−0.2
36.	Maine	−0.3
37.	Delaware	−0.4
38.	Louisiana	−0.4
39.	Pennsylvania	−0.5
40.	Maryland	−0.6
41.	Oregon	−0.6
42.	Hawaii	−0.7
43.	Rhode Island	−0.7
44.	Washington	−0.8
45.	New Jersey	v0.8
46.	California	−0.8
47.	Illinois	−0.9
48.	Alaska	−0.9
49.	Massachusetts	−2.1
50.	New York	−4.1

GOVERNMENT DEBT

2.1% The problem with state and local debt, above a modest level, is that it worsens credit ratings and increases yields paid on government bonds.[29] Poterba and Rueben give readily interpretable coefficient estimates for our purposes. They find that a one-standard-deviation increase in state debt as a percentage of personal income is associated with a 7.6-basis-point increase in bond yield. The present value of the additional interest payments into the indefinite future that are generated by this increase in the bond yield rate is $0.00076*debt*i$, where i is the social discount rate. Following Office of Management and Budget standards, we set $i=0.07$. We also set *debt* equal to the state average.

The defense of state debt is that some voters value the services funded by debt, even at the expense of higher default risk and interest payments. Accordingly, we follow the solution we used for taxation and divide the number arrived at in the manner described in the previous paragraph by 3.6.

For debt, we use the latest fiscal year data from the Census Bureau (FY 2012) and carry forward to 2014 for the provisional index for that year.

---

29. James M. Poterba and Kim Rueben, "State Fiscal Institutions and the U.S. Municipal Bond Market," in *Fiscal Institutions and Fiscal Performance*, ed. James M. Poterba (Chicago: University of Chicago Press, 1999), pp. 181–208; Craig L. Johnson and Kenneth A. Kriz, "Fiscal Institutions, Credit Ratings, and Borrowing Costs," *Public Budgeting and Finance* 25, no. 1 (2005): 84–103.

TABLE 6

Rank	State	Government Debt Ranking		Rank	State	Government Debt Ranking
1.	Wyoming	2.5		26.	Louisiana	0.1
2.	Idaho	1.8		27.	Minnesota	0.1
3.	North Dakota	1.6		28.	Indiana	−0.1
4.	Oklahoma	1.6		29.	Michigan	−0.1
5.	Arkansas	1.2		30.	Connecticut	−0.1
6.	Montana	1.2		31.	Arizona	−0.1
7.	North Carolina	1.1		32.	Delaware	−0.1
8.	Iowa	1.1		33.	New Jersey	−0.3
9.	Mississippi	1.0		34.	Kansas	−0.4
10.	Tennessee	0.9		35.	Colorado	−0.4
11.	Maryland	0.9		36.	New Mexico	−0.5
12.	South Dakota	0.9		37.	Pennsylvania	−0.6
13.	Georgia	0.9		38.	Oregon	−0.6
14.	Maine	0.7		39.	Hawaii	−0.6
15.	Vermont	0.6		40.	California	−0.7
16.	Virginia	0.6		41.	Texas	−0.8
17.	West Virginia	0.5		42.	Washington	−0.8
18.	Alabama	0.4		43.	South Carolina	−0.9
19.	Nebraska	0.4		44.	Illinois	−1.0
20.	Ohio	0.4		45.	Massachusetts	−1.0
21.	New Hampshire	0.4		46.	Rhode Island	−1.2
22.	Wisconsin	0.3		47.	Nevada	−1.4
23.	Florida	0.2		48.	Alaska	−1.5
24.	Missouri	0.1		49.	Kentucky	−1.5
25.	Utah	0.1		50.	New York	−2.5

OVERALL FISCAL POLICY RANKING

29.7% The fiscal policy ranking is available in Table 7. New Hampshire edges out Tennessee and South Dakota for the top slot. The latter two states have lower overall tax burdens, but New Hampshire's high level of fiscal decentralization puts it ahead.

Since the two taxation variables make up the lion's share of fiscal policy's weight, it is unsurprising that low-tax states dominate the top of the fiscal policy rankings, while high-tax states fall at the bottom. In Table 7, the numbers represent the number of weighted standard deviations each state is above the average. For instance, New York's 2014 score of –0.54 means that even if New York were exactly average on regulatory policy and personal freedom (garnering a total score of 0 on them), it would still be, on average, half a standard deviation less free than the average for every policy.

A state that is one standard deviation better than average on every single policy will end up with an overall freedom score of 1, and a state that is one standard deviation worse than average on every single policy will end up with an overall freedom score of –1. Since fiscal policy represents less than a third of the overall index, New York's score of –0.54 means that it is on average more than one and a half standard deviations worse than average on every fiscal policy.

In general, right-of-center states dominate the top of the fiscal policy ranking, while left-of-center states occupy the bottom. The next chapter looks at the relationship between public ideology and freedom in more detail.

Figure 3 shows how the average fiscal policy score has changed for all 50 states since 2000. It appears that the Great Recession has actually improved states' fiscal policies, mostly from declining tax burdens and spending cuts.

FIGURE 3 State Average Fiscal Policy Scores over Time

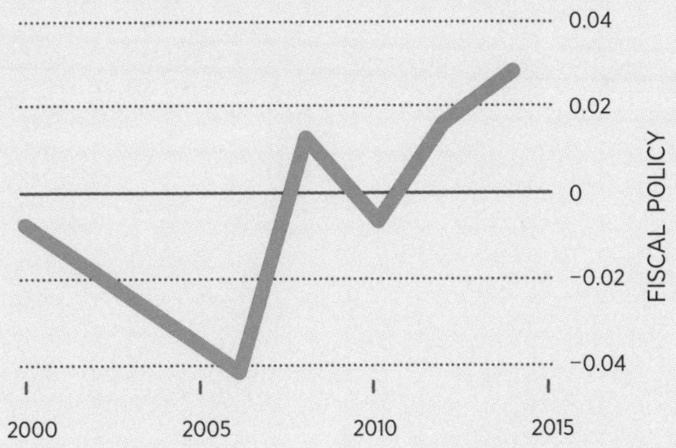

TABLE 7

Rank	State	Overall Fiscal Policy Ranking, 2014 Provisional		Rank	State	Overall Fiscal Policy Ranking, 2014 Provisional
1.	New Hampshire	0.29		26.	Indiana	0.03
2.	Tennessee	0.28		27.	Arkansas	0.03
3.	South Dakota	0.27		28.	Kentucky	0.03
4.	Florida	0.23		29.	Delaware	0.03
5.	Oklahoma	0.20		30.	Iowa	0.02
6.	Alabama	0.18		31.	West Virginia	0.02
7.	Montana	0.16		32.	Nebraska	0.01
8.	Idaho	0.16		33.	Kansas	0.01
9.	Missouri	0.15		34.	Maryland	0.00
10.	Texas	0.15		35.	Washington	0.00
11.	Alaska	0.15		36.	Massachusetts	−0.01
12.	Virginia	0.14		37.	Wisconsin	−0.01
13.	Pennsylvania	0.12		38.	Rhode Island	−0.02
14.	Georgia	0.11		39.	Oregon	−0.04
15.	North Dakota	0.10		40.	New Jersey	−0.06
16.	Arizona	0.09		41.	Mississippi	−0.06
17.	North Carolina	0.09		42.	New Mexico	−0.07
18.	Michigan	0.08		43.	Maine	−0.10
19.	Louisiana	0.07		44.	Connecticut	−0.11
20.	Utah	0.06		45.	Minnesota	−0.14
21.	Wyoming	0.06		46.	California	−0.15
22.	Colorado	0.06		47.	Vermont	−0.15
23.	South Carolina	0.05		48.	Illinois	−0.16
24.	Ohio	0.03		49.	Hawaii	−0.30
25.	Nevada	0.03		50.	New York	−0.54

TABLE 8

Rank	State	Overall Fiscal Policy Ranking, 2012		Rank	State	Overall Fiscal Policy Ranking, 2012
1.	South Dakota	0.29		26.	Kentucky	0.02
2.	New Hampshire	0.27		27.	Indiana	0.01
3.	Tennessee	0.27		28.	Maryland	0.01
4.	Florida	0.22		29.	Nebraska	0.01
5.	Oklahoma	0.19		30.	Massachusetts	0.01
6.	Alabama	0.17		31.	Ohio	0.00
7.	Montana	0.15		32.	Iowa	0.00
8.	Texas	0.15		33.	Washington	0.00
9.	Missouri	0.14		34.	Oregon	−0.02
10.	Idaho	0.14		35.	West Virginia	−0.03
11.	Virginia	0.13		36.	Delaware	−0.03
12.	Georgia	0.11		37.	Wisconsin	−0.04
13.	Pennsylvania	0.11		38.	Rhode Island	−0.04
14.	Alaska	0.09		39.	Kansas	−0.04
15.	Louisiana	0.07		40.	New Jersey	−0.06
16.	North Dakota	0.06		41.	Mississippi	−0.06
17.	North Carolina	0.06		42.	New Mexico	−0.07
18.	Wyoming	0.06		43.	Minnesota	−0.13
19.	Arizona	0.06		44.	Maine	−0.13
20.	Colorado	0.06		45.	Connecticut	−0.13
21.	Michigan	0.05		46.	Vermont	−0.14
22.	Nevada	0.04		47.	California	−0.16
23.	Arkansas	0.04		48.	Illinois	−0.17
24.	South Carolina	0.04		49.	Hawaii	−0.34
25.	Utah	0.03		50.	New York	−0.53

Table 8 contains the fiscal policy ranking for 2012, using only publicly available data without projections.

REGULATORY POLICY

The regulatory policy dimension includes categories for land-use freedom and environmental policy, health insurance freedom, labor-market freedom, occupational freedom, lawsuit freedom, cable and telecommunications freedom, and miscellaneous regulations that do not fit under another category. Figure 4 shows the weights for health insurance policies now controlled by the federal government (7.4 percent) and for only those health insurance policies that states can still control after the Patient Protection and Affordable Care Act (PPACA) (2.8 percent), altogether summing to 10.2 percent of the index.

FIGURE 4 Regulatory Policy Weights

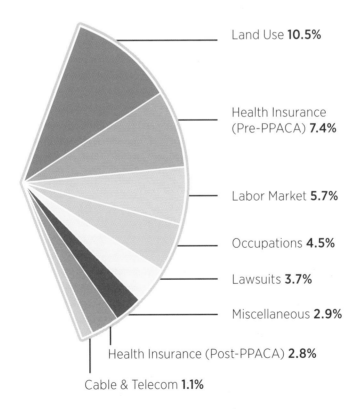

Land Use **10.5%**

Health Insurance
(Pre-PPACA) **7.4%**

Labor Market **5.7%**

Occupations **4.5%**

Lawsuits **3.7%**

Miscellaneous **2.9%**

Health Insurance (Post-PPACA) **2.8%**

Cable & Telecom **1.1%**

The calculated freedom scores do not allow weights to vary by year, even when variation across states disappears. In other words, the weights for all the variables have to add up to 100 percent for every year, even when a variable no longer contributes to differences across states because every state has the same policy. That happened when the PPACA passed, and states could no longer choose whether or not to have a community rating, guaranteed issue, and the individual mandate. As a result of our methodological choice, the data show the PPACA as a large negative shock to all states' regulatory policy. We take this approach to avoid variables' entering and leaving the data set at different years and variable weights' not summing to 100 percent.

Regulations that seem to have a mainly paternalistic justification are placed under the personal freedom dimension. They include laws such as private school and homeschool regulations and smoking bans.

To take into account the wider, unmeasured costs of insecure rights, this index increases the weights on variables representing policies encoded in state constitutions or the federal Constitution. It does so because the fact that a policy has been encoded within a constitution is prima facie evidence that the policy is widely considered to affect a "fundamental" freedom—a freedom with consequences for the security of the citizenry that extend beyond citizens under its immediate purview.

Within the regulatory policy dimension, the weights of certain variables are boosted as follows:

1. The victim cost/freedom value is multiplied by two if a closely related policy is encoded in the U.S. Constitution, or has been recognized by at least some courts as relating to a fundamental right. Examples of such policies include eminent domain reform, rent control, regulatory taking restrictions, and mandatory permission of political speech on private property, which we view as compelled speech implicating the First Amendment.

2. The victim cost/freedom value is multiplied by 1.5 if the policy is encoded in state constitutions but not the federal Constitution and has not otherwise been recognized judicially as a fundamental right. Right-to-work laws are the only such policies in the regulatory dimension.

We believe this sort of boost is necessary to capture the particular importance Americans have attached to certain fundamental freedoms, even if it necessarily involves an element of judgment. Freedoms are more fundamental the more widely people consider them part of their flourishing and autonomy, and policies potentially infringing on them are therefore subject to stricter judicial scrutiny than policies that would restrict freedoms that, although potentially valuable, are not as fundamental. By relying on existing judicial interpretations of fundamental[30] rights, the freedom index avoids at least one possible source of subjectivity as it "upgrades" these policies.

30. Legal Information Institute, "Fundamental Right," Cornell University Law School, August 19, 2010, http://www.law.cornell.edu/wex/fundamental_right.

LAND-USE FREEDOM AND ENVIRONMENTAL POLICY

10.5% The category for land-use freedom and environmental policy includes eminent domain rules, land-use regulations, renewable portfolio standards, and regulations requiring employers to let their employees bring guns onto company-owned parking lots. Most of its weight comes from three variables: local rent control laws (6.2 percent of the overall index) and two indices of residential land-use regulations, also known as zoning (together 3.3 percent of the index). One of the zoning indices comes from researchers at the Wharton School of Business and does not vary over time,[31] while the other comes from two economists at Harvard and does vary over time.[32] According to the best evidence, a one-standard-deviation increase in residential zoning restrictions would directly cost victims over $13 billion a year, if imposed nationwide.[33] Rather than impose such costs, states should allow property owners to solve most land-use externalities with various contractual arrangements, such as homeowners' associations, or at most what Dartmouth economist William Fischel calls "good housekeeping" zoning.[34]

Renewable portfolio standards (RPS), which mandate that power companies buy certain proportions of their energy from (usually) wind and solar sources, are worth 1.0 percent of the overall index. Our variable tracks the stringency of these requirements. The average RPS raises electricity prices by 0.8–0.9 percent, with bigger effects likely for more stringent programs.[35] To promote cleaner electricity generation, states could help limit pollution that creates significant, direct, negative externalities through means other than command-and-control regulations.

The remainder of this category takes into account whether compensation or an economic assessment is required before a regulatory taking, an index of eminent domain reform; whether companies must allow employees' guns on their property; and whether free speech is mandated on private property.

31. Joseph Gyourko, Albert Saiz, and Anita Summers, "A New Measure of the Local Regulatory Environment for Housing Markets: The Wharton Residential Land Use Regulatory Index," *Urban Studies* 45, no. 3 (2008): 693–729.

32. Peter Ganong, "Why Has Regional Income Convergence in the U.S. Stopped?" HKS Working Paper no. RWP12-028, Harvard Kennedy School, July 8, 2015, http://www.people.fas.harvard.edu/~ganong/motion.html.

33. Edward L. Glaeser, Joseph Gyourko, and Raven Saks, "Why Is Manhattan So Expensive? Regulation and the Rise in Housing Prices," *Journal of Law and Economics* 48, no. 2 (2005): 331–69; Stephen Malpezzi, "Housing Prices, Externalities, and Regulation in US Metropolitan Areas," *Journal of Housing Research* 7, no. 2 (1996): 209–41.

34. William A. Fischel, *Zoning Rules!* (Cambridge, MA: Lincoln Institute of Land Policy, 2015).

35. Cliff Chen, Ryan Riser, and Mark Bolinger, "Weighing the Costs and Benefits of State Renewables Portfolio Standards in the United States: A Comparative Analysis of State-Level Policy Impact Projections," *Renewable & Sustainable Energy Reviews* 13, no. 3 (2009): 552–66; J. Heeter et al., "A Survey of State-Level Cost and Benefit Estimates of Renewable Portfolio Standards," technical report, National Renewable Energy Laboratory, Golden, CO, May 2014.

(The federal courts require compensation for regulatory takings only when they destroy the value of the affected land; therefore, states were coded only for having protections stronger than the federal one.) It may surprise readers that eminent domain reform comprises only 0.1 percent of the freedom index, given that it affects a fundamental right, and given how salient the issue was—especially among property rights advocates—following the Supreme Court's *Kelo* decision.[36] However, the estimated victim cost of eminent domain abuse is relatively low, at roughly $754 million a year ($377 million without the "constitutional weight" boost), though admittedly this may underestimate losses due to insecurity of tenure, attorneys' fees, opportunity costs of legal challenges, and so on.[37] It is worth noting that most states that have reformed eminent domain have kept open a wide "blight loophole" that could still allow public takings for private interests. Therefore, the eminent domain index has been coded to take blight reform into account, as well as the incorporation of eminent domain restrictions into the state constitution.

Both of the final two variables have to do with property rights. We hold that businesses may permissibly require employees to leave guns at home, just as we defend the right of malls and community associations to prohibit any or all political messages. That view might perplex some gun rights advocates. However, the only consistent property rights–respecting position is that gun rights stop at the boundary of someone else's property; to think otherwise is to impose one's own view on another without his consent. Although symbolically significant, however, these policies do not generally cause severe inconvenience to their victims and therefore are not worth much in the index.

36. See *Kelo v. City of New London*, 545 U.S. 469 (2005).

37. "Building Empires, Destroying Homes: Eminent Domain Abuse in New York," Institute for Justice, October 2009, http://www.ij.org/images/pdf_folder/other_pubs/buildingempires.pdf.

TABLE 9

| | | Land-Use Freedom and Environmental | | | | |
Rank	State	Policy Ranking		Rank	State	
1.	Louisiana	0.06		26.	Virginia	0.03
2.	Alabama	0.05		27.	Idaho	0.02
3.	Indiana	0.05		28.	Nevada	0.02
4.	Mississippi	0.05		29.	Wisconsin	0.02
5.	Arkansas	0.05		30.	Michigan	0.02
6.	Oklahoma	0.05		31.	Pennsylvania	0.02
7.	Tennessee	0.04		32.	Arizona	0.02
8.	Iowa	0.04		33.	New Mexico	0.01
9.	Missouri	0.04		34.	Montana	0.01
10.	Nebraska	0.04		35.	Colorado	0.00
11.	Florida	0.04		36.	Minnesota	0.00
12.	Kansas	0.04		37.	Oregon	0.00
13.	Texas	0.04		38.	Delaware	−0.01
14.	South Dakota	0.04		39.	Vermont	−0.01
15.	North Dakota	0.04		40.	Massachusetts	−0.02
16.	Kentucky	0.04		41.	Washington	−0.02
17.	West Virginia	0.04		42.	Rhode Island	−0.05
18.	South Carolina	0.04		43.	Connecticut	−0.05
19.	Georgia	0.04		44.	Hawaii	−0.06
20.	Ohio	0.04		45.	New Hampshire	−0.07
21.	North Carolina	0.03		46.	Maine	−0.15
22.	Alaska	0.03		47.	New York	−0.20
23.	Wyoming	0.03		48.	California	−0.23
24.	Illinois	0.03		49.	Maryland	−0.25
25.	Utah	0.03		50.	New Jersey	−0.26

HEALTH INSURANCE FREEDOM

7.4%　The PPACA (Obamacare) nationalized most health insurance regulation. We treat such nationalizations, as have also occurred in a pro-freedom direction on certain gun laws, as changes in state policies. This choice allows us to compare the state of freedom over time, using the same policies. We do the same thing with sodomy laws, which have also been nationalized (in a pro-freedom direction).

All states are now required to have small-group adjusted community rating (2.7 percent of the index), individual market-adjusted community rating (0.5 percent), individual market-guaranteed issue (0.7 percent), bans on elimination riders (<0.1 percent), mandated external review of grievances (<0.1 percent), the individual health insurance mandate (2.7 percent), small-group prior approval of rates (0.6 percent), and nongroup prior approval of rates (0.1 percent) and are forbidden from offering mandate-free or mandate-light plans (<0.1 percent). States are still able to vary somewhat on the extent of mandated benefits (2.4 percent), standing referrals to specialists (<0.1 percent), direct access to specialists (0.4 percent), and bans on financial incentives to providers from insurers (<0.1 percent).

Community rating and the individual mandate get the highest weights because they represent a large transfer of wealth from the healthy to the unhealthy, approximately $10 billion a year.[38] State-level mandated coverages raise premium costs for consumers. Unfortunately, data on these policies are not available after 2010, because the organization that produced them, the Council for Affordable Health Insurance, has folded. The HMO regulations have low victim costs because public backlash against particular practices, such as financial incentives to providers, drove them from the marketplace even before laws were passed.[39] In this case, public opinion drove both market practice and state law. Nevertheless, research suggests that public opinion on this issue may be misinformed. In their heyday in the 1990s, when many of the now widely banned practices were widespread, HMOs successfully suppressed health care costs.[40]

---

38. These numbers are derived from estimates in Mark V. Pauly and Bradley Herring, "Risk Pooling and Regulation: Policy and Reality in Today's Individual Health Insurance Market," *Health Affairs* 26, no. 3 (2007): 770–79.

39. Mark A. Hall, "The Death of Managed Care: A Regulatory Autopsy," *Journal of Health Politics, Policy, and Law* 30, no. 3 (2005): 427–52.

40. Maxim L. Pinkovskiy, "The Impact of the Managed Care Backlash on Health Care Costs: Evidence from State Regulation of Managed Care Cost Containment Practices," November 13, 2012, http://economics.mit.edu/files/8448.

TABLE 10

Rank	State	Health Insurance Freedom Ranking		Rank	State	Health Insurance Freedom Ranking
1.	Idaho	−0.021		26.	Vermont	−0.086
2.	Michigan	−0.028		27.	Kansas	−0.086
3.	Delaware	−0.041		28.	Oregon	−0.088
4.	Utah	−0.044		29.	Maine	−0.091
5.	Alabama	−0.049		30.	Kentucky	−0.092
6.	Wyoming	−0.054		31.	Massachusetts	−0.094
7.	South Dakota	−0.054		32.	Georgia	−0.095
8.	Hawaii	−0.054		33.	Pennsylvania	−0.095
9.	South Carolina	−0.055		34.	North Carolina	−0.096
10.	Iowa	−0.056		35.	New Jersey	−0.096
11.	Indiana	−0.058		36.	Missouri	−0.100
12.	Mississippi	−0.059		37.	Arkansas	−0.100
13.	Ohio	−0.064		38.	Louisiana	−0.102
14.	Oklahoma	−0.070		39.	California	−0.102
15.	Florida	−0.071		40.	Nebraska	−0.106
16.	Nevada	−0.075		41.	Minnesota	−0.112
17.	Tennessee	−0.076		42.	Washington	−0.116
18.	Arizona	−0.078		43.	New Mexico	−0.117
19.	Alaska	−0.078		44.	Virginia	−0.117
20.	North Dakota	−0.081		45.	Maryland	−0.120
21.	New Hampshire	−0.082		46.	New York	−0.122
22.	Montana	−0.082		47.	Colorado	−0.125
23.	Wisconsin	−0.083		48.	Rhode Island	−0.125
24.	Illinois	−0.085		49.	Connecticut	−0.127
25.	West Virginia	−0.086		50.	Texas	−0.131

LABOR-MARKET FREEDOM

5.7% Right-to-work laws make up nearly half of the labor regulation category and nearly 3 percent of the entire freedom index. They are valued at over $10 billion a year.[41] Right-to-work laws are controversial among libertarians because they override collective-bargaining contracts reached between employers and employee unions, allowing employers to hire workers who do not pay agency fees to a union. On the other hand, right-to-work laws can be justified as a means of employer and employee self-defense against the mechanisms of the Wagner Act (the National Labor Relations Act), which essentially allows an "agency shop" to form if a majority of workers votes in favor.

From the libertarian point of view, the Wagner Act violates the fundamental freedom of association and basic property rights, and right-to-work laws somewhat restore those freedoms, since few employers would voluntarily agree to an agency shop in the absence of the Wagner Act. Although right-to-work laws violate the rights of some workers and employers, they restore freedom of association to a far greater number. In an ideal world, both the National Labor Relations Act and right-to-work laws would be repealed, and employees and employers would be free to negotiate as they saw fit, collectively or individually.

For those who disagree with our logic, we have for the first time produced alternative indices to the freedom index that exclude right-to-work laws. See Appendix B.

Other policy variables in this category, in descending order of importance, are short-term disability insurance requirements (costs being lower labor productivity[42] and administrative expenses for businesses[43]), policies dealing with workers' compensation (funding mechanisms and mandated coverages), state minimum-wage laws (figures adjusted for median private wages), requirements for employer verification of legal resident status, stricter-than-federal private employment discrimination laws (smoker status, marital status, age, etc.), and mandated paid family leave.

---

41. Steven E. Abraham and Paula B. Voos, "Right-to-Work Laws: New Evidence from the Stock Market," *Southern Economic Journal* 67, no. 2 (2000): 345–62; David T. Ellwood and Glenn Fine, "The Impact of Right-to-Work Laws on Union Organizing," *Journal of Political Economy* 95, no. 2 (1987): 250–73; William J. Moore, "The Determinants and Effects of Right-to-Work Laws: A Review of the Recent Literature," *Journal of Labor Research* 19, no. 3 (1998): 445–69; Robert Krol and Shirley Svorny, "Unions and Employment Growth: Evidence from State Economic Recoveries," *Journal of Labor Research* 28, no. 3 (2007): 525–35.

42. John Bound et al., "The Welfare Implications of Increasing Disability Insurance Benefit Generosity," *Journal of Public Economics* 88, no. 12 (2004): 2487–514.

43. In other words, the funding mechanism (taxation) does not count here; it counts as part of the tax burden.

TABLE II

Rank	State	Labor-Market Freedom Ranking		Rank	State	Labor-Market Freedom Ranking
1.	Texas	0.061		26.	Maine	−0.015
2.	Tennessee	0.051		27.	Missouri	−0.017
3.	Georgia	0.047		28.	New Mexico	−0.019
4.	Virginia	0.047		29.	New Hampshire	−0.020
5.	North Carolina	0.047		30.	Minnesota	−0.020
6.	Arkansas	0.045		31.	Pennsylvania	−0.020
7.	Indiana	0.043		32.	Kentucky	−0.020
8.	Iowa	0.043		33.	Illinois	−0.021
9.	Kansas	0.043		34.	Delaware	−0.021
10.	Alabama	0.043		35.	Massachusetts	−0.025
11.	Mississippi	0.043		36.	Maryland	−0.028
12.	Oklahoma	0.043		37.	Colorado	−0.029
13.	Florida	0.042		38.	Vermont	−0.029
14.	Nevada	0.038		39.	Alaska	−0.031
15.	Michigan	0.038		40.	Connecticut	−0.032
16.	Nebraska	0.037		41.	West Virginia	−0.033
17.	Utah	0.036		42.	Montana	−0.036
18.	Louisiana	0.035		43.	Ohio	−0.042
19.	South Carolina	0.034		44.	Oregon	−0.045
20.	South Dakota	0.033		45.	Washington	−0.047
21.	Idaho	0.029		46.	New York	−0.059
22.	North Dakota	0.019		47.	New Jersey	−0.061
23.	Wyoming	0.012		48.	Hawaii	−0.065
24.	Arizona	0.012		49.	Rhode Island	−0.068
25.	Wisconsin	−0.009		50.	California	−0.075

OCCUPATIONAL FREEDOM

4.5% Occupational licensing is difficult to measure. Some of the literature uses listings of licensed occupations by state at America's Career InfoNet,[44] but we have found those listings to be highly unreliable, often excluding certain licensed occupations or including others that are privately certified, not regulated by the government. We use three redundant measures of the prevalence of licensure to reduce measurement error.

Our first measure of licensure prevalence is a weighted sum for 64 occupations, where each occupation's weight is its proportion of the total employment in these 64 occupations. Our second measure is a simple count of the number of licensed occupations within a set reported in *Book of the States* for various years.[45] A third measure is available only for 2014 and is carried back to other years. It counts the number of mentions of certain phrases in each state's statutes, such as "shall not practice." We do find that these three variables correlate together modestly *(0.2<r<0.3)* in 2014, with the first measure looking to be the most reliable one. The three variables together are worth about 2.4 percent of the index, apportioned half to the first, most reliable measure and one-quarter each to the other two.

The "intensity" of licensure is measured by three variables from the Institute for Justice's study *License to Work:* the sum of educational, examination, and fee requirements for all coded occupations.[46] Those variables do not vary over time. Together, they are worth 0.9 percent of the index. The direct victim cost of a nationwide, one-standard-deviation increase in occupational licensing education or experience requirements in just the occupations tracked by this index would be worth about $2.6 billion a year. A similar change in examination requirements would be worth about $0.9 billion a year. Licensing fees also constitute a small portion of occupational regulation costs.

We also include sunrise and sunset provisions for occupational licensing, but because of a lack of evidence regarding their effectiveness, they are worth less than 0.1 percent of the index. ("Sunrise" refers to independent review requirements before a new licensing board is created; "sunset" refers to automatic expiration of licensing boards after several years so that the legislature must reauthorize them.)

---

44. For instance, Morris M. Kleiner and Alan B. Krueger, "The Prevalence and Effects of Occupational Licensing," *British Journal of Industrial Relations* 48, no. 4 (2010): 676–87.

45. *The Book of the States* (Lexington, KY: Council of State Governments, various years).

46. Dick M. Carpenter et al., *License to Work: A National Study of Burdens from Occupational Licensing* (Arlington, VA: Institute for Justice, 2012).

The remaining occupational freedom variables have to do with medical scope of practice. Nurse practitioner scope of practice is the most important, making up 0.9 percent of the index. Dental hygienist independent practice is worth 0.1 percent of the index, followed by three more minor variables: (a) membership in the Nurse Licensure Compact, (b) nursing consultation exception, and (c) physician assistant prescription authority.

TABLE 12

Rank	State	Occupational Freedom Ranking	Rank	State	Occupational Freedom Ranking
1.	Idaho	0.039	26.	Michigan	−0.007
2.	Colorado	0.038	27.	Washington	−0.007
3.	Wyoming	0.035	28.	New Mexico	−0.007
4.	Minnesota	0.023	29.	Wisconsin	−0.008
5.	Vermont	0.021	30.	Hawaii	−0.009
6.	Kansas	0.020	31.	Georgia	−0.009
7.	Maine	0.020	32.	New Jersey	−0.010
8.	New Hampshire	0.017	33.	West Virginia	−0.011
9.	Rhode Island	0.016	34.	Delaware	−0.011
10.	Missouri	0.015	35.	Utah	−0.012
11.	Pennsylvania	0.014	36.	Ohio	−0.014
12.	Alaska	0.010	37.	North Carolina	−0.020
13.	Montana	0.009	38.	Arizona	−0.020
14.	North Dakota	0.007	39.	South Carolina	−0.021
15.	Nebraska	0.006	40.	Virginia	−0.021
16.	Massachusetts	0.005	41.	Illinois	−0.027
17.	South Dakota	0.003	42.	Tennessee	−0.028
18.	Indiana	0.001	43.	Oregon	−0.029
19.	Iowa	0.001	44.	Louisiana	−0.031
20.	Mississippi	−0.001	45.	Nevada	−0.036
21.	Alabama	−0.001	46.	Texas	−0.037
22.	Oklahoma	−0.002	47.	Florida	−0.037
23.	Connecticut	−0.002	48.	Arkansas	−0.038
24.	Kentucky	−0.003	49.	Maryland	−0.043
25.	New York	−0.007	50.	California	−0.053

LAWSUIT FREEDOM

3.7%   Deciding tort claims among private parties is an important function of a decentralized legal system that provides justice to victims of the unjust, harmful acts of others. In an efficient civil liability system, the costs that defendants have to pay are merely compensation for wrongs and not a limitation on their freedom. Moreover, the liability insurance costs that businesses have to pay reflect, in an efficient system, the likelihood that they will impose harms on others.

In practice, however, the United States' civil liability system imposes vastly higher costs on everyone than every other developed country's system. [47] Moreover, the costs of the system vary widely by state. In fact, it is more appropriate to think of there being 50 separate civil liability systems in the United States than one national system, and "bad" state systems can impose significant costs above those necessary to remedy wrongs. That is especially the case when defendants are from another state. [48]

The civil liability index captures risks and costs to property and contract freedoms that businesses must pass on to consumers as higher prices. Unfortunately for consumers—and that means everyone—tort abuse's overall cost to the economy is quite high. In fact, according to policy analysts Lawrence J. McQuillan, Hovannes Abramyan, and Anthony P. Archie, the nationwide "tort tax" amounts to $328 billion annually in direct costs and $537 billion annually in indirect costs. [49] Not all of those indirect costs are relevant to this variable in our index: administration costs show up in state spending and taxation, and the costs of lost innovation (42 percent of all tort costs according to McQuillan, Abramyan, and Archie) seem too higher-order to be included here. That is consistent with our overall approach, since we do not include the cost of economic growth forgone for any other variable.

One of the most significant improvements to the index that we have made in this edition has to do with state civil liability systems. The freedom index includes a single variable, an index of how plaintiff-friendly each state's civil liability system is, which depends in turn upon eight variables. We use principal component analysis to find the common variance among each of them: (a) ratings of lawsuit climate by businesses (previously the only variable used), [50] (b) partisan elections for the supreme court, (c) partisan elections

47. For a good overview, see the contributions to F. H. Buckley, ed., *The American Illness: Essays on the Rule of Law* (New Haven, CT: Yale University Press, 2013).

48. For evidence, see Alexander Tabarrok and Eric Helland, "Court Politics: The Political Economy of Tort Awards," *Journal of Law and Economics* 42, no. 1 (1999): 157–88.

49. Lawrence J. McQuillan, Hovannes Abramyan, and Anthony P. Archie, *Jackpot Justice: The True Cost of America's Tort System* (San Francisco: Pacific Research Institute, 2007).

50. See Institute for Legal Reform, "Ranking the States: Lawsuit Climate 2010," U.S. Chamber of Commerce, https://www.uschamber.com/sites/default/files/documents/files/2010LawsuitClimateReport.pdf. New reports can be found at http://www.instituteforlegalreform.com/states.

for trial courts, (d) lawyer concentration index, (e) legal services share of GDP, (f) blanket punitive or noneconomic damages cap, (g) burden of proof for conduct justifying punitive damages, and (h) joint and several liability abolition.

Even though the U.S. tort system is largely at the state level, certain nationwide features affect the tort environment in every state. Even the "best" state will have a "tort tax" of some kind. Moreover, a state's poor tort environment affects out-of-state defendants, creating an interjurisdictional externality. [51] Nevertheless, Crain et al. find that adopting all recommended tort reforms could reduce a state's tort losses by 49 percent and annual insurance premiums by 16 percent. [52] Using an econometric model of insurance costs and tort system perceptions, Hinton, McKnight, and Miller find a potential reduction in tort costs ranging from $20 million in Vermont to $5.3 billion in California, due to comprehensive tort reform. [53] We use their estimates to come up with an estimate of how nationwide tort reform amounting to a standard-deviation change on our variable would affect liability insurance premiums. Then, we divide by 0.55 to take into account deadweight loss and costs of legal representation, which are 45 percent of the tort tax (excluding administration and lost innovation costs) according to McQuillan, Abramyan, and Archie.

51. Tabarrok and Helland, "Court Politics."

52. Nicole V. Crain et al., "Tort Law Tally: How State Tort Reforms Affect Tort Losses and Tort Insurance Premiums," Pacific Research Institute, San Francisco, April 2009.

53. Paul J. Hinton, David McKnight, and Ronald I. Miller, "Determinants of State Tort Costs: The Predictive Power of the Harris State Liability Systems Ranking Study," NERA Economic Consulting, White Plains, NY, October 2012.

TABLE 13

Rank	State	Lawsuit Freedom Ranking
1.	Nebraska	0.076
2.	New Hampshire	0.066
3.	North Dakota	0.063
4.	Alaska	0.058
5.	Colorado	0.044
6.	Idaho	0.043
7.	Kansas	0.038
8.	Wisconsin	0.038
9.	South Carolina	0.036
10.	Wyoming	0.035
11.	Arizona	0.035
12.	Iowa	0.032
13.	South Dakota	0.032
14.	New Jersey	0.030
15.	Oklahoma	0.029
16.	Mississippi	0.025
17.	Indiana	0.025
18.	Utah	0.023
19.	Hawaii	0.023
20.	Tennessee	0.022
21.	Oregon	0.021
22.	Nevada	0.019
23.	Arkansas	0.018
24.	Maine	0.017
25.	Montana	0.016
26.	Florida	0.013
27.	Georgia	0.011
28.	Kentucky	0.010
29.	Virginia	0.009
30.	Minnesota	0.009
31.	California	0.006
32.	Maryland	0.006
33.	Washington	0.002
34.	Vermont	−0.001
35.	Delaware	−0.003
36.	Missouri	−0.006
37.	Connecticut	−0.007
38.	Rhode Island	−0.011
39.	North Carolina	−0.013
40.	Massachusetts	−0.016
41.	Ohio	−0.019
42.	Michigan	−0.026
43.	Texas	−0.030
44.	New Mexico	−0.045
45.	Alabama	−0.049
46.	Pennsylvania	−0.059
47.	New York	−0.068
48.	Louisiana	−0.069
49.	West Virginia	−0.070
50.	Illinois	−0.077

MISCELLANEOUS REGULATORY FREEDOM

2.9% Miscellaneous regulations include, in declining order of importance, certificate-of-need requirements for new hospital construction, auto insurance rate filing requirements, homeowner's insurance rate filing requirements, price-gouging laws, general unfair-pricing and sales-below-cost laws, rate classification prohibitions for some classes of insurance, membership in the Interstate Insurance Product Regulation Compact, life insurance form-filing requirements, direct-to-consumer auto sales, minimum-markup and sales-below-cost laws for gasoline, workers' comp insurance rate filing requirements, moving company entry regulations, and mandatory product labeling laws.

Certificate-of-need regulations land their first-place slot in this category on the basis of the over $3 billion in extra costs they impose on hospitals, customers, and potential market entrants.[54] Next come state personal auto insurance rate-filing requirements. These regimes range from Massachusetts's old "fixed and established" system (scrapped in 2008)—in which all car insurance premiums were dictated by law—to no rate-filing requirement whatsoever in Wyoming. A one-standard-deviation change on this −1 to 4 scale, about 1.2 points, would be worth $2 billion nationwide. The main problem with strict rate regulation regimes is that they encourage insurers to stop insuring some drivers altogether, forcing those drivers to find coverage in a state-guaranteed, "residual" market. [55]

Homeowner's insurance rate-filing regulations range from "prior approval" to "no file." A one-standard-deviation shift on this variable would be worth $1.3 billion nationwide. The other insurance variables matter quite a bit less. Although states do not regulate life insurance and annuity rates, they do regulate forms, that is, the nature of products and customer disclosures. The Interstate Insurance Product Regulation Compact makes it easier to sell the same life insurance policy or annuity across state lines. Some states do not require prior approval of life insurance forms before companies begin selling them. Prohibitions on the use of certain criteria for insurance rating purposes, such as age, gender, territory, and credit rating, redistribute wealth from low risks to high risks and drive some consumers out of the market altogether.

---

54. Christopher J. Conover and Frank A. Sloan, "Does Removing Certificate-of-Need Regulations Lead to a Surge in Health Care Spending?" *Journal of Health Politics, Policy, and Law* 23, no. 3 (1998): 455–81; Jon M. Ford and David L. Kaserman, "Certificate-of-Need Regulation and Entry: Evidence from the Dialysis Industry," *Southern Economic Journal* 59, no. 4 (1993): 783–91; Patrick A. Rivers, Myron D. Fottler, and Mustafa Zeedan Younis, "Does Certificate of Need Really Contain Hospital Costs in the United States?" *Health Education Journal* 66, no. 3 (2007): 229–44.

55. Scott E. Harrington and Helen I. Doerpinghaus, "The Economics and Politics of Automobile Insurance Rate Classification," *Journal of Risk and Insurance* 60, no. 1 (1993): 59–84.

Price-gouging laws, which have gained in popularity recently, try to repeal the laws of supply and demand. They impose price controls on necessary products after disasters, making them even scarcer by disincentivizing supply and incentivizing demand. [56] According to David Montgomery, Robert Baron, and Mary Weisskopf, a price-gouging law on gasoline could be expected to reduce economic welfare by at least $1.9 billion in the wake of a major disaster on the scale of Hurricanes Rita and Katrina.[57]

TABLE 14

Rank	State	Misc. Regulatory Freedom Ranking	Rank	State	Misc. Regulatory Freedom Ranking
1.	Wyoming	0.034	26.	New York	−0.001
2.	Idaho	0.028	27.	California	−0.002
3.	Utah	0.027	28.	Maryland	−0.002
4.	Arizona	0.024	29.	Montana	−0.004
5.	New Mexico	0.023	30.	Michigan	−0.004
6.	Texas	0.023	31.	Louisiana	−0.004
7.	Indiana	0.022	32.	Maine	−0.004
8.	North Dakota	0.022	33.	Pennsylvania	−0.004
9.	Minnesota	0.020	34.	Rhode Island	−0.005
10.	Wisconsin	0.019	35.	Nevada	−0.006
11.	Kansas	0.018	36.	Kentucky	−0.006
12.	Colorado	0.017	37.	Arkansas	−0.007
13.	South Dakota	0.016	38.	Alabama	−0.010
14.	Illinois	0.011	39.	Mississippi	−0.010
15.	Ohio	0.009	40.	Tennessee	−0.011
16.	New Hampshire	0.008	41.	Delaware	−0.011
17.	Vermont	0.008	42.	Hawaii	−0.012
18.	Nebraska	0.005	43.	New Jersey	−0.013
19.	Missouri	0.004	44.	Massachusetts	−0.013
20.	Georgia	0.004	45.	Washington	−0.014
21.	Oregon	0.003	46.	South Carolina	−0.014
22.	Alaska	0.001	47.	Florida	−0.015
23.	Oklahoma	0.001	48.	Connecticut	−0.016
24.	Iowa	0.000	49.	West Virginia	−0.019
25.	Virginia	0.000	50.	North Carolina	−0.019

56. Michael Giberson, "The Problem with Price Gouging Laws," *Regulation*, Spring 2011, pp. 48–53.

57. W. David Montgomery, Robert A. Baron, and Mary K. Weisskopf, "Potential Effects of Proposed Price Gouging Legislation on the Cost and Severity of Gasoline Supply Interruptions," *Journal of Competition Law and Economics* 3, no. 3 (2007): 357–97.

CABLE AND TELECOM FREEDOM

1.1% The least important category in the regulatory policy dimension is cable and telecommunications market freedom. It is important to note that they are the only public utility regulation areas included in the freedom index, because some utility "deregulation" is not truly deregulatory, as in the case of procompetitive "reregulation" that has restructured the electricity and natural gas markets in certain states. Although these services are important for household budgets, it is not at all clear that "deregulation" results in a net increase in individual freedom. The utilities are all characterized by physical connections to the consumer. Because of the monopoly element in transmission (parallel connections are judged infeasible), even under deregulation, governments maintain "common carrier" regulations that require the regulated owner of the transmission grid to allow open access to competing providers at a regulated price. The transmission grid then becomes a commons with no profit incentive for the owner to expand, upgrade, or maintain the network. In many cases, retail competition is tightly managed by state governments to prevent anticompetitive manipulation of the market. For those reasons, many analysts insist on the term "restructuring" as opposed to "deregulation" for these industries. [58]

Telecommunications deregulation accounts for roughly two-thirds of the weight for this category, and the remainder is accounted for by statewide cable franchising, which eases the entry of telecom firms into the video cable market. [59]

---

58. Peter Van Doren and Jerry Taylor, "Rethinking Electricity Restructuring," Cato Institute Policy Analysis no. 530, November 30, 2004, http://www.cato.org/pub_display.php?pub_id=2609.

59. Adam Summers, "Cable Franchise Reform: Deregulation or Just New Regulators?" *Freeman* 57, no. 3 (2007): 31–34; Cecil Bohanon and Michael Hicks, "Statewide Cable Franchising and Broadband Connections," Digital Policy Institute, Ball State University, Muncie, IN, 2010.

TABLE 15

Rank	State	Cable and Telecom Freedom Ranking	Rank	State	Cable and Telecom Freedom Ranking
1.	Arkansas	0.013	23.	Kentucky	0.005
1.	California	0.013	23.	Maine	0.005
1.	Florida	0.013	23.	Massachusetts	0.005
1.	Georgia	0.013	23.	Mississippi	0.005
1.	Idaho	0.013	23.	Montana	0.005
1.	Illinois	0.013	23.	Nebraska	0.005
1.	Indiana	0.013	23.	New Hampshire	0.005
1.	Iowa	0.013	23.	New Mexico	0.005
1.	Kansas	0.013	23.	North Dakota	0.005
1.	Louisiana	0.013	23.	Oklahoma	0.005
1.	Michigan	0.013	23.	Oregon	0.005
1.	Missouri	0.013	23.	Pennsylvania	0.005
1.	Nevada	0.013	23.	South Dakota	0.005
1.	North Carolina	0.013	23.	Utah	0.005
1.	Ohio	0.013	23.	Wyoming	0.005
1.	Rhode Island	0.013	41.	Alaska	−0.001
1.	South Carolina	0.013	41.	Connecticut	−0.001
1.	Tennessee	0.013	41.	Hawaii	−0.001
1.	Texas	0.013	41.	New Jersey	−0.001
1.	Vermont	0.013	45.	Arizona	−0.009
1.	Virginia	0.013	45.	Maryland	−0.009
1.	Wisconsin	0.013	45.	Minnesota	−0.009
23.	Alabama	0.005	45.	New York	−0.009
23.	Colorado	0.005	45.	Washington	−0.009
23.	Delaware	0.005	45.	West Virginia	−0.009

38.7% As with fiscal policy, there is a correlation between the overall regulatory policy ranking and state ideology, but it is weaker. States that rank highest on regulatory policy are mostly conservative, but they tilt toward midwestern more than southern. In general, they are "good-government" states that score well on variables such as the liability system variable. As the "Politics of Freedom" chapter will show, regulatory policy is the most important policy variable for explaining economic growth in the states. Although it is worth only about 25 percent more than fiscal policy in the index, it is far more important for explaining economic growth patterns across the states over almost every time period we examine.

We validate our regulatory policy measure by examining its correlation to small businesses' ratings of their states' regulatory environments. Thumbtack.com conducts an annual survey of independent businesses in each state, funded by the Kauffman Foundation.[60] We average each state's rank out of 45 for 2012, 2013, and 2014 (5 states lack data). Smaller numbers are better, indicating a higher rank. The correlation between the 2014 regulatory index score and the Thumbtack.com regulatory survey rank is −0.67, a strong negative correlation that suggests that our index captures most of what small businesses think about when it comes to regulations that affect their business.

Figure 5 shows how average regulatory policy has changed over time. Again, the big drop in 2012 is due to the PPACA.

FIGURE 5 State Average Regulatory Policy Scores over Time

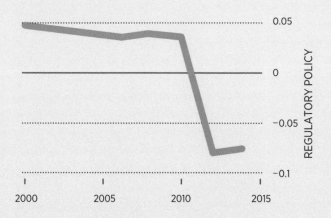

60. The survey is available at https://www.thumbtack.com/survey#/2015/1/states.

TABLE 16

Rank	State	Overall Regulatory Policy Ranking		Rank	State	Overall Regulatory Policy Ranking
1.	Idaho	0.15		26.	North Carolina	−0.05
2.	Indiana	0.10		27.	Texas	−0.06
3.	Wyoming	0.10		28.	Kentucky	−0.07
4.	Kansas	0.09		29.	New Hampshire	−0.08
5.	Iowa	0.08		30.	Montana	−0.08
6.	North Dakota	0.08		31.	Ohio	−0.08
7.	South Dakota	0.08		32.	Vermont	−0.08
8.	Nebraska	0.07		33.	Delaware	−0.09
9.	Utah	0.06		34.	Minnesota	−0.09
10.	Oklahoma	0.05		35.	Louisiana	−0.10
11.	Mississippi	0.05		36.	Oregon	−0.14
12.	South Carolina	0.03		37.	Pennsylvania	−0.14
13.	Tennessee	0.02		38.	New Mexico	−0.15
14.	Georgia	0.01		39.	Massachusetts	−0.15
15.	Michigan	0.01		40.	Illinois	−0.16
16.	Alabama	−0.01		41.	Hawaii	−0.18
17.	Wisconsin	−0.01		42.	West Virginia	−0.19
18.	Alaska	−0.01		43.	Washington	−0.21
19.	Florida	−0.01		44.	Maine	−0.22
20.	Arizona	−0.02		45.	Rhode Island	−0.23
21.	Arkansas	−0.02		46.	Connecticut	−0.24
22.	Nevada	−0.03		47.	New Jersey	−0.41
23.	Virginia	−0.04		48.	California	−0.44
24.	Missouri	−0.05		49.	Maryland	−0.45
25.	Colorado	−0.05		50.	New York	−0.47

Although we believe that a composite freedom index that includes both economic and personal freedom is most valuable and best represents the actual state of freedom in the states, readers may wish to compare and contrast the states solely by their overall economic freedom, particularly for empirical analysis of income growth. We invite researchers to use the economic freedom variable as a tool to investigate income growth and related phenomena. Economic freedom is calculated as the sum of the fiscal and regulatory freedom indices. Here, we use the 2014 fiscal policy projections.

We validate our economic freedom index by correlating it to state scores for taxes and regulations as rated by chief executives of for-profit companies for *Chief Executive* magazine.[61] We use the average scores for 2013 and 2014 for all 50 states. The correlation between our economic freedom index and the chief executives' ratings is 0.85, indicating an extremely strong relationship between what we measure as economic freedom and what entrepreneurs are concerned about when it comes to state policy. [62]

Figure 6 shows the evolution of state average economic freedom over time. Despite some improvements in 2007–8 and 2013–14, the overall trend in economic freedom is negative, especially because of the PPACA's coming into force in 2011–12.

FIGURE 6 State Average Economic Freedom Scores over Time

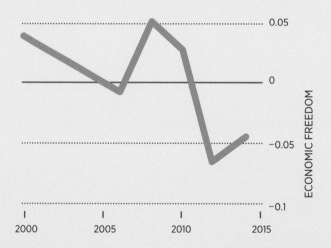

61. The rankings are announced on *Chief Executive's* website, http//chiefexecutive.net, but are no longer available.

62. We also correlated chief executives' ratings to the Economic Freedom of North America (EFNA) index, as measured in 2012 (latest available year) for the subnational level. That correlation is 0.67, which is strong but not as strong as the correlation between our index and chief executives' ratings. EFNA also has a weaker correlation with the Thumbtack.com survey results than our index. EFNA and our economic freedom index correlate at a moderately strong 0.59.

TABLE 17

Rank	State	Overall Economic Freedom Ranking		Rank	State	Overall Economic Freedom Ranking
1.	South Dakota	0.35		26.	Nevada	0.01
2.	Idaho	0.31		27.	Colorado	0.00
3.	Tennessee	0.30		28.	Mississippi	−0.01
4.	Oklahoma	0.25		29.	Wisconsin	−0.02
5.	New Hampshire	0.22		30.	Pennsylvania	−0.02
6.	Florida	0.22		31.	Louisiana	−0.03
7.	Alaska	0.19		32.	Kentucky	−0.04
8.	North Dakota	0.17		33.	Ohio	−0.05
9.	Alabama	0.17		34.	Delaware	−0.07
10.	Wyoming	0.15		35.	Massachusetts	−0.16
11.	Indiana	0.13		36.	West Virginia	−0.17
12.	Georgia	0.12		37.	Oregon	−0.17
13.	Utah	0.12		38.	Washington	−0.21
14.	Missouri	0.11		39.	New Mexico	−0.22
15.	Virginia	0.10		40.	Minnesota	−0.23
16.	Iowa	0.10		41.	Vermont	−0.23
17.	Arizona	0.10		42.	Rhode Island	−0.25
18.	Kansas	0.09		43.	Maine	−0.31
19.	Texas	0.09		44.	Illinois	−0.32
20.	South Carolina	0.08		45.	Connecticut	−0.35
21.	Montana	0.08		46.	Maryland	−0.45
22.	Michigan	0.08		47.	New Jersey	−0.47
23.	Nebraska	0.07		48.	Hawaii	−0.48
24.	North Carolina	0.04		49.	California	−0.59
25.	Arkansas	0.01		50.	New York	−1.00

PERSONAL FREEDOM

The personal freedom versus paternalism dimension consists of the following categories: (a) incarceration and arrests for victimless crimes, (b) marriage freedom, (c) educational freedom, (d) gun rights, (e) alcohol freedom, (f) cannabis freedom, (g) gaming freedom, (h) asset forfeiture, (i) tobacco freedom, (j) travel freedom, (k) campaign finance freedom, and (l) other mala prohibita and miscellaneous civil liberties. Weighting these categories (Figure 7) was a challenge because the observable financial impacts of these policies do not often include the full harms to victims.

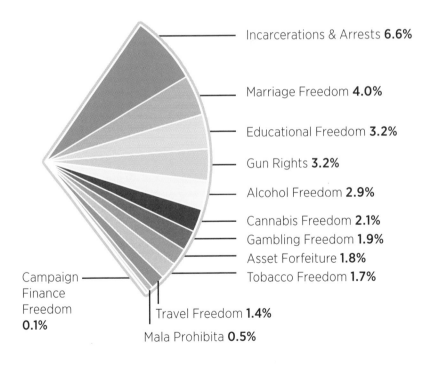

FIGURE 7 Personal Freedom Weights

Incarcerations & Arrests **6.6%**

Marriage Freedom **4.0%**

Educational Freedom **3.2%**

Gun Rights **3.2%**

Alcohol Freedom **2.9%**

Cannabis Freedom **2.1%**

Gambling Freedom **1.9%**

Asset Forfeiture **1.8%**

Tobacco Freedom **1.7%**

Campaign Finance Freedom **0.1%**

Travel Freedom **1.4%**

Mala Prohibita **0.5%**

With some assumptions, one can use results in the academic literature to measure, for instance, the lost consumer surplus from marijuana prohibition, or even to make a plausible guess at the disutility incurred by a year in prison. However, it is much more difficult to measure the risks that prohibitionist policies pose to individuals who are not imprisoned—especially those who may not even engage in the activity prohibited, but who legitimately fear further restrictions on their freedoms.

An example may help illustrate the problem. Imagine two countries, each the size of the United States. In Country A, the average tax rate is 1 percent (of income) lower than in Country B, but unlike Country B, Country A prohibits the practice of a minor religion—say, Zoroastrianism. Assuming personal income of $12 trillion, as in the United States, the lower tax rate in Country B allows for more freedom worth $33 billion a year, by the method of calculation used in this book.

Now suppose 10,000 Zoroastrians go to prison for their beliefs. There are few estimates of the cost of prison, including opportunity cost and psychological harms, but the estimates that exist range between $30,000 and $50,000 per year for the average prisoner.[63] Taking the higher figure, the prohibition of Zoroastrianism is found to have a victim cost of approximately $500 million per year: far, far lower than the benefit of lower taxes.

Is the country with slightly lower taxes but a blatant infringement of religious freedom truly freer? Surely, the calculation above has missed some very significant costs to freedom from the infringement of religious liberty. This calculation problem is related to the discussion of fundamental rights in the "Regulatory Policy" section above. Freedom to believe (or disbelieve) in any religion and freedom to practice peacefully (or refuse to practice) any religion seem to be freedoms that every person rationally desires. They are fundamental rights. Many personal freedoms have this character, and it needs to be recognized in the freedom index.

Therefore, the index applies constitutional weights to personal freedoms—as with regulatory policies—but uses different values, because the direct, measurable costs to victims of policies that infringe on personal freedoms are generally a smaller percentage of true costs than the direct, measurable costs to victims of regulatory policies. Put another way, measuring the economic consequences that regulatory policies have on their full victim class is a relatively simple procedure, but the full costs of policies that infringe on personal freedoms are measurable only in part. Further, as mentioned in the discussion of fiscal policy, taxes and economic regulations do not necessarily infringe on the rights of all apparent victims, unlike poli-

---

63. John J. Donohue, "Assessing the Relative Benefits of Incarceration: The Overall Change over the Previous Decades and the Benefits on the Margin," in Do Prisons Make Us Safer? The Benefits and Costs of the Prison Boom, ed. Steven Raphael and Michael Stoll (New York: Russell Sage Foundation, 2008); Innocence Project, "Compensating the Wrongly Convicted," http://www.innocenceproject.org/Content/Compensating_The_Wrongly_Convicted.php (accessed January 25, 2012).

cies that affect personal freedoms.

Again, the index takes constitutional provisions relating to certain freedoms as prima facie evidence of a freedom's "basicness," indicating that the full victim class should be thought of as quite broad. Therefore, variables relating to fundamental, high-salience rights are multiplied by a factor of 10, based on their inclusion in the federal Constitution. Variables relating to rights specified only in at least one state constitution are multiplied by a factor of 5. Variables that receive the "constitutional weights" are noted in the text below. There is of course nothing magical about these numbers, but they bring the personal freedom dimension into rough parity with the fiscal and regulatory policy dimensions as nearly one-third of the overall index.

The following sections introduce each category within the personal freedom dimension, in order of weight.

INCARCERATION AND ARRESTS FOR VICTIMLESS CRIMES

6.6%   The most heavily weighted category in the personal free-dom dimension is the law enforcement statistics category, which consists of data on incarceration rates adjusted for violent and property crime rates,[64] nondrug victimless crime arrests, and the drug enforcement rate. This category is worth over one-quarter of the personal freedom index. Given that the United States is frequently lambasted for having more prisoners per capita than almost every other country, and that the incarceration rate varies widely across states, it is perhaps no surprise that this category should be so important. The personal freedom dimension also includes laws that create or reduce victimless crimes in other categories, such as marijuana, gun, and prostitution laws. Our philosophy for assigning weights to those categories is to consider the forgone consumer and producer surplus due to prohibitions, while we consider within the law enforcement statistics category the costs of arrest and prison time.

A one-standard-deviation nationwide reduction in incarceration rates adjusted for crime rates would yield about $17 billion in new value for prisoners. This figure excludes the fiscal benefits of incarcerating fewer people.

A similar reduction in drug arrests per reported drug user would benefit arrestees by $5.8 billion. Other victimless crime arrests are calculated in two different ways, since there is no direct, state-by-state measure of the number of people who engage in these activities, as there is for drug arrests. Instead, the index takes the arrests of people over age 18 for weapons, prostitution, gambling, loitering, and liquor law violations as a percentage of the population and as a percentage of total arrests. The former figure is an imperfect measure of a citizen's risk of being arrested for one of these offenses (except that states may differ in the percentage of citizens who engage in these activities), whereas the latter is more of a measure of police priorities. Both variables are equally weighted and together amount to $4 billion of benefit to potential arrestees.

---

64. The adjustment involves regressing the incarceration rate on violent and property crime rates and taking the residuals. States with high scores will be those that lock up more people than would be expected given their crime rates.

TABLE 18

Rank	State	Incarceration and Arrests for Victimless Crimes Ranking		Rank	State	
1.	Massachusetts	0.111		26.	Michigan	0.003
2.	Rhode Island	0.098		27.	Nevada	0.003
3.	Washington	0.081		28.	Tennessee	0.002
4.	Maine	0.074		29.	Illinois	−0.002
5.	Minnesota	0.072		30.	Arkansas	−0.003
6.	New Mexico	0.072		31.	West Virginia	−0.010
7.	New Hampshire	0.049		32.	Indiana	−0.010
8.	New York	0.047		33.	Oregon	−0.012
9.	Vermont	0.035		34.	Ohio	−0.012
10.	Alaska	0.031		35.	Wisconsin	−0.012
11.	New Jersey	0.029		36.	Pennsylvania	−0.017
12.	California	0.028		37.	Florida	−0.025
13.	North Dakota	0.027		38.	Missouri	−0.029
14.	Iowa	0.026		39.	Georgia	−0.033
15.	Utah	0.026		40.	Arizona	−0.038
16.	Hawaii	0.022		41.	Alabama	−0.039
17.	Connecticut	0.021		42.	Oklahoma	−0.045
18.	North Carolina	0.021		43.	Texas	−0.050
19.	Kansas	0.020		44.	Kentucky	−0.057
20.	Nebraska	0.016		45.	Wyoming	−0.058
21.	Montana	0.006		46.	South Dakota	−0.060
22.	Maryland	0.006		47.	Virginia	−0.063
23.	Colorado	0.005		48.	Idaho	−0.077
24.	South Carolina	0.004		49.	Louisiana	−0.092
25.	Delaware	0.004		50.	Mississippi	−0.107

MARRIAGE FREEDOM

4.0% Most of the weight of the marriage freedom category is tied to the availability of same-sex partnerships, both civil unions and marriage. The remainder is tied to waiting periods and blood test requirements, availability of cousin marriage and covenant marriage, and sodomy laws, which were struck down by the Supreme Court in 2003. In our view, state governments should treat marriage as a contract that is "registered" or "recorded," rather than as a personal status that is "licensed."

States that prohibited same-sex couples from entering private contracts that provide the benefits of marriage (whether termed "marriages" or "civil unions") clearly took away an important contract right from such couples. Some states merely refrained from providing a convenient mechanism, such as civil unions or marriage, for same-sex couples to make contracts covering inheritance, hospital visitation, medical power of attorney, and so on. Other states went further and expressly prohibited any private contracts intended to provide benefits equivalent to marriage. For instance, the Virginia constitution states that "this Commonwealth and its political subdivisions shall not create or recognize a legal status for relationships of unmarried individuals that intends to approximate the design, qualities, significance, or effects of marriage." These state laws are sometimes called "super-DOMAs," after the federal Defense of Marriage Act. Other states that, by statute or constitution, prohibit all marriage-like private contracts for same-sex couples are Alabama, Arkansas, Florida, Georgia, Idaho, Kansas, Kentucky, Louisiana, Michigan, Nebraska, North Carolina, North Dakota, Ohio, Oklahoma, South Carolina, South Dakota, Texas, Utah, and Wisconsin (which is a curious example of a state that has limited domestic partnerships but also a super-DOMA, banning contracts offering benefits "equal to marriage").

Now that the Supreme Court has nationalized same-sex marriage, those distinctions among states are irrelevant. However, as of year-end 2014, a few states still had not had court rulings overturning their prohibitions on same-sex marriage: Alabama, Arkansas, Florida, Georgia, Kentucky, Louisiana, Michigan, Mississippi, Missouri, Nebraska, North Dakota, Ohio, South Dakota, Tennessee, and Texas. Those states occupy the bottom sector of this index's ranking. But in future years, the ranking on this variable will be driven mostly by cousin marriage, which at 0.3 percent of the index is more than four times as important as covenant marriage and vastly more important than blood tests and waiting periods.[65] In Appendix B, we present an alternative index of personal freedom assuming that every state has same-sex marriage and no super-DOMA.

---

65. Though cousin marriage is rare, bans on the practice receive the constitutional weight of 10 because they prevent certain couples from marrying altogether. Covenant marriage, waiting periods, and blood tests, by contrast, do not receive the constitutional weight.

The freedom index estimates that the freedom to marry is worth about $2,500 per year to same-sex couples, and that about 900,000 couples would take advantage of that opportunity were it available nationwide.[66] In previous editions of the index, we gave states equal scores on this variable for same-sex civil unions and marriage, considering the difference somewhat terminological at the time. However, after the Supreme Court decision striking down the federal Defense of Marriage Act (*United States v. Windsor*, 570 U.S. 12 [2013]), a window of time opened up in which states with full same-sex marriage actually afforded those couples greater freedom than available under civil unions, since the federal government was required to extend certain rights to married couples that they did not have to extend to civil unions, such as exemption from inheritance tax. Therefore, in this edition of the index, we give a small benefit to states that enacted same-sex marriage vis-à-vis same-sex civil unions, even as we advocate, like many other libertarians, that government cease to define "marriage" at all.

66. M. V. Lee Badgett, "The Economic Value of Marriage for Same-Sex Couples," *Drake Law Review* 58 (2010): 1081–116.

TABLE 19

Rank	State	Marriage Freedom Ranking		Rank	State	Marriage Freedom Ranking
1.	California	0.054		22.	West Virginia	0.046
1.	Colorado	0.054		22.	Wyoming	0.046
1.	Connecticut	0.054		28.	Delaware	0.046
1.	Hawaii	0.054		29.	Iowa	0.046
1.	New Mexico	0.054		29.	Kansas	0.046
1.	North Carolina	0.054		29.	Oregon	0.046
1.	Rhode Island	0.054		29.	Pennsylvania	0.046
1.	Vermont	0.054		29.	Washington	0.046
1.	Virginia	0.054		34.	Minnesota	0.046
1.	South Carolina	0.054		35.	Montana	0.046
1.	Maryland	0.054		36.	Tennessee	-0.001
1.	Alaska	0.054		37.	Mississippi	-0.009
1.	Massachusetts	0.054		37.	Missouri	-0.009
1.	New Jersey	0.054		39.	Alabama	-0.024
15.	New York	0.053		39.	Georgia	-0.024
16.	Arizona	0.053		41.	Florida	-0.024
17.	Indiana	0.050		42.	Arkansas	-0.028
17.	Maine	0.050		43.	Louisiana	-0.028
17.	Utah	0.050		44.	Kentucky	-0.031
20.	Illinois	0.050		44.	Nebraska	-0.031
21.	Wisconsin	0.050		44.	North Dakota	-0.031
22.	Idaho	0.046		44.	Ohio	-0.031
22.	Nevada	0.046		44.	South Dakota	-0.031
22.	New Hampshire	0.046		49.	Michigan	-0.031
22.	Oklahoma	0.046		49.	Texas	-0.031

EDUCATIONAL FREEDOM

3.2% Educational policy is worth more of the index in this edition than in the last edition. One reason is that we have added more variables. Previously, we had not counted public school choice and private school voucher programs as pro-freedom, in a nod to libertarian concerns that merely "marketizing" the delivery of public services might make them more efficient but still preserve the problems of tax funding.

We disagree with those concerns, however. It seems clear that when a state allows a recipient of public funding who also pays taxes to decide how that funding is used, that person's freedom is enhanced. Home-owning families that pay property taxes enjoy more freedom when they can decide to use their property taxes to send their kids to a school outside their district.

The second reason that educational policy has increased in weight is our new tax credit/deduction for private scholarship funds or educational expenses variable. The variable now takes into account the legislated scope and size of each state's program, and as a result the variable is worth more. At 1.2 percent of the index, it is the most important single variable for educational freedom. Although we generally deplore attempts to change behavior through the tax code, tax credits for scholarship contributions for private education are a second-best policy response to educational savings accounts, full school privatization, or both; they break up territorial monopolies in education.

Other important variables for educational freedom include publicly funded voucher law size and scope (0.7 percent), mandatory state licensure of private school teachers (0.6 percent), mandatory state approval of private schools (0.2 percent), years of compulsory schooling (0.2 percent), and extent of private school curriculum control (0.1 percent). Vouchers are worth less than tax credit scholarship funds because extant programs are generally more narrowly targeted and come with more strings attached. Were a state to enact general, unrestricted school choice, such a policy would have a heavy weight in our index.

Less significant are public school choice, mandatory registration of private schools, existence of a homeschool law, homeschool curriculum control, homeschool teacher qualifications, homeschool standardized testing, homeschool notification index, and homeschool record-keeping index. All the homeschool variables combined make up 0.15 percent of the index.

Note that although Nevada ranks second to last in this category, we have not yet included the state's "universal educational choice" law enacted in 2015. That change will significantly raise Nevada's ranking in this index, assuming the courts lift the injunction in place as of this writing.

Rank	State	Educational Freedom Ranking		Rank	State	Educational Freedom Ranking
1.	Arizona	0.052		26.	New Jersey	−0.001
2.	Indiana	0.049		27.	Arkansas	−0.001
3.	Florida	0.044		28.	Texas	−0.002
4.	Georgia	0.043		29.	Colorado	−0.002
5.	Louisiana	0.034		30.	Delaware	−0.002
6.	North Carolina	0.033		31.	Oregon	−0.003
7.	Virginia	0.030		32.	Kentucky	−0.003
8.	New Hampshire	0.024		33.	New Mexico	−0.003
9.	Rhode Island	0.022		34.	California	−0.004
10.	Oklahoma	0.022		35.	Alaska	−0.005
11.	Pennsylvania	0.021		36.	New York	−0.005
12.	Iowa	0.018		37.	Connecticut	−0.006
13.	Wisconsin	0.017		38.	Hawaii	−0.006
14.	Vermont	0.017		39.	West Virginia	−0.007
15.	Illinois	0.015		40.	Massachusetts	−0.009
16.	Ohio	0.014		41.	Maine	−0.010
17.	Minnesota	0.010		42.	Wyoming	−0.011
18.	South Carolina	0.009		43.	South Dakota	−0.012
19.	Utah	0.007		44.	Tennessee	−0.014
20.	Mississippi	0.007		45.	Nebraska	−0.016
21.	Alabama	0.006		46.	Michigan	−0.018
22.	Kansas	0.004		47.	North Dakota	−0.024
23.	Idaho	0.003		48.	Washington	−0.024
24.	Montana	0.002		49.	Nevada	−0.026
25.	Missouri	0.002		50.	Maryland	−0.028

GUN RIGHTS

3.2% Gun rights are worth much less in this edition than in the last edition—though still an ample 3.2 percent—for two reasons. First, we disaggregate gun policies in this edition rather than using a single variable constructed through principal components analysis as in prior editions. That change allowed us to investigate the costs of each firearms policy separately. Our weight for the policy category as a whole should therefore be more accurate.

Second, we consider only some firearms policies to trigger Second Amendment scrutiny, and they are the only ones to get the full "times 10" constitutional weighting factor. We follow recent case law in our judgments on this point. Supreme Court decisions in *D.C. v. Heller*[67] and *McDonald v. Chicago*[68] held that federal, state, and local governments are not allowed to ban gun ownership for self-defense purposes altogether, and state and federal appeals court decisions have also held that the Second Amendment protects a right to carry a firearm outside the home. On the other hand, the Supreme Court has opined that the U.S. Constitution permits bans on certain types of firearms and reasonable regulations on how someone may qualify to carry a weapon for self-defense. However, since the Louisiana constitution provides that all firearms-related restrictions should be subject to strict scrutiny, we apply a "times 5" constitutional weighting factor to all those firearms policies not receiving the "times 10" boost. Variables falling into this latter category include concealed-carry permit costs, concealed-carry permit terms, nonpowder gun regulations, restrictions on multiple purchases of handguns, licensing or regulation of gun dealers, universal background checks, registration of firearms, locking device requirements, ammunition microstamping, duty-to-retreat laws, and laws relating to National Firearms Act weapons (machine guns, sound suppressors, short-barreled rifles, short-barreled shotguns, and "any other weapon").

The most significant variable in the gun rights category is the existence of a local gun ban (1.0 percent of the index), which only Illinois had, until struck down in *McDonald v. Chicago*. At about 0.4 percent of the index, we find the cost of a concealed-carry permit and our index of concealed-carry laws, which takes into account shall-issue versus may-issue, "peaceable journey" (carry in vehicles), local preemption, availability of nonresident permits, and the scope of places where concealed carry is allowed. Our index of firearms owner licensing requirements and waiting periods on firearms purchases are worth just slightly less (0.3 percent). At 0.2 percent of the

---

67. *D.C. v. Heller*, 554 U.S. 570 (2008).
68. *McDonald v. Chicago*, 561 U.S. 742 (2010).

index is whether a state has a stricter minimum age to purchase or possess firearms than the federal standard.

Other variables included in this category, and worth far less than those discussed in the previous paragraph, are our index of open-carry laws, assault weapons bans, "design safety standards" (bans on cheap handguns), large-capacity magazine bans, and .50-caliber rifle bans.

If every state improved by one standard deviation on each variable in this category, we estimate the move would create about $13 billion annually in new value for owners, buyers, and sellers of firearms.

TABLE 21

Rank	State	Gun Rights Ranking	Rank	State	Gun Rights Ranking
1.	Vermont	0.025	26.	Oregon	0.007
2.	Wyoming	0.024	27.	Oklahoma	0.007
3.	Arizona	0.023	28.	New Mexico	0.006
4.	Alaska	0.022	29.	Missouri	0.006
5.	New Hampshire	0.016	30.	Ohio	0.006
6.	South Dakota	0.014	31.	Texas	0.006
7.	Georgia	0.013	32.	Arkansas	0.006
8.	Kentucky	0.012	33.	North Carolina	0.005
9.	Alabama	0.012	34.	Nebraska	0.005
10.	Tennessee	0.011	35.	Wisconsin	0.003
11.	Virginia	0.011	36.	Michigan	0.002
12.	North Dakota	0.011	37.	Louisiana	0.002
13.	Colorado	0.010	38.	Florida	0.002
14.	West Virginia	0.010	39.	Minnesota	0.000
15.	Kansas	0.010	40.	Iowa	−0.002
16.	Maine	0.010	41.	Delaware	−0.007
17.	Indiana	0.009	42.	New York	−0.015
18.	Idaho	0.009	43.	Connecticut	−0.018
19.	Washington	0.009	44.	Maryland	−0.022
20.	Pennsylvania	0.009	45.	Illinois	−0.023
21.	Utah	0.008	46.	New Jersey	−0.023
22.	Nevada	0.008	47.	Massachusetts	−0.023
23.	Montana	0.008	48.	Rhode Island	−0.026
24.	Mississippi	0.008	49.	California	−0.034
25.	South Carolina	0.007	50.	Hawaii	−0.047

ALCOHOL FREEDOM

2.9% With this edition, we have expanded our alcohol policy variables and coded them back in time as far as possible. Some of our variables even go back to the 1930s.

The alcohol distribution system ("control"—which means that the state has a monopoly on distribution—versus "license"—which means that the state licenses distributors) makes up 1.1 percent of the whole index on its own. Research shows that state distribution of alcohol imposes significant costs on consumers in time and inconvenience.[69]

The freedom index assumes a "full-price elasticity" (including formal and informal prices) of –0.2 for all alcohol types, which is similar to what has been discovered in the literature cited above. Reducing consumption of alcohol by 5 percent with a state monopoly, according to University of California, Los Angeles, professors Stanley I. Ornstein and Dominique M. Hanssens, therefore implies a 25 percent "tax" due to transaction cost.[70] According to the U.S. Department of Agriculture, packaged alcoholic beverage sales in 2010 amounted to $91 billion. If all such sales had to go through state monopolies, then one might expect a transaction-cost "tax" of close to $23 billion.[71]

Blue laws (bans on Sunday sales) would, if implemented nationwide, reduce consumer welfare by over $4.5 billion and are worth 0.4 percent of the index. Preventing wine, spirits, or in a few states even beer from being sold in grocery stores, a new variable in this edition, has a similar cost. Taxes on beer, wine, and spirits each make up 0.2–0.3 percent of the index as a whole, followed by direct wine shipment bans, keg registration/bans, and "happy hour" bans. Mandatory server training, worth less than 0.01 percent of the index, rounds out this category.

With its strong brewing industry, it is no surprise that Wisconsin finishes first in this ranking. Nor is Utah's last-place finish shocking.

---

69. Stanley I. Ornstein and Dominique M. Hanssens, "Alcohol Control Laws and the Consumption of Distilled Spirits and Beer," *Journal of Consumer Research* 12, no. 2 (1985): 200–213.

70. Ibid.

71. Björn Trolldal and William Ponicki, "Alcohol Price Elasticities in Control and License States in the United States, 1982–1999," *Addiction* 100, no. 8 (2005): 1158–65. Our comparison here is from minimum to maximum values for this variable.

TABLE 22

Rank	State	Alcohol Freedom Ranking	Rank	State	Alcohol Freedom Ranking
1.	Wisconsin	0.021	26.	West Virginia	0.003
2.	Missouri	0.021	27.	Michigan	0.003
3.	Nevada	0.020	28.	Georgia	0.003
4.	California	0.020	29.	Arkansas	0.002
5.	Arizona	0.018	30.	Delaware	0.002
6.	Louisiana	0.017	31.	Washington	0.001
7.	New Mexico	0.015	32.	Ohio	−0.001
8.	Texas	0.014	33.	Iowa	−0.001
9.	South Dakota	0.013	34.	New Hampshire	−0.001
10.	Massachusetts	0.013	35.	North Carolina	−0.005
11.	Hawaii	0.013	36.	Minnesota	−0.006
12.	Maryland	0.013	37.	Oregon	−0.007
13.	Colorado	0.012	38.	Alaska	−0.007
14.	Nebraska	0.012	39.	Virginia	−0.007
15.	North Dakota	0.011	40.	Kentucky	−0.007
16.	Florida	0.010	41.	Maine	−0.007
17.	Illinois	0.010	42.	Tennessee	−0.008
18.	New Jersey	0.010	43.	Mississippi	−0.008
19.	New York	0.010	44.	Oklahoma	−0.008
20.	Rhode Island	0.009	45.	Alabama	−0.014
21.	Connecticut	0.009	46.	Vermont	−0.017
22.	Wyoming	0.005	47.	Montana	−0.018
23.	Indiana	0.005	48.	Idaho	−0.024
24.	South Carolina	0.004	49.	Pennsylvania	−0.029
25.	Kansas	0.004	50.	Utah	−0.065

CANNABIS FREEDOM

2.1% Unlike the last edition, this edition of the index develops weights for each policy variable in the cannabis freedom category. As mentioned earlier in the section "Incarceration and Arrests for Victimless Crimes," we consider here only the lost consumer and producer surplus due to prohibition, not the costs of arrests and incarceration.

Recent work has yielded inconsistent findings on marijuana policy and consumption. Rand Corporation economist Rosalie Liccardo Pacula and her coauthors[72] find that marijuana penalties have a small effect on marijuana use among youth (a one-standard-deviation increase in minimum jail time is associated with a 1.2 percent decline in annual risk of use), but "decriminalization" or "depenalization" as such retains a small (about 2 to 3 percent) effect even when these penalty variables are controlled for, which the authors cannot explain. In a different study, Pacula and her colleagues[73] find that reduced penalties for users increase consumption and therefore price, resulting in higher profits for sellers. They also calculate that prohibition probably doubles the price of a pound of marijuana, at least (adding $200 to $300 to the cost).

A reasonable estimate of the amount of marijuana sold in the United States in a year is 50 million pounds.[74] Unfortunately, absolutely no evidence exists on the consequences of supplier penalties. We conservatively assume total seller profits of $200 per pound (including compensation for risk). We estimate the new consumer surplus conservatively, assuming a price elasticity of demand of –0.2 (like alcohol) and unit elasticity of supply.

Looking at decriminalization of small-scale possession first, we assume this policy boosts consumption by 3 percent, which implies a transaction-cost tax of roughly 15 percent. We then calculate the deadweight loss and the forgone producer surplus, assuming a price per pound of $330. This underestimate is small because decriminalization also correlates with strength of criminal penalties, which Pacula et al.[75] find affect consumption. Moving from criminalization to decriminalization nationwide should then increase consumer and producer welfare by about $2.3 billion. Our coding of this variable assumes that the benefits of full legalization of possession are about five times as large.

72. Rosalie Liccardo Pacula et al., "Marijuana Decriminalization: What Does It Mean in the United States?," NBER Working Paper no. 9690, National Bureau of Economic Research, Cambridge, MA, May 2003, http://www.nber.org/papers/w9690.

73. Rosalie Liccardo Pacula et al., "Risks and Prices: The Role of User Sanctions in Marijuana Markets," NBER Working Paper no. 13415, National Bureau of Economic Research, Cambridge, MA, September 2007, http://www.nber.org/papers/w13415.

74. Jon Gettman, "Lost Taxes and Other Costs of Marijuana Laws," DrugScience.org, 2007, http://www.drugscience.org/Archive/bcr4/5Supply.html.

75. Pacula et al., "Marijuana Decriminalization."

The most important variable in the cannabis freedom category is our index of medical marijuana laws, which takes into account the scope of qualifying conditions, the maximum amount permitted, whether home cultivation is permitted, and whether dispensaries are permitted. Pacula et al. find that some features of medical marijuana laws, such as home cultivation and (especially) dispensaries, may increase overall consumption, but their results are not easily interpretable in a supply-and-demand model, nor are they generally statistically significant.[76] Other research has found no effect on consumption.[77] But several studies now seem to show that legal dispensaries result in lower prices by shifting out the supply curve. Wen, Hockenberry, and Cummings find that allowing nonspecific pain as a reason for medical marijuana recommendations increases use by those over age 21 significantly.[78] The bottom line is that the total effect of medical marijuana laws on consumption is modest, probably a bit more than decriminalization, but much is unknown. We choose a weight for this variable of 1.5 times that for decriminalization.

The next most important variable is the maximum penalty for a single marijuana offense not involving a minor, which in some states is life imprisonment. These penalties depress supply and raise price. We also include whether high-level possession or cultivation of cannabis is a misdemeanor or felony and any mandatory minimum sentence for "low-level" cultivation or sale. All these variables are assumed together to have a similar effect on decriminalization of possession.

The next most important variable is whether some recreational cannabis sales are legal. Recreational sales of marijuana in Colorado, the first state to implement legal recreational sale, have not decreased medical marijuana sales.[79] It is unclear what the effect has been on total sales, that is, whether legalization simply reduces the black market or also increases total consumption. Even under the former scenario, the big increase in recreational sales over time suggests that many consumers benefit by buying on the legal rather than the black market. In the 12 months through June 2015, legal recreational sales amounted to about $450 million in Colorado. Assume 20 percent of that reflects producer costs (a common statistic is that in the absence of prohibition and any taxes, the price of marijuana would fall by 80 per-

76. Rosalie Liccardo Pacula et al., "Assessing the Effects of Medical Marijuana Laws on Marijuana and Alcohol Use: The Devil Is in the Details," NBER Working Paper no. 19302, National Bureau of Economic Research, Cambridge, MA, August 2013.

77. Rosalie Liccardo Pacula and Eric L. Sevigny, "Marijuana Legalization Policies: Why We Can't Learn Much from Policy Still in Motion," *Journal of Policy Analysis and Management* 33, no. 1 (2014): 212–21.

78. Hefei Wen, Jason M. Hockenberry, and Janet R. Cummings, "The Effect of Medical Marijuana Laws on Adolescent and Adult Use of Marijuana, Alcohol, and Other Substances," *Journal of Health Economics* 42, issue C (2015): 64–80.

79. Ricardo Baca, "Colorado Pot Sales Spike in June, Top $50 Million for First Time," *Cannabist*, August 13, 2015, http://www.thecannabist.co/2015/08/13/colorado-marijuana-taxes-recreational-sales-june-2015-50-million/39384/.

cent). The remainder reflects producer and consumer surplus. We assume one-quarter of that surplus is due to legalization of sales specifically, rather than possession and cultivation. After adjusting to the national population, we estimate then that legalizing some marijuana sales would create $5.4 billion of benefit nationally.

Finally, we consider the impact of *Salvia divinorum* bans within this category. A 2006 study found that 750,000 people used salvia in that year, compared with 26 million marijuana users per year.[80] Therefore, we add together all the marijuana weights and multiply by 0.75/26. An objection to this strategy is that the variance among states is greater on salvia policy, so this weight understates the importance of the policy (in no state is marijuana completely unregulated). On the other hand, the per-user quantity of salvia consumed is surely much lower than for marijuana, so this weight may overstate the importance of the policy. Since we cannot assess the relative magnitudes of these biases, we simply assume that they cancel out. Salvia bans are therefore worth less than 0.1 percent of the index.

80. National Survey on Drug Use and Health, "Use of Specific Hallucinogens: 2006," *NSDUH Report*, February 14, 2008, http://archive.samhsa.gov/data/2k8/hallucinogens/hallucinogens.htm.

TABLE 23

Rank	State	Cannabis Freedom Ranking		Rank	State	Cannabis Freedom Ranking
1.	Washington	0.065		26.	Pennsylvania	−0.003
2.	Colorado	0.062		27.	Utah	−0.005
3.	Alaska	0.053		28.	Kansas	−0.005
4.	Maine	0.030		29.	Nebraska	−0.005
5.	California	0.026		30.	Indiana	−0.006
6.	Massachusetts	0.024		31.	West Virginia	−0.006
7.	Oregon	0.020		32.	Idaho	−0.006
8.	Vermont	0.017		33.	Wisconsin	−0.006
9.	Maryland	0.016		34.	Kentucky	−0.007
10.	Rhode Island	0.013		35.	Wyoming	−0.007
11.	Michigan	0.012		36.	Mississippi	−0.008
12.	Nevada	0.012		37.	North Dakota	−0.008
13.	New Mexico	0.012		38.	South Dakota	−0.009
14.	Hawaii	0.011		39.	South Carolina	−0.009
15.	New York	0.011		40.	Florida	−0.010
16.	Delaware	0.010		41.	Iowa	−0.010
17.	Arizona	0.009		42.	Arkansas	−0.011
18.	Connecticut	0.008		43.	Georgia	−0.011
19.	Illinois	0.007		44.	Tennessee	−0.012
20.	Minnesota	0.007		45.	Texas	−0.013
21.	Montana	0.005		46.	Missouri	−0.014
22.	New Hampshire	0.003		47.	Alabama	−0.015
23.	New Jersey	0.003		48.	Oklahoma	−0.015
24.	Ohio	0.001		49.	Virginia	−0.015
25.	North Carolina	−0.003		50.	Louisiana	−0.019

GAMBLING FREEDOM

1.9% Annual nationwide commercial casino net profits ("win") are about $39 billion,[81] so gambling is big business. Unfortunately, no state has a free market in gaming enterprises, but a monopolistic, state-licensed system at least permits more freedom than a total ban.

We do not have figures on all-source gambling revenues by state, so we use the tax data to infer them, since it seems reasonable to assume that most states try to levy the revenue-maximizing tax rate. The freedom index uses the Australian Productivity Commission's admittedly flawed method [82] (but a creditable and unique attempt) for deriving the consumer surplus, as follows:

$$S = \frac{p(1-t)q}{2e}$$

where S is the surplus, $p(1-t)q$ is price including tax times quantity (we use total state tax revenues), and e is the price elasticity of demand, assumed to be −1.3 following the academic literature and the APC's estimate for nonproblem gamblers. [83] Thus, the total gambling revenues figure is divided by 2.6 to get the consumer surplus. For the purposes of the freedom index, producer surplus is irrelevant, because the producer side of the industry is heavily oligopolistic or monopolistic because of state control.

Although gambling revenue is worth 1.8 percent of the index, the remaining variables in this category have very small weights. A social gambling exception and whether "aggravated gambling" is a felony or not each make up 0.02 percent of the freedom index. Express prohibitions on Internet gambling, which are redundant on federal prohibitions, are worth less than 0.01 percent.

81. UNLV Center for Gaming Research, "United States Commercial Casino Gaming: Monthly Revenues," http://gaming.unlv.edu/reports/national_monthly.pdf.

82. Brian Dollery and John Storer, "Assessing the Impact of Electronic Gaming Machines: A Conceptual Critique of the Productivity Commission's Methodology," *Gambling Research* 20, no. 1 (2008): 1–12.

83. Australian Gaming Council, "Estimating Consumer Surplus," http://www.austgamingcouncil.org.au/images/pdf/eLibrary/2330.pdf (accessed January 25, 2013).

TABLE 24

Rank	State	Gambling Freedom Ranking		Rank	State	Gambling Freedom Ranking
1.	Nevada	0.078		26.	Washington	−0.002
2.	Louisiana	0.053		27.	North Dakota	−0.003
3.	Indiana	0.047		28.	Texas	−0.009
4.	Pennsylvania	0.042		29.	Virginia	−0.010
5.	Iowa	0.039		30.	Nebraska	−0.010
6.	Missouri	0.035		31.	California	−0.011
7.	Mississippi	0.035		32.	North Carolina	−0.011
8.	Connecticut	0.033		33.	New York	−0.011
9.	Montana	0.028		34.	Idaho	−0.012
10.	Illinois	0.026		35.	Kentucky	−0.012
11.	West Virginia	0.025		36.	Alabama	−0.012
12.	Oklahoma	0.021		37.	Oregon	−0.012
13.	Michigan	0.020		38.	Arizona	−0.012
14.	New Mexico	0.016		39.	Massachusetts	−0.012
15.	New Jersey	0.011		40.	Delaware	−0.012
16.	Maine	0.010		41.	Tennessee	−0.012
17.	Colorado	0.008		42.	Rhode Island	−0.012
18.	South Dakota	0.005		43.	New Hampshire	−0.013
19.	Ohio	0.003		44.	Wyoming	−0.013
20.	Maryland	0.002		45.	Vermont	−0.013
21.	Arkansas	0.002		46.	Hawaii	−0.013
22.	Minnesota	0.000		47.	Kansas	−0.013
23.	South Carolina	0.000		48.	Wisconsin	−0.014
24.	Alaska	−0.001		49.	Georgia	−0.014
25.	Florida	−0.002		50.	Utah	−0.014

ASSET FORFEITURE

1.8% Civil asset forfeiture is the government's ability to take a person's property by accusing him or her of a crime. Often the seized cash or proceeds of auctioning the property accrue to the seizing agency, providing incentives for "policing for profit." Typically, the person whose property is seized must file suit and prove innocence to get the property back. Both federal and state/local law enforcement engage in asset forfeiture.

This category is worth a lot more in this edition of the freedom index (1.8 percent). The last edition gave asset forfeiture a low weight because it measured only state asset forfeiture laws. And evidence suggested that state asset forfeiture laws did little to curb the practice, because state and local law enforcement cooperated with the Department of Justice to seize and forfeit under federal procedures, which are generally less citizen-friendly than state procedures, and receive a cut of the proceeds.

In this edition, asset forfeiture is worth more because we measure not only state laws, including the extent to which a few states limit federal "adoption" of state-initiated forfeiture cases, but also the amount of "equitable-sharing" revenue that the Department of Justice gives state/local law enforcement in each state. A standard-deviation change in equitable-sharing forfeitures nationwide amounts to $3.7 billion. We give state forfeiture laws the same weight even though we have no consistent data on state-level forfeitures.

TABLE 25

Rank	State	Asset Forfeiture Ranking		Rank	State	Asset Forfeiture Ranking
1.	Oregon	0.024		26.	Arizona	−0.003
2.	Minnesota	0.020		27.	Tennessee	−0.003
3.	Maine	0.017		28.	Alaska	−0.004
4.	Colorado	0.017		29.	Arkansas	−0.005
5.	South Dakota	0.016		30.	New York	−0.006
6.	North Dakota	0.014		31.	Idaho	−0.006
7.	Connecticut	0.013		32.	Alabama	−0.007
8.	New Mexico	0.012		33.	Montana	−0.007
9.	Wyoming	0.012		34.	Delaware	−0.007
10.	Maryland	0.012		35.	Texas	−0.007
11.	Wisconsin	0.010		36.	Iowa	−0.007
12.	North Carolina	0.009		37.	South Carolina	−0.008
13.	California	0.009		38.	West Virginia	−0.008
14.	Vermont	0.007		39.	Kansas	−0.008
15.	Indiana	0.006		40.	Kentucky	−0.008
16.	Florida	0.005		41.	Virginia	−0.008
17.	Michigan	0.005		42.	New Hampshire	−0.008
18.	Missouri	0.005		43.	Ohio	−0.008
19.	Utah	0.005		44.	Pennsylvania	−0.009
20.	Louisiana	0.003		45.	New Jersey	−0.009
21.	Nebraska	0.002		46.	Mississippi	−0.010
22.	Nevada	0.000		47.	Massachusetts	−0.010
23.	Hawaii	0.000		48.	Illinois	−0.016
24.	Oklahoma	−0.001		49.	Georgia	−0.017
25.	Washington	−0.002		50.	Rhode Island	−0.046

TOBACCO FREEDOM

1.7% In the tobacco freedom category, representing 1.7 percent of the index, we consider the effect of cigarette taxes, smoking bans (in privately owned workplaces, restaurants, and bars), vending machine bans, and Internet sales regulations on freedom.

Cigarette taxes are the most important variable in this category. A $1-per-pack tax increase is associated with a 0.375–standard deviation increase in the variable and about a 16.7 percent increase in the price of a pack.[84] Nobel Prize–winning economist Gary S. Becker and his colleagues calculate that the long-run price elasticity of demand for cigarettes is about −0.75. [85] In 2010, 303 billion cigarettes were sold in the United States, typically at 20 cigarettes per pack. [86] These facts are sufficient to calculate the deadweight loss (dividing by two under the assumption of perfectly elastic supply) and the total cost to consumers. As with alcohol taxes, we divide the latter element by 2.5 to capture the fact that taxes have the conditional consent of some taxpayers, but not by 4 as we did for general taxes (see discussion in the "Fiscal Policy" section), because "sin taxes" disproportionately hit consumers of these products, who are more likely to be opposed to high taxes on the goods they consume. Cigarette taxes are worth 1.3 percent of the freedom index.

Economics professor Michael L. Marlow examines the consequences of Ohio's comprehensive smoking ban for its losers. State and local governments issued 33,347 citations, with an average expense of about $1,250 per citation (given that each cited location averaged about five citations). [87] Extrapolating from Ohio's population supplies the national numbers for the freedom index.

The second set of costs from smoking bans has to do with lost business and the associated disutility to smokers. There is an unfortunate lack of good studies with quasi-random treatment; however, a reasonable assumption is that the costs of bans must be at least as high as (and possibly much greater than) the fines establishments are willing to risk to permit smoking. Thus, a simple approach is to multiply an estimate of this amount by 2.5, assuming that the lost revenue is slightly greater than the fines businesses are willing to incur. Because bars are affected by smoking bans much more

84. Ann Boonn, "State Cigarette Excise Tax Rates and Rankings," Campaign for Tobacco-Free Kids, Washington, DC, December 13, 2012, http://www.tobaccofreekids.org/research/factsheets/pdf/0097.pdf.

85. Gary S. Becker, Michael Grossmann, and Kevin M. Murphy, "Rational Addiction and the Effect of Price on Consumption," *American Economic* Review 81, no. 2 (1991): 237–41.

86. "Economic Facts about U.S. Tobacco Production and Use," Centers for Disease Control and Prevention, Atlanta, November 15, 2012, http://www.cdc.gov/tobacco/data_statistics/fact_sheets/economics/econ_facts/.

87. Michael L. Marlow, "The Economic Losers from Smoking Bans," *Regulation*, Summer 2010, pp. 14–19, http://www.cato.org/sites/cato.org/files/serials/files/regulation/2010/6/regv33n2-4.pdf.

than restaurants and workplaces, we assign 80 percent of the weight to smoking bans in bars and 10 percent each to the latter bans.

Vending machine and Internet sales regulations are together worth less than 0.1 percent of the index.

TABLE 26

Rank	State	Tobacco Freedom Ranking	Rank	State	Tobacco Freedom Ranking
1.	Missouri	0.017	26.	Iowa	−0.004
2.	Georgia	0.014	27.	Oregon	−0.004
3.	Virginia	0.012	28.	Pennsylvania	−0.005
4.	Louisiana	0.012	29.	South Dakota	−0.007
5.	Idaho	0.012	30.	New Mexico	−0.008
6.	Alabama	0.012	31.	Delaware	−0.008
7.	Kentucky	0.011	32.	New Hampshire	−0.009
8.	Wyoming	0.011	33.	Montana	−0.010
9.	West Virginia	0.010	34.	Utah	−0.010
10.	South Carolina	0.010	35.	Alaska	−0.010
11.	Nevada	0.010	36.	Maine	−0.013
12.	Mississippi	0.010	37.	Illinois	−0.014
13.	North Carolina	0.008	38.	Arizona	−0.014
14.	Tennessee	0.008	39.	Maryland	−0.014
15.	North Dakota	0.008	40.	Michigan	−0.014
16.	Nebraska	0.006	41.	Wisconsin	−0.021
17.	Arkansas	0.004	42.	New Jersey	−0.023
18.	California	0.004	43.	Vermont	−0.025
19.	Colorado	0.004	44.	Minnesota	−0.026
20.	Oklahoma	0.003	45.	Washington	−0.028
21.	Indiana	0.003	46.	Hawaii	−0.031
22.	Kansas	0.003	47.	Connecticut	−0.033
23.	Florida	−0.002	48.	Massachusetts	−0.034
24.	Texas	−0.002	49.	Rhode Island	−0.034
25.	Ohio	−0.004	50.	New York	−0.047

TRAVEL FREEDOM

1.4% Two new variables to this edition—the use and retention of automated license plate reader data and the availability of driver's licenses to those without Social Security numbers (such as undocumented workers)—make up together about half of the travel freedom category's total weight in the index, helping explain its greater prominence in this edition, now worth 1.4 percent of the total.

About 11.1 million undocumented immigrants are in the United States, and we assume that 60 percent of them would be willing to get driver's licenses, slightly lower than the rate of licensed drivers in the general population. We then assume the mean value of a license per driver per year is $750. For automated license plate readers, we assume that the average driver, of whom there are 210 million in the United States, would be willing to pay $15 a year to avoid being subject to their unlimited use. This variable is worth 0.3 percent of the index.

Suspicionless sobriety checkpoints invade privacy and create anxiety among those stopped and searched. Extrapolating from two different sources, we estimate that about 9 million drivers a year are searched at sobriety checkpoints nationwide, or would be if they were legal nationwide. We assume a cost of $50 per driver searched in lost time, privacy, and anxiety. We multiply the variable by five since some state constitutions prohibit these checkpoints. It is worth 0.2 percent of the freedom index.

Seat belt laws are worth a little less, about 0.15 percent of the index, based on estimated costs of tickets. A new variable to this edition, a fingerprint or thumbprint required for a driver's license, is worth 0.13 percent of the index. After that come uninsured/underinsured motorist insurance coverage requirements, motorcycle helmet laws, open-container laws, and bans on driving while using a cell phone, in that order.

These variables were included in previous editions of *Freedom in the 50 States,* and some of them generated a fair number of comments by readers and audience members at public presentations. In particular, it was argued that some of these variables seem to be justified on the grounds of enhancing public safety. But not every measure that enhances public safety is morally justifiable—consider random searches of pedestrians. A preferable approach would use penalties for "distracted driving" of whatever cause, rather than a blanket ban on using a handheld phone while driving, which does not always pose a risk to others. Likewise, it would be better to focus on penalties for drunk driving rather than punishing people for having opened beverage containers in their vehicles, another behavior that does not necessarily pose a direct risk to others. In states with a federally conforming open-container law, having an unsealed but closed wine bottle on the floor of the passenger side of a car is sufficient to trigger a misdemeanor violation and possible jail time.

No state does extremely well on travel freedom. Washington scores at the top despite having no restrictions on the use of automated license plate readers, a primary handheld cell phone ban, an open-container law, a motorcycle helmet law, and a secondary seat belt law, because it is one of the few states that allows someone to obtain a driver's license without a Social Security number and, unlike number two Vermont, does not authorize sobriety checkpoints.

TABLE 27

Rank	State	Travel Freedom Ranking	Rank	State	Travel Freedom Ranking
1.	Washington	0.011	26.	Ohio	−0.002
2.	Vermont	0.011	27.	Pennsylvania	−0.002
3.	Oregon	0.010	28.	Tennessee	−0.002
4.	Colorado	0.009	29.	Virginia	−0.003
5.	Utah	0.009	30.	North Dakota	−0.004
6.	Nevada	0.008	31.	South Dakota	−0.004
7.	Maryland	0.008	32.	Missouri	−0.004
8.	Connecticut	0.007	33.	Texas	−0.005
9.	New Hampshire	0.007	34.	Delaware	−0.005
10.	New Mexico	0.007	35.	Indiana	−0.005
11.	Illinois	0.006	36.	Kentucky	−0.005
12.	California	0.004	37.	Oklahoma	−0.005
13.	Idaho	0.003	38.	Massachusetts	−0.005
14.	Wyoming	0.003	39.	Nebraska	−0.005
15.	Arkansas	0.003	40.	South Carolina	−0.006
16.	Maine	0.001	41.	Mississippi	−0.006
17.	Alaska	0.000	42.	New Jersey	−0.006
18.	Iowa	0.000	43.	Alabama	−0.006
19.	Michigan	0.000	44.	Georgia	−0.006
20.	Rhode Island	0.000	45.	Louisiana	−0.006
21.	Minnesota	−0.001	46.	Kansas	−0.007
22.	Wisconsin	−0.001	47.	West Virginia	−0.007
23.	Florida	−0.001	48.	New York	−0.007
24.	Arizona	−0.002	49.	North Carolina	−0.008
25.	Montana	-0.002	50	Hawaii	−0.008

MALA PROHIBITA

0.5% The term *mala prohibita* refers to acts defined as criminal in statute, even though they are not harms in common law (*mala in se*). This category is a grab bag of mostly unrelated policies, including raw milk laws, fireworks laws, prostitution laws, physician-assisted suicide laws, religious freedom restoration acts, rules on taking DNA samples from criminal suspects without a probable-cause hearing, trans-fat bans, and, new to this edition, state equal rights amendments, and mixed martial arts legalization.[88]

Of these, the policies with the greatest potential cost to victims are prostitution prohibition and trans-fat bans. If Nevada-style policies legalizing but regulating brothels were in effect nationwide, the industry would garner an estimated $5 billion in revenue.[89] Next most important is California's restaurant trans-fat ban, which if implemented nationwide would cost consumers—at a reasonable estimate—over $3.5 billion worth of pleasure a year.[90] Next is the legalization of raw milk, then legalization of mixed martial arts, followed closely by fireworks laws. Then comes physician-assisted suicide, which receives the "times five" constitutional weighting factor, since the Montana constitution has been held to protect a right thereto. Rounding out this category, in order, are state equal rights amendments, state DNA database laws, and religious freedom restoration acts.

---

88. To be clear, we do not necessarily condone prostitution, but we defend the rights of willing adults to engage in the consensual exchange of sex. We completely condemn all nonconsensual sex trafficking as unjust and deserving of legal prohibition.

89. Daria Snadowsky, "The Best Little Whorehouse Is Not in Texas: How Nevada's Prostitution Laws Serve Public Policy, and How Those Laws May Be Improved," *Nevada Law Journal* 6, no. 1 (2005): 217–19.

90. *The Becker-Posner Blog*, "Comment on the New York Ban on Trans Fats," blog entry by Gary Becker, December 21, 2006, http://www.becker-posner-blog.com/2006/12/comment-on-the-new-york-ban-on-trans-fats--becker.html.

TABLE 28

Rank	State	Mala Prohibita Ranking		Rank	State	Mala Prohibita Ranking
1.	Nevada	0.0117		26.	South Dakota	0.0004
2.	New Mexico	0.0029		27.	Oklahoma	0.0004
3.	Washington	0.0022		28.	Virginia	0.0004
4.	Oregon	0.0018		29.	Kansas	0.0002
5.	Vermont	0.0012		30.	Colorado	0.0002
6.	Pennsylvania	0.0012		31.	Kentucky	0.0001
7.	New Hampshire	0.0011		32.	Massachusetts	0.0000
8.	Connecticut	0.0011		33.	North Dakota	−0.0002
9.	Wyoming	0.0010		34.	Wisconsin	−0.0002
10.	South Carolina	0.0010		35.	Hawaii	−0.0002
11.	Missouri	0.0010		36.	Maryland	−0.0002
12.	Texas	0.0010		37.	Mississippi	−0.0003
13.	Utah	0.0009		38.	Louisiana	−0.0004
14.	Montana	0.0008		39.	Rhode Island	−0.0004
15.	Tennessee	0.0008		40.	Florida	−0.0005
16.	Maine	0.0007		41.	Georgia	−0.0006
17.	Minnesota	0.0007		42.	North Carolina	−0.0006
18.	Arkansas	0.0007		43.	West Virginia	−0.0006
19.	Illinois	0.0007		44.	Alabama	−0.0007
20.	Indiana	0.0006		45.	Ohio	−0.0009
21.	Arizona	0.0006		46.	Iowa	−0.0010
22.	Alaska	0.0006		47.	New York	−0.0016
23.	Idaho	0.0006		48.	Delaware	−0.0017
24.	Nebraska	0.0005		49.	New Jersey	−0.0019
25.	Michigan	0.0005		50.	California	−0.0089

CAMPAIGN FINANCE

0.1% Citizens should have the right to express and promote their political opinions in a democracy, including their support for or opposition to candidates for office. By regulating contributions to parties and candidates, governments effectively limit citizens' ability to spread their ideas.

The campaign finance policy category covers public financing of campaigns and contribution limits (individuals to candidates, individuals to parties, an index of individuals to political action committees (PACs) and PACs to candidates, and an index of individuals to PACs and PACs to parties). Although these policies receive "constitutional weights" boosting them by a factor of 10 because of their First Amendment implications, they receive low weights even so because there is little evidence that current contribution limits significantly reduce private actors' involvement in politics, unless the limits are extremely low (and Vermont's extremely low limits were struck down by the U.S. Supreme Court in 2006).[91]

Also, there is just not much money in state elections, even in states without contribution limits. According to the National Institute on Money in State Politics, in the last three election cycles nationwide individual contributions to state legislative candidates amounted to about $850 million per two-year cycle, or less than $3 per person in the country.[92] Finally, even being prevented from making, say, a $1,000 donation to a candidate does not result in a $1,000 loss to the frustrated donor, since the donor can put those funds to a different use. The freedom index assumes a utility loss equivalent to 10 percent of the planned contribution when calculating victim cost. In sum, the nationwide victim losses from state campaign finance restrictions come to a figure in the tens of millions of dollars a year, at most.

91. *Randall v. Sorrell*, 548 U.S. 230 (2006).
92. National Institute on Money in State Politics website, http://www.followthemoney.org.

TABLE 29

Rank	State	Campaign Finance Freedom Ranking		Rank	State	Campaign Finance Freedom Ranking
1.	Indiana	0.00108		26.	North Carolina	−0.00024
1.	Mississippi	0.00108		27.	Ohio	−0.00024
1.	Missouri	0.00108		28.	Illinois	−0.00025
1.	North Dakota	0.00108		29.	South Carolina	−0.00025
1.	Oregon	0.00108		30.	New York	−0.00025
1.	Pennsylvania	0.00108		31.	Maryland	−0.00026
1.	Texas	0.00108		32.	Michigan	−0.00026
8.	Virginia	0.00106		33.	California	−0.00027
9.	Alabama	0.00104		34.	Arizona	−0.00043
9.	Iowa	0.00104		35.	Delaware	−0.00046
9.	Utah	0.00104		36.	Louisiana	−0.00047
12.	Nebraska	0.00089		37.	Vermont	−0.00051
13.	Wyoming	0.00012		38.	Rhode Island	−0.00057
14.	Nevada	−0.00001		39.	Kansas	−0.00061
15.	Georgia	−0.00002		40.	Hawaii	−0.00062
16.	New Mexico	−0.00003		41.	Alaska	−0.00063
17.	Tennessee	−0.00004		42.	New Jersey	−0.00063
18.	Idaho	−0.00006		43.	New Hampshire	−0.00065
19.	Montana	−0.00006		44.	Oklahoma	−0.00072
20.	Washington	−0.00007		45.	Wisconsin	−0.00074
21.	Florida	−0.00008		46.	West Virginia	−0.00075
22.	South Dakota	−0.00011		47.	Kentucky	−0.00076
23.	Minnesota	−0.00015		48.	Massachusetts	−0.00077
24.	Maine	−0.00016		49.	Colorado	−0.00077
25.	Arkansas	−0.00022		50.	Connecticut	−0.00083

29% The top states in the personal freedom dimension tend to be more western and northeastern, while the bottom states are mostly socially conservative and southern. In past editions, we have found a strong rural–urban division, but that factor has diminished with the new weights, particularly on gun rights and asset forfeiture. One reason for the rural–urban relationship is likely voters' fears of crime, which lead them to support harsh policing and prosecutorial tactics, stricter drug and gun laws, and more limits on civil liberties. However, no statistical relationship exists between personal freedom and actual crime rates. It is well known that public perceptions of crime can diverge widely from the truth.[93] An alternative explanation is that more negative externalities of personal behavior exist in urban settings. But if that were the case, one would also expect urbanized states to have more economic regulation and higher taxation, and they do not. Socially conservative states tend to restrict alcohol, gambling, marijuana, and marriage freedoms but permit greater freedom in education and have more respect for gun rights and for private property on smoking policy.

Figure 8 shows state average personal freedom scores over time. After personal freedom plunged nationwide between 2000 and 2008, partially due to a wave of new tobacco restrictions, it has grown substantially since 2010, due in large part to judicial engagement on gun and marriage rights and to ballot initiatives loosening cannabis regulations.

FIGURE 8 Personal Freedom Weights

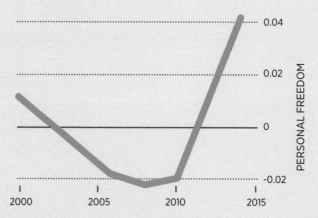

93. Lydia Saad, "Perceptions of Crime Problem Remain Curiously Negative," Gallup, October 22, 2007, http://www.gallup.com/poll/102262/perceptions-crime-problem-remain-curiously-negative.aspx; University of Texas, "Public Perception of Crime Remains out of Sync with Reality, Criminologist Contends," November 10, 2008, http://news.utexas.edu/2008/11/10/crime.

TABLE 30

Rank	State	Overall Personal Freedom Ranking		Rank	State	Overall Personal Freedom Ranking
1.	New Mexico	0.183		26.	Maryland	0.045
2.	Colorado	0.177		27.	New Jersey	0.041
3.	Nevada	0.172		28.	Missouri	0.034
4.	Maine	0.162		29.	New York	0.027
5.	Washington	0.160		30.	Oklahoma	0.025
6.	Indiana	0.151		31.	Delaware	0.018
7.	Alaska	0.132		32.	Wyoming	0.015
8.	Minnesota	0.122		33.	Utah	0.014
9.	New Hampshire	0.114		34.	Virginia	0.003
10.	Vermont	0.110		35.	North Dakota	0.002
11.	Massachusetts	0.106		36.	Florida	−0.003
12.	Iowa	0.105		37.	Hawaii	−0.008
13.	North Carolina	0.101		38.	Michigan	−0.015
14.	Arizona	0.088		39.	Louisiana	−0.025
15.	Connecticut	0.087		40.	Nebraska	−0.025
16.	California	0.085		41.	Arkansas	−0.030
17.	Rhode Island	0.075		42.	Tennessee	−0.031
18.	Oregon	0.072		43.	Georgia	−0.034
19.	South Carolina	0.065		44.	Ohio	−0.035
20.	Illinois	0.060		45.	Idaho	−0.049
21.	Montana	0.059		46.	South Dakota	−0.072
22.	West Virginia	0.057		47.	Mississippi	−0.087
23.	Pennsylvania	0.056		48.	Alabama	−0.087
24.	Kansas	0.053		49.	Texas	−0.096
25.	Wisconsin	0.045		50.	Kentucky	−0.106

FIGURE 9 Freedom Evolution of Selected States

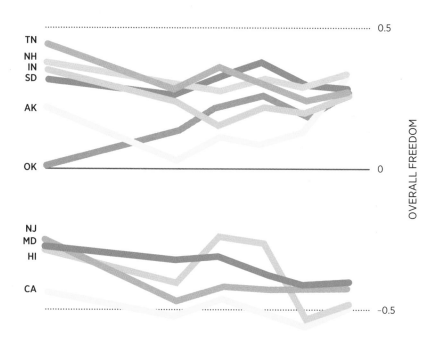

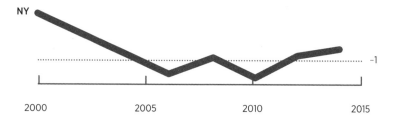

OVERALL
FREEDOM RANKING

The weighted sum of all the variables is used to produce the overall freedom ranking of the states. The overall freedom scores rate states on how free they are relative to other states. A score of 1 would correspond to a state's being one standard deviation above average in every single variable, although in reality, every state scores better on some variables and worse on others. A score of 0 would be equivalent to a state's being absolutely average on every variable, and a score of –1 to a state's being one standard deviation below average on every variable. Table 31 presents the overall freedom rankings as of year-end 2014.

New Hampshire, Alaska, Oklahoma, Indiana, and South Dakota make up a quintet at the top of the ranking; Tennessee and Idaho follow closely behind. New York is by far the least free state, followed by California, Hawaii, New Jersey, and Maryland. Since states' freedom scores represent their situation at the beginning of the year 2015, they include changes made by legislatures that in most states were elected in November 2012. Figure 9 shows the evolution of the top and bottom states over time.

The Granite State began at number two at the start of our time series in 2000; then, it narrowly took the top spot over Tennessee in 2006. It slipped further in 2007–8, made up some ground in 2009–10, and improved relative to other states even while falling back in absolute terms during the PPACA implementation years 2011–12. In other words, New Hampshire improved substantially on policies under its own control following the 2010 elections. With further improvement in 2013–14, the state was able to take the crown narrowly from a faltering South Dakota.

South Dakota has scored generally high throughout our period and was a clear number one in 2010 and 2012. Most of South Dakota's improvements occurred during the 2007–10 period. Although the state has fallen to number five, it remains very close to the top spot.

Indiana has risen to the number four slot with slow and steady reform. The Hoosier State began well enough in 2000, fell off the pace in the years to 2008, and then has climbed upward since 2009, even as most other states have fallen back. Educational freedom is one area where Indiana has truly been a national leader in recent years.

Alaska finds itself in the top five for the first time. The Last Frontier had fallen well off the pace of the leaders in 2006–10, but since then it has rocketed upward, partly on the strength of cannabis legalization in 2014, but also because of substantial improvements in fiscal policy, such as tax cuts at the state level and large reductions in state debt. However, Alaska's fiscal policy score is significantly overstated in 2014 due to collapsing corporate tax revenues following oil price declines.

Oklahoma presents the most positive picture of improvement over time. The state shot up significantly between 2000 and 2006, gains that the state built upon in 2007–10. After sharing in the decline that hit virtually every state in 2011–12, Oklahoma bounced back strongly in 2013–14.

Tennessee's record is one of modest but secular decline (a consistent negative trend sustained over the long run). From a clear number one in 2000, Tennessee fell just behind New Hampshire in 2006, narrowly regained top billing in 2008, and has fallen since then. Still, even at number six, it is not far behind number one New Hampshire.

Although none of the top six states is considered a highly desirable locale by coastal elites, residents of these states have much to be proud of, and the rest of us should be more willing to look to states like New Hampshire, South Dakota, Indiana, and Oklahoma as models to emulate.

What might be most remarkable about these rankings and the overall freedom scores is how much worse New York is than even the next-lowest-ranking state. Indeed, the Empire State scores about half a point worse than almost every other state in the Union, and almost a point and a half worse than the freest states. The difference between New York's and New Hampshire's scores corresponds to one and a third standard deviations on every single variable. New York also performs poorly across the board, ranking at or near the bottom in all three dimensions of freedom. Thus, New Yorkers feel the heavy hand of government in every area of their lives. Is it any wonder that people are fleeing the state in droves? According to the Internal Revenue Service state-to-state migration data, about 1.3 million people, on net, fled New York for other states between 2000 and 2012, 9.3 percent of the state's 2000 population (the IRS's measure of "people" is exemptions claimed on tax filings). Fortunately, the state remains a magnet for foreign immigrants. Otherwise, it might be facing some of the same problems bedeviling demographically challenged countries outside the United States.

Of the top 20 states in the overall freedom ranking, 15 were carried by Republican Party candidate Mitt Romney in 2012. The outliers are New Hampshire, Virginia, Colorado, Iowa, and Florida, all of which are moderate "swing" states. This pattern is replicated in reverse for the bottom 20 states.

OVERALL FREEDOM RANKING

TABLE 31

Rank	State	Overall Freedom Score	Rank	State	Overall Freedom Score
1.	New Hampshire	0.33	26.	Pennsylvania	0.03
2.	Alaska	0.33	27.	Wisconsin	0.03
3.	Oklahoma	0.28	28.	Texas	0.00
4.	Indiana	0.28	29.	Arkansas	-0.02
5.	South Dakota	0.28	30.	New Mexico	-0.03
6.	Tennessee	0.26	31.	Delaware	-0.05
7.	Idaho	0.26	32.	Washington	-0.05
8.	Florida	0.21	33.	Massachusetts	-0.06
9.	Iowa	0.20	34.	Louisiana	-0.06
10.	Arizona	0.18	35.	Ohio	-0.08
11.	Colorado	0.18	36.	Mississippi	-0.10
12.	Nevada	0.18	37.	Oregon	-0.10
13.	North Dakota	0.18	38.	Minnesota	-0.11
14.	Wyoming	0.17	39.	West Virginia	-0.12
15.	South Carolina	0.15	40.	Vermont	-0.12
16.	Kansas	0.15	41.	Kentucky	-0.15
17.	Montana	0.14	42.	Maine	-0.15
18.	Missouri	0.14	43.	Rhode Island	-0.17
19.	North Carolina	0.14	44.	Illinois	-0.26
20.	Utah	0.14	45.	Connecticut	-0.26
21.	Virginia	0.10	46.	Maryland	-0.40
22.	Georgia	0.09	47.	New Jersey	-0.43
23.	Alabama	0.09	48.	Hawaii	-0.49
24.	Michigan	0.06	49.	California	-0.50
25.	Nebraska	0.05	50.	New York	-0.98

Sixteen of the 20 (and all bottom 9) were carried by the Democratic Party nominee and presidential election winner Barack Obama. Still, some deeply Republican states do poorly: Louisiana, Mississippi, West Virginia, and Kentucky. That factor would suggest that the so-called red state–blue state divide in American politics affects freedom. In the next chapter, we analyze this relationship more systematically.

Figure 10 shows the evolution of overall freedom scores over time. Although there is no trend in the data since 2006 despite the PPACA's big impact in 2011–12, the trend going back to 2000 is clearly negative. Americans have become less free over the past decade and a half because of intervention at the state level. Similar trends have been found at the central level in other studies.[94] We discuss some of the reasons for the decline in 2011–12 and the rebound in 2013–14 in the next section, "Change over Time." One interesting point we will note here is that if we exclude health insurance altogether, every state but two would have posted overall freedom gains in 2011–12.

FIGURE 10 State Average Overall Freedom over Time

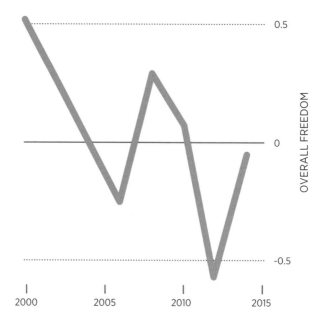

94. James Gwartney, Robert Lawson, and Joshua Hall, "Economic Freedom of the World: Lessons for the U.S.," *Huffington Post*, September 25, 2011, http://www.huffingtonpost.com/james-gwartney/economic-freedom-of-the-w_b_980441.html.

CHANGE OVER TIME

The following list pulls out the most improved and worsened states from year-end 2012 to year-end 2014 (Table 32). It is important to recognize that short-term changes will be caused by a great deal of noise in the fiscal data that may or may not be due to significant policy changes, especially since our fiscal year 2015 tax data are budget projections. Nonetheless, it is worth noting which states saw the most change in individual freedom in the period covered by our newest data.

Alaska tops the list as most improved, but its presence here is misleading. Half of Alaska's measured freedom gain was due to what appears in the data to have been a massive tax cut, but in fact no statutory changes occurred to cause tax collections to fall in fiscal years 2014 and 2015. Instead, the falling price of oil drove down corporate profits and cut corporate income tax collections in half. The state made up the difference by withdrawing massive sums from its huge rainy-day fund. As we have seen in previous editions of this index, resource-dependent "rentier" states like Alaska and Wyoming are especially volatile on fiscal policy.

Kansas's high score is also a bit misleading. About 40 percent of its increase in 2013–14 is due to phased-in tax cuts that were not initially paid for and resulted in a credit rating downgrade.[95] Subsequent tax increases to close the gap do not yet show up in our index. [96] However, the remaining 60 percent of Kansas's growth came from same-sex marriage legalization and enactment of a tax credit scholarship program.

Interestingly, every state but South Dakota increased on freedom in 2013–14. The most important single reason for the nationwide gain in freedom over this period was improvements on marriage policy, driven by legislative and judicial initiatives to grant gay couples access to the institution. However, other personal freedoms also increased, including educational freedom and gun rights. As we have already seen, state fiscal policies also jumped upward in this period, as more states cut than raised taxes in FY 2015.

Our second list shows changes from year-end 2010 to year-end 2012 (Table 33). Those changes occurred from the date of the last edition of the freedom index (published in 2013), which had a data cutoff of December 31, 2010, through the next two years. As repeatedly noted in the text, most states fell during these years because of PPACA implementation, and if that policy had not occurred, most states would have gained in freedom. States that already had community rating and guaranteed issue for nongroup and small-group

95. *Cato at Liberty,* "Governor Brownback's Tax Cuts," blog entry by Chris Edwards, October 10, 2014, http://www.cato .org/blog/governor-brownbacks-tax-cuts.

96. "Kansas House, Senate Pass Tax Increases, End 113-Day Session," *Wichita Eagle,* June 12, 2015, http://www.kansas.com /news/politics-government/article23827492.html.

TABLE 32

Rank	State	Freedom Growth, 2013–14			
1.	Alaska	0.19	26.	Rhode Island	0.05
2.	Kansas	0.14	27.	Florida	0.04
3.	Wisconsin	0.11	28.	Ohio	0.04
4.	North Carolina	0.11	29.	New Hampshire	0.04
5.	Arizona	0.11	30.	Alabama	0.04
6.	Utah	0.11	31.	Maine	0.04
7.	South Carolina	0.10	32.	Washington	0.03
8.	Oklahoma	0.10	33.	Iowa	0.03
9.	Montana	0.09	34.	Tennessee	0.03
10.	Idaho	0.09	35.	Louisiana	0.02
11.	Virginia	0.09	36.	Oregon	0.02
12.	West Virginia	0.08	37.	Missouri	0.02
13.	Indiana	0.08	38.	Texas	0.02
14.	Illinois	0.08	39.	New York	0.01
15.	Delaware	0.08	40.	Michigan	0.01
16.	Colorado	0.08	41.	Arkansas	0.01
17.	New Mexico	0.07	42.	Mississippi	0.01
18.	Wyoming	0.07	43.	Georgia	0.01
19.	Pennsylvania	0.07	44.	Vermont	0.01
20.	Minnesota	0.06	45.	Maryland	0.01
21.	Hawaii	0.05	46.	New Jersey	0.01
22.	Connecticut	0.05	47.	Kentucky	0.0
23.	California	0.05	48.	Massachusetts	0.0
24.	Nevada	0.05	49.	Nebraska	0.0
25.	North Dakota	0.05	50.	South Dakota	−0.02

TABLE 33

Rank	State	Freedom Growth, 2011-12		Rank	State	Freedom Growth, 2011-12
1.	Washington	0.08		26.	Arizona	-0.07
2.	New York	0.08		27.	Nevada	-0.08
3.	Alaska	0.05		28.	Nebraska	-0.08
4.	Massachusetts	0.05		29.	New Mexico	-0.08
5.	Vermont	0.02		30.	Illinois	-0.08
6.	Maine	0.01		31.	Connecticut	-0.08
7.	Michigan	0.00		32.	Ohio	-0.09
8.	Wyoming	-0.01		33.	Kansas	-0.09
9.	New Jersey	-0.01		34.	South Carolina	-0.10
10.	Rhode Island	-0.01		35.	North Dakota	-0.10
11.	Louisiana	-0.02		36.	Iowa	-0.10
12.	Indiana	-0.02		37.	Texas	-0.10
13.	New Hampshire	-0.02		38.	Minnesota	-0.11
14.	Oregon	-0.03		39.	Missouri	-0.11
15.	Colorado	-0.03		40.	Montana	-0.11
16.	California	-0.03		41.	Kentucky	-0.11
17.	Maryland	-0.04		42.	Georgia	-0.11
18.	West Virginia	-0.04		43.	Alabama	-0.11
19.	Arkansas	-0.05		44.	Idaho	-0.11
20.	Wisconsin	-0.06		45.	Virginia	-0.11
21.	North Carolina	-0.06		46.	Utah	-0.12
22.	Florida	-0.07		47.	Mississippi	-0.12
23.	Tennessee	-0.07		48.	Pennsylvania	-0.12
24.	Oklahoma	-0.07		49.	Delaware	-0.13
25.	South Dakota	-0.07		50.	Hawaii	-0.28

health insurance—and in the case of Massachusetts, an individual mandate—
were not much affected by the federal law. Thus, New York had already
destroyed its nongroup health insurance market with regulation and did
not suffer a big fall in measured health insurance freedom during 2011–12.
In fact, New York's fiscal policy improved noticeably, and its personal freedom increased significantly, mostly because of same-sex marriage, but also
because of improvements across the board in victimless crime arrests and
incarceration rates.

Washington similarly regulated health insurance strictly before the
PPACA, and so its enactment did not harm the state much. Washington
improves so much because of the legalization of cannabis possession for personal use, which took effect immediately in 2012; privatization of the state
liquor monopoly and legalization of grocery store sales of spirits; expansion
of legal gambling; reductions in victimless crime arrests and incarceration
rate; and moderate reductions in taxes, government debt, subsidies, and
public employment.

By contrast, Hawaii was our previous top state for health insurance freedom, and the PPACA was responsible for over 50 percent of its measured
decline in these two years. However, Hawaii also experienced one of the
largest tax increases in the country under Governor Neil Abercrombie, raising income, excise, and rental car sales taxes.[97] Even without the PPACA,
Hawaii would have been our biggest loser for these two years.

The last list showing changes over time (Table 34) highlights the big picture since our first comprehensive set of data in 2000. Thus, this list covers
policies from year-end 2000 until year-end 2014. Between those two years,
inclusive, we now have six data points for each state (2000, 2006, 2008,
2010, 2012, and 2014).

Over this long period, Oklahoma is by far the biggest gainer. The state
posted tremendous gains on regulatory policy between 2000 and 2006,
improving yet further to 2010. The state also improved massively on fiscal
policy in 2007–8, as well as in every other interval we measure. On personal
freedom, the state improved during every interval except 2000–2006, with
its biggest gains coming in 2010–14. Legal gambling was a big part of its
personal freedom improvement in 2011–12. Tax credit scholarships and a
voucher program for students with disabilities also boosted the state's educational freedom. Oklahoma is even beginning to shed its civil-authoritarian
reputation as local police departments reduce their participation in asset
forfeiture equitable sharing and it has cut its drug enforcement rate over the
past 14 years by more than 50 percent. A 2012 prison reform bill (the Justice
Reinvestment Initiative, HB 3052) and a 2015 law (the Justice Safety Valve

97. Chris Edwards, *Fiscal Policy Report Card on America's Governors 2012* (Washington, DC: Cato Institute, 2012), p. 6.

TABLE 34

Rank	State	Freedom Growth, 2000–2014		Rank	State	Freedom Growth, 2000–2014
1.	Oklahoma	0.27		26.	California	-0.06
2.	Alaska	0.11		27.	Iowa	-0.07
3.	Maine	0.11		28.	Ohio	-0.07
4.	Idaho	0.09		29.	Indiana	-0.07
5.	Utah	0.04		30.	Texas	-0.08
6.	Wisconsin	0.03		31.	Delaware	-0.09
7.	Florida	0.01		32.	Arkansas	-0.09
8.	Michigan	0.01		33.	Minnesota	-0.09
9.	Montana	0.01		34.	Missouri	-0.10
10.	Washington	0.00		35.	Nevada	-0.10
11.	Arizona	0.00		36.	Alabama	-0.11
12.	South Carolina	0.00		37.	Kansas	-0.11
13.	Louisiana	0.00		38.	Pennsylvania	-0.11
14.	Colorado	-0.01		39.	Maryland	-0.12
15.	New Mexico	-0.02		40.	Mississippi	-0.12
16.	Georgia	-0.02		41.	New York	-0.13
17.	Virginia	-0.03		42.	Oregon	-0.14
18.	South Dakota	-0.04		43.	Rhode Island	-0.14
19.	North Dakota	-0.04		44.	Connecticut	-0.16
20.	Massachusetts	-0.04		45.	New Jersey	-0.16
21.	New Hampshire	-0.04		46.	Tennessee	-0.17
22.	Wyoming	-0.06		47.	Nebraska	-0.20
23.	North Carolina	-0.06		48.	Hawaii	-0.21
24.	West Virginia	-0.06		49.	Kentucky	-0.22
25.	Vermont	-0.06		50.	Illinois	-0.22

Act, HB 1518) should continue to reduce the state's future incarceration rate by giving judges more flexibility over sentencing and drug treatment options and separating minor parole offenders from the general prison population. Federal courts have struck down the state's sodomy law and same-sex marriage ban (which was a super-DOMA prohibiting all marriage-like private contracts).

Kentucky is our second biggest loser over this 14-year period. However, we believe its decline is overstated. The state posted a massive loss in personal freedom between 2000 and 2006 (about 0.15 points). Part of that loss is due to the enactment of a harsh anti-gay-marriage law, but part of it is due to a huge measured increase in drug arrests. But the Federal Bureau of Investigation data we use for drug arrests are probably flawed for Kentucky in 2000, because the state is such an outlier that year, and the data are based on law enforcement unit surveys with incomplete response rates and therefore are not necessarily representative of the whole state. Kentucky has improved on fiscal policy, mostly in the years 2007–8. However, it has gradually declined on regulatory policy.

Illinois is the "biggest loser" over the 2000–2014 period. Although the state did improve significantly on personal freedom, it lost a tremendous amount of economic freedom, especially because of its fiscal policies. In 2000, Illinois was an above-average state on both fiscal and regulatory policy. The biggest declines occurred in the 2009–12 period, when taxes were hiked repeatedly. State and local government debt rose by 9 percentage points of personal income between FY 2000 and FY 2011. State and local employment rose steadily from 2001 to 2010 and has fallen back since. Local taxes rose faster than the national average in the 2001–8 period, however. On regulatory policy, the state's biggest losses came in health insurance, labor policy (repeat minimum-wage hikes), and occupational licensing (increase in extent and coverage of licenses).

Lastly, it is worth pointing out policy areas that have received significant attention throughout the 2000–2014 period. Tobacco policy is the most notable area in which state policies have become more restrictive of personal freedom, with significant increases in taxes as well as greater and greater restrictions on where one can smoke. Laws dealing with domestic partnerships, civil unions, and gay marriage also changed dramatically, especially in the years 2010–14. Cannabis laws are undergoing liberalization, first in states with citizen ballot initiatives. Gun laws and educational policies have been gradually liberalized across the country. On the regulatory side, eminent domain reform occurred in some fashion in most states following the infamous *Kelo v. City of New London* decision by the U.S. Supreme Court in 2005. Indiana, Michigan, and Wisconsin (after our data cutoff) have recently enacted right-to-work laws, and that area seems likely to remain active, as other states such as New Hampshire have passed bills only to see them vetoed. Policies dealing with new technologies, such as DNA databases and automated license plate readers, are new issues and will continue to evolve.

One ongoing feature of policy change is the displacement of state discretion with federal mandates, for both good and ill with regard to pure individual liberty (leaving aside the damage done to federalism, a long-term institutional bulwark of freedom). Federal courts have forced states to liberalize gun laws, sodomy laws, and marriage laws, though in all those areas state governments were reforming long before the federal courts chose to intervene conclusively. In health insurance regulation, all three branches of the federal government have acted in concert to dramatically raise the regulatory threshold, mostly via the PPACA. States may still choose to regulate health insurance even more tightly than the federal government, but they may not choose more market-oriented models of regulation.

INDEX OF CRONYISM

For the first time, we present a separate "freedom from cronyism" state ranking that takes into account blatantly anti-competitive business and alcohol regulations and subsidies. In addition to subsidies as a share of the state economy, this index draws on the following variables: (a) general sales-below-cost/minimum-markup law, (b) sales-below-cost/minimum-markup law for gasoline, (c) certificate of public convenience and necessity for household goods movers, (d) direct auto sales bans, (e) certificate of need for hospital construction, (f) all occupational licensing variables, (g) eminent domain laws, (h) bans on direct shipment of wine, and (i) alcohol sales blue laws.

Table 35 shows how the states come out on cronyism in 2014 (higher values/lower rankings indicate less cronyism). The numbers in the table represent the weights of each variable multiplied by the standardized value (number of standard deviations greater than the mean). As noted in the previous chapter, a state that is one standard deviation better—freer—than the average on every single policy will score 1 on overall freedom. Since the index of cronyism draws on a subset of the freedom index, the values in this table fall within a much smaller range. Wyoming's score of 0.078, therefore, means that, taking cronyist policies into account, Wyoming's positions on those issues contribute 0.078 to its overall freedom score. Wyoming is the least cronyist state.

We compare our cronyism scores with state corruption scores based on a survey of statehouse journalists.[98] The correlation between the two is −0.38,

98. Bill Marsh, "Illinois Is Trying. It Really Is. But the Most Corrupt State Is Actually ...," *New York Times*, December 14, 2008, http://www.nytimes.com/2008/12/14/weekinreview/14marsh.html.

TABLE 35

Rank	State	Freedom from Cronyism Ranking		Rank	State	Freedom from Cronyism Ranking
1.	Wyoming	0.078		26.	Michigan	−0.004
2.	Idaho	0.072		27.	Georgia	−0.005
3.	Kansas	0.056		28.	Texas	−0.005
4.	Colorado	0.046		29.	Rhode Island	−0.010
5.	Minnesota	0.045		30.	Connecticut	−0.010
6.	North Dakota	0.038		31.	Virginia	−0.011
7.	South Dakota	0.036		32.	Alaska	−0.011
8.	New Hampshire	0.032		33.	South Carolina	−0.015
9.	Indiana	0.025		34.	North Carolina	−0.017
10.	Missouri	0.021		35.	Ohio	−0.017
11.	Nebraska	0.020		36.	Delaware	−0.022
12.	New Mexico	0.018		37.	Nevada	−0.026
13.	Iowa	0.018		38.	Tennessee	−0.026
14.	Vermont	0.018		39.	Arkansas	−0.028
15.	Wisconsin	0.018		40.	Washington	−0.030
16.	Mississippi	0.017		41.	Hawaii	−0.031
17.	Montana	0.016		42.	Florida	−0.036
18.	Pennsylvania	0.014		43.	New Jersey	−0.036
19.	Alabama	0.011		44.	Oregon	−0.042
20.	Kentucky	0.007		45.	Louisiana	−0.048
21.	Maine	0.005		46.	Illinois	−0.049
22.	Utah	0.003		47.	Massachusetts	−0.053
23.	Oklahoma	0.003		48.	California	−0.060
24.	Arizona	0.003		49.	Maryland	−0.064
25.	West Virginia	−0.003		50.	New York	−0.107

indicating that states scoring higher on freedom from cronyism score lower on corruption. In other words, cronyist states are more corrupt.

We also compare our cronyism scores with state lobbyist-to-legislator ratios from the mid-2000s. [99] The correlation between the two is −0.48, indicating that states with more lobbyists relative to legislators are more cronyist. Figure 11 shows how the freedom from cronyism index relates to the logged number of lobbyists per legislator for all 49 states for which lobbyist data are available (Nevada is excluded).

FIGURE 11

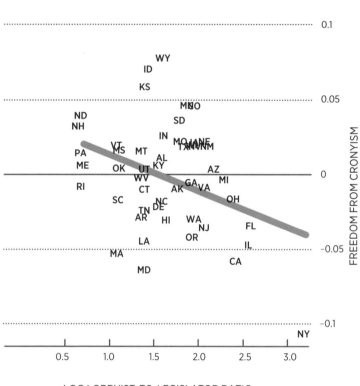

LOG LOBBYIST-TO-LEGISLATOR RATIO

99. Center for Public Integrity, "Ratio of Lobbyists to Legislators 2006," December 21, 2007, http://www.publicintegrity.org/2007/12/21/5913/ratio-lobbyists-legislators-2006.

When freedom from cronyism is regressed on both the corruption and lobbyist ratio, each independent variable enters the equation with a negative sign and is statistically significant. The relationship is stronger with the raw lobbyist ratio, but it holds up very well when the log value of lobbyist ratio is used to deal with outliers like New York.

Political economist Mancur Olson famously argued that states that had been in the Union longer would have more organized, distributive coalitions, more complex regulation, and therefore lower economic growth.[100] He also makes an exception for former Confederate states, which he claims experienced a complete replacement of their political systems, first through Reconstruction and then through desegregation and the Voting Rights Act of 1965. We will consider this and other institutional and cultural explanations for freedom in the next chapter.

---

100. Mancur Olson, *The Rise and Decline of Nations: Economic Growth, Stagflation, and Social Rigidities* (New Haven, CT: Yale University Press, 1982).

PART 2
POLITICS OF FREEDOM

In this chapter, we consider the causes and consequences of freedom in the states. First, we examine the relationship between public opinion and freedom. Next, we investigate how freedom and policy ideology relate to each other. Third, we consider whether political institutions and culture affect freedom. Fourth, we consider the consequences of freedom for economic growth and migration. Finally, we sum up with some observations about the political economy of freedom at the state level.

PUBLIC OPINION AND FREEDOM

Figure 12 is a scatter plot of state economic and personal freedom scores for year-end 2012. A quarter of the states are loosely clustered in the lower-right quadrant of the figure with positive economic freedom scores but negative personal freedom. However, the outlier states are instructive. In the bottom part of the lower-right quadrant, we see economically freer, personally less free states, such as Idaho, South Dakota, Oklahoma, Georgia, Texas, Alabama, and Virginia. Idaho is the paradigmatic conservative state here.

FIGURE 12

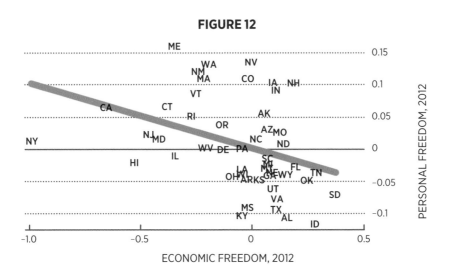

In the upper right are economically and personally free states, such as New Hampshire, Iowa, Alaska, Indiana, Arizona, Colorado, and Missouri. Tennessee, and Florida are mediocre on personal freedom but strong on economic freedom. In the upper center are Nevada, Washington, New Mexico, and Massachusetts, not particularly economically free but strong on personal freedom.

At the bottom center are Mississippi and Kentucky, relatively weak on personal freedom but mediocre on economic freedom. Far out on the left is New York, which scores quite poorly on economic freedom and is middling on personal freedom. New Jersey, Hawaii, Maryland, and Illinois are not as extreme as New York on economic freedom but still score quite badly on economic freedom while hovering around zero on personal freedom.

Finally, the upper left is fairly bare, with California, Connecticut, Maine, and Vermont performing poorly on economic freedom but doing a bit better on personal freedom (or in the case of Maine, a lot better). These are the stereotypical left-liberal states that do well on personal freedom but are economically collectivist. Generally, then, conservative states do better than left-liberal states on economic freedom and rural/western/New England states do better than urban/southern/Mid-Atlantic states on personal freedom. It is notable that clustering is not as dense around zero as it was in the last version of the freedom index, which captured policies as of year-end 2010.

As shown in Figure 13, at the end of 2014, fewer than a third of the states scored below zero on personal freedom, demonstrating how personal freedom has grown over the period our study covers. States such as Oklahoma, Idaho, Colorado, Indiana, Minnesota, and Washington improved substantially on personal freedom in 2013–14. No such trend is visible in economic freedom, and as already demonstrated, the nationwide downward trend in economic freedom has swamped the growth in average personal freedom.

FIGURE 13

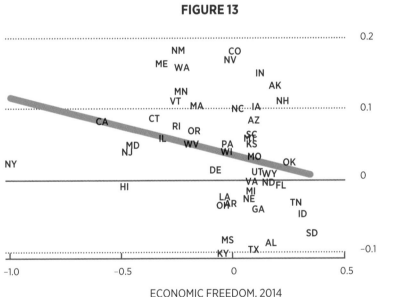

The negative correlation between economic and personal freedom also weakens in 2014 compared with 2012. Some would argue that from a libertarian point of view, conservative governance is good for economic freedom but bad for personal freedom, whereas the opposite is true of left-liberal governance. Conservative states, with some notable exceptions, do tend to have higher economic freedom than left-liberal states, but left-liberal states' advantage over conservative states on personal freedom is modest on average and "noisy."

As the scatter plots show, a group of states rank relatively highly on the overall year-end 2014 freedom index, are mostly moderately right-of-center, and are not especially controlling in the personal freedom dimension: New Hampshire (1st overall, 8th personal), Alaska (2nd overall, 7th personal), Indiana (4th overall, 6th personal), and Iowa (9th overall, 12th personal). Personal freedom includes both policies on which conservative states tend to be better than progressive states, such as education, guns, and tobacco, and policies on which progressive states tend to be better, such as marriage, cannabis, and incarceration rates and victimless crime arrests. Progressive states do not necessarily conform to the stereotype of enjoying greater personal freedom despite less economic freedom.

Several "blue" states, such as Hawaii, New York, Delaware, Wisconsin, and Michigan, score below the median on personal freedom in 2014, and more will join them now that the Supreme Court has nationalized same-sex marriage, thus ending an advantage they enjoyed over many "red" states. Indeed, another reason why economic freedom differentiates states better than personal freedom is the significant role played by the federal government on social policies that relate to personal freedom issues (especially given the decline in federalism in the arenas of marriage and guns), thus allowing conservative states' advantage on economic freedom to drive a measured difference in overall freedom.

We now move to analyzing in a more systematic fashion the relationship between public opinion ideology, as measured by presidential election results by state, and economic, personal, and overall freedom.

Figure 14 is a scatter plot of economic freedom in 2000 against presidential voting in 1996. (We choose presidential elections before the year that the policy is measured, because we think a lag exists between changes in public opinion and changes in law.) The x-axis measures the number of percentage points to the left of each state's popular vote, summing up Democratic and Green vote shares for the state minus the same for the country as a whole. We see a strong negative relationship between the leftward lean in the electorate and economic freedom. However, strongly conservative states are no more economically free on average than mildly conservative or centrist states, such as Tennessee, New Hampshire, Missouri, and Florida.

Figure 15 shows the same scatter plot for 2014, allowing us to see how the relationship between ideology and economic freedom has changed over the entire range of our time series. Now, the relationship between ideology and freedom looks more linear, rather than curved. Centrist states have fallen

FIGURE 14

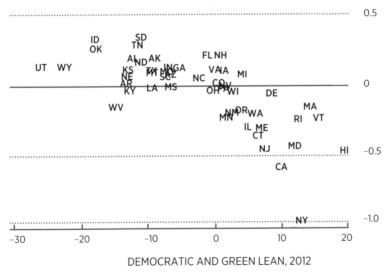

FIGURE 14 scatter plot. Y-axis: ECONOMIC FREEDOM, 2000 (0.5, 0, -0.5, -1.0). X-axis: DEMOCRATIC AND GREEN LEAN, 1996 (-20, -10, 0, 10, 20).

FIGURE 15

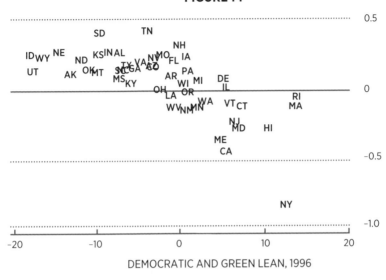

FIGURE 15 scatter plot. Y-axis: ECONOMIC FREEDOM, 2014 (0.5, 0, -0.5, -1.0). X-axis: DEMOCRATIC AND GREEN LEAN, 2012 (-30, -20, -10, 0, 10, 20).

on economic freedom, including Missouri and Iowa, while Tennessee has moved to the right in voting, yielding more consistency with its economic freedom position. West Virginia now looks like a big outlier, having moved substantially to the right since 2000. If right-wing ideology leads to more economic freedom, economic freedom should rise in West Virginia in future years. However, other poor, southern states tend not to do well on economic freedom (e.g., Mississippi, Arkansas, and Kentucky), suggesting West Virginia's room for improvement may be limited.

Figure 16 plots personal freedom in 2000 against partisan lean in 1996. The relationship between partisanship and personal freedom in that year was extremely noisy. Centrist New Mexico topped the charts, followed by right-wing Alaska. Left-leaning Illinois did badly, but it was outdone by deeply conservative Oklahoma, Idaho, South Dakota, Texas, and Alabama. All New England states except Connecticut were near the top.

FIGURE 16

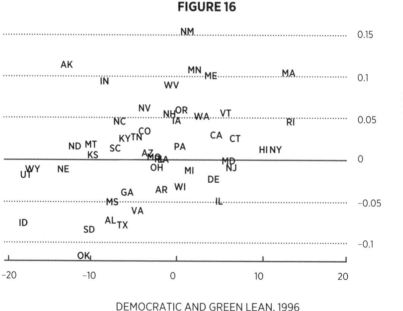

DEMOCRATIC AND GREEN LEAN, 1996

Figure 17 shows the relationship between partisanship and personal freedom at the end of our time series. Now, left-liberal states enjoy a clearer advantage on personal freedom, but the relationship is still much noisier than the one between partisanship and economic freedom. The bottom four states on personal freedom are southern: Kentucky, Alabama, Texas, and Mississippi.

FIGURE 17

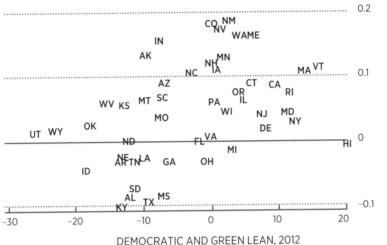

DEMOCRATIC AND GREEN LEAN, 2012

Figure 18 puts economic and personal freedom together to show how partisanship relates to overall freedom. Again, we see a curvilinear relationship in which conservative and moderate states do much better than strongly leftist ones. New York sits in a class of its own at the bottom of the scale.

FIGURE 18

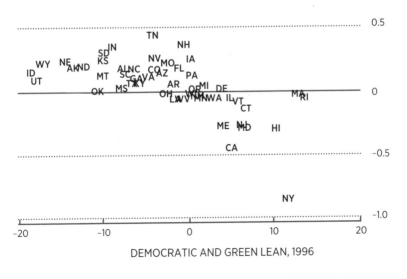

DEMOCRATIC AND GREEN LEAN, 1996

Figure 19 shows the overall freedom and partisanship relationship at the end of our time series. A distinct negative relationship exists between leftward tilt and overall freedom. However, the outliers are still noteworthy. New York is still abysmal even for a strongly left-wing state. West Virginia, Kentucky, Mississippi, Louisiana, and Arkansas all underperform other conservative states. Colorado, Nevada, and especially New Hampshire outperform the center. Massachusetts does better than one would expect for such a progressive state.

FIGURE 19

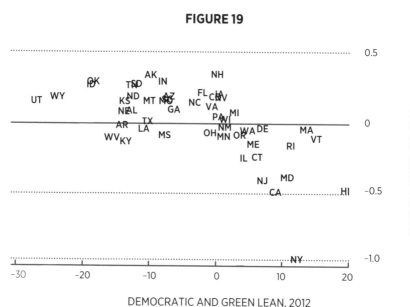

DEMOCRATIC AND GREEN LEAN, 2012

To study the dynamics of public opinion and freedom over time, we regressed, for each state, its overall freedom score on partisanship (Democratic and Green lean) from two years ago and from four years ago. (For years between presidential elections, we interpolate partisanship linearly.) The regression includes fixed state and year effects and covers the years 2008–14. This time period is short, so the results need to be taken as tentative. The "fixed effects" specification forces the regression to focus on over-time change within each state.[101] The results are shown in Table 36.

---

101. Despite Nickell bias, we also tried including a lagged dependent variable, but it was not statistically significant.

TABLE 36

Partisanship and Overall Freedom

Variable	Coefficient	Std. Error
Partisanship$_{t-2}$	0.009	0.001
Partisanship$_{t-4}$	−0.0120	0.001
R^2	97.7%	
N	200	

Note: Panel-corrected standard errors reported.

The statistically significant results suggest that when public opinion in a state moves left, freedom initially increases, then falls below where it was initially. Adding together the coefficients on both partisanship variables yields an estimate of −0.004 (statistically significant), which means that a one-point increase in leftward tilt reduces freedom by 0.004 permanently. For instance, if a state begins at 2 percentage points to the left of the national median voter in presidential elections, then moves to 6 percentage points to the left, the predicted change in freedom over the next two years is $4*0.008=0.032$. However, the change in freedom over four years is $4*0.008-4*0.012=-0.016$. This finding is consistent with the claim that state-level politicians are more sensitive to public opinion on hot-button social issues than they are on economics, perhaps because of the competitive dynamic between states, if leftward moves at first boost personal freedom and only later cut economic freedom. However, we caution that with such a short time series, this odd up-and-down pattern might be a statistical artifact, but the results are consistent with the cross-sectional data showing that more left-wing states tend to have somewhat less overall freedom.

FREEDOM AND POLICY IDEOLOGY

In this section, we explore how states' systematic variation in policies relates to freedom. By "systematic variation," we are referring to the fact that states similar in some characteristic tend to have similar policies across a range of different policies. For instance, Alabama and Idaho both tend to have more laws regulating abortion than most other states, and they also both have right-to-work laws, which most states do not have. California and New York have few laws regulating abortion but many laws regulating landlords (and no right-to-work laws). The underlying characteristic that accounts for the systematic similarities and differences across states over a wide range of public policies is what political scientists call "policy ideology."[102]

Policy ideology relates to public opinion ideology. If democratic representation is working as we expect, then states with more left-wing (respectively, right-wing) public opinion should also have more left-wing (right-wing) policies. A large body of literature in political science assesses the relationship between these two variables, conditional on other factors.[103]

In our earlier work, we found two dimensions of policy ideology: policy conservatism-progressivism and civil libertarianism-communitarianism.[104] More conservative states tend to have more abortion restrictions, fewer firearms restrictions, higher sales taxes, lower income taxes, fewer labor regulations, more restrictions on same-sex partnerships, stricter drug laws, and laxer driving laws than more progressive states. More civil-libertarian states tend to have laxer gun and drug laws, lower incarceration rates, and more state government involvement in the distribution of alcohol than civil-communitarian states. (The last relationship might be surprising to some readers. It reflects the fact that state alcohol distribution is still largely a relic of the immediate post-Prohibition regulatory systems that states adopted. Civil libertarian, clean-government states have historically "moralistic" political cultures favorable to the regulation of alcohol.)

In this edition of the index, we are for the first time presenting some evidence on how policy ideology relates to freedom. We derived our policy ideology estimates in two different ways. First, we used only those variables for which we have complete data on each of the years 2000, 2006, 2008, 2010, 2012, and 2014. That means dropping policies for which we lack complete data, including all the fiscal policy and law enforcement variables. (For this exercise, we do not use the data forecasting and imputation techniques we use to get complete data for the freedom index.) Second, we relaxed that

102. Robert S. Erikson, Gerald C. Wright Jr., and John P. McIver, *Statehouse Democracy* (Cambridge: Cambridge University Press, 1993).

103. Ibid.; Jeffrey R. Lax and Justin H. Phillips, "Gay Rights in the States: Public Opinion and Policy Responsiveness," *American Political Science Review* 103, no. 3 (2009): 367–86; John G. Matsusaka, "Popular Control of Public Policy: A Quantitative Approach," *Quarterly Journal of Political Science* 5, no. 2 (2010): 133–67.

104. Jason Sorens, Fait Muedini, and William P. Ruger, "US State and Local Public Policies in 2006: A New Database," *State Politics & Policy Quarterly* 8, no. 3 (2008): 309–26.

approach and included all variables for which we have at least "nearly complete" data for all those years except 2014, which allowed us to include the law enforcement variables and a few fiscal policies.

We again find significant evidence of two dimensions of policy ideology. Figure 20 shows how the states stack up on each dimension in 2014, using the narrow set of complete variables. By construction, the two dimensions of policy ideology are totally uncorrelated with each other.

FIGURE 20

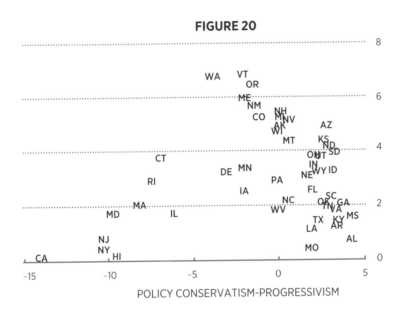

According to these data, California, New Jersey, New York, Hawaii, and Maryland are the most progressive states, while Alabama, Mississippi, Idaho, Arkansas, Tennessee, Georgia, South Carolina, Oklahoma, and the Dakotas are the most conservative states. These findings certainly do not beggar belief. The most civil-libertarian states are found in northern New England (Vermont, Maine, and New Hampshire), the Pacific Northwest (Washington and Oregon), and the Southern Rockies (Colorado and New Mexico). The most civil-communitarian states are Hawaii, California, Missouri, New York, Alabama, and New Jersey.

Figure 21 shows policy ideology in 2012 using a broader range of variables. The values for the two dimensions in Figures 20 and 21 are not directly comparable, because they are based on different inputs. Still, the state ranks are quite similar. Essentially, the same groups of states anchor the far left and far right. The list of most civil-communitarian states differs somewhat, with

Louisiana taking top spot and New York and Hawaii falling well back. The list of most civil-libertarian states now includes Alaska and Montana along with those previously mentioned.

FIGURE 21

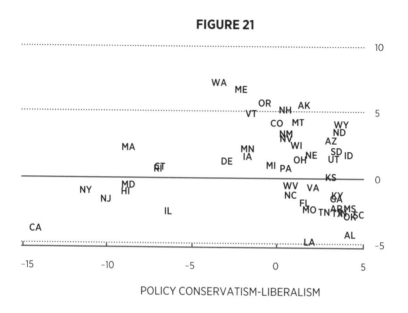

We now turn to the relationship between freedom and policy ideology. Figure 22 again suggests that left-liberal, progressive states are less economically free. Again, New York is far less free than we would expect even given its ideology. Massachusetts, Iowa, New Hampshire, and South Dakota are above the line of best fit, suggesting that they do better than one would expect given their ideology. Part of the reason might be their institutions, which we will examine in the next section, or their competition with neighboring, freer states.

Figure 23 shows the relationship between civil libertarianism and personal freedom in 2014. Interestingly, we find a strong, positive relationship between the two. States that are more civil libertarian also tend to have more personal freedom. The relationship between civil libertarianism and personal freedom is, however, noisier than that between left–right ideology and economic freedom. More states are farther away from the line of best fit. The reason is that personal freedom appears to be driven in part by left–right ideology as well. Thus, strongly left-wing states like California and Massachusetts are well above the regression line, whereas their counterparts on the right—South Dakota, Mississippi, Kentucky, and Texas—are far below the regression line in Figure 23.

FIGURE 22

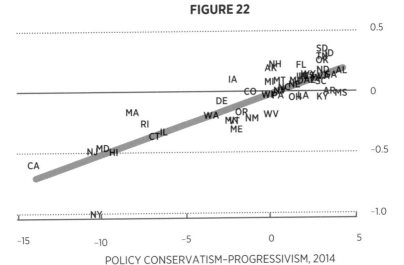

POLICY CONSERVATISM–PROGRESSIVISM, 2014

ECONOMIC FREEDOM, 2014

FIGURE 23

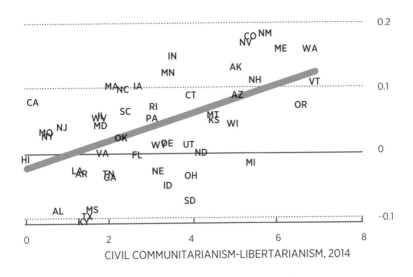

CIVIL COMMUNITARIANISM-LIBERTARIANISM, 2014

PERSONAL FREEDOM, 2014

In conclusion, we have more evidence that conservative states have more economic freedom and less personal freedom than progressive states, although the former relationship is much stronger than the latter. Moreover, we find good evidence of a civil libertarian versus civil communitarian dimension in state policies, which independently relates to personal freedom.

INSTITUTIONS, CULTURE, AND FREEDOM

Having already examined the relationship between public opinion and freedom in each state, we now look at the interesting issue of how political institutions, political culture, and freedom relate to each other. There is a long-standing debate in the social sciences between "institutionalists"[105] and "culturalists," most famously between the Weberians, stressing culture, and the new institutionalists. We cannot resolve this (basically unresolvable) debate here, but since it is obvious to us that both types of variables matter and interact, we draw on both traditions to try to understand how greater freedom comes about in the American states.

In the "Index of Cronyism" section, we found that more corrupt states with more lobbyists tend to have less freedom, even controlling for public opinion. But what causes states to have more corruption and more lobbyists? Part of the answer might be state culture, rooted in historical experience, but part of the answer might lie in formal state institutions, the rules of the political game. In this section, we specifically consider state age, legislative professionalism, constitutional complexity, and the ballot initiative as institutional correlates of freedom.

Our model of how state policy comes about begins with political institutions and political culture. The previous paragraph lists our institutional variables. Under the heading of political culture, we group lobbyists per legislator, corruption perceptions, and partisanship ("Democratic plus Green lean"). Institutions and culture together affect policy, but they can also affect each other. In this study, we investigate how these different variables relate together statistically. Correlation does not directly imply causation, but strong correlations among variables can suggest possible causal pathways and rule out others.

Table 37 presents correlations in the data for all these variables, measured as of 2014 unless otherwise noted. Some of the variables require further comment. We include two indicators of state age. One is the logged number of years since a state attained statehood. The other is the same, except that it considers former Confederate states to have been "born" in 1965, the year of the Voting Rights Act, which is Mancur Olson's preferred measure. Constitutional complexity is the logged number of words in the state constitution as of the start of 2013, taken from the *Book of the States* website. [106]

105. Douglass C. North, "The New Institutional Economics," *Journal of Institutional and Theoretical Economics* 142, no. 1 (1986): 230–37; Douglass C. North and Barry R. Weingast, "Constitution and Commitment: The Evolution of Institutions Governing Public Choice in 17th Century England," *Journal of Economic History* 49 (1989): 803–32; Douglass C. North, *Institutions, Institutional Change and Economic Performance* (Cambridge: Cambridge University Press, 1990); Daron Acemoglu, Simon Johnson, and James A. Robinson, "Institutions as a Fundamental Cause of Long-Run Growth," *Handbook of Economic Growth* 1 (2005): 385–472; Raymond Fisman and Edward Miguel, "Corruption, Norms, and Legal Enforcement: Evidence from Diplomatic Parking Tickets," *Journal of Political Economy* 115, no. 6 (2007): 1020–48; Joel Mokyr, *The Enlightened Economy: An Economic History of Britain 1700–1850* (New Haven, CT: Yale University Press, 2010).

106. Council of State Governments, *The Book of the States 2013* (Washington, DC: Council of State Governments, 2013), Table 1.1, http://bit.ly/1T8p422.

Legislative professionalism is an index incorporating legislator salary, staff, and session lengths and is measured as of 2007. [107] "Initiative" is a 0–1 dummy variable for whether a state contains a ballot initiative process whereby citizens may legislate directly into either the statutes or the constitution, excluding New Mexico's public-veto referendum. Lobbyists per legislator and journalists' corruption perceptions were discussed in the "Index of Cronyism" section, and "Partisanship" is the adjusted Democratic plus Green lean from the 2012 presidential election.

Looking first at the correlations within each group of variables, we see that the institutional variables mostly do not correlate strongly with each other. Even the two state age variables correlate less than might be supposed. The cultural variables also correlate little with each other, with the strongest link being between more left-leaning states and more lobbyists per legislator. Economic freedom is modestly negatively correlated with personal freedom, as already noted, while overall freedom is extremely closely correlated with economic freedom but not at all with personal freedom. Although personal freedom is one-third of the overall index, it is much "noisier" than economic freedom and has a much narrower range of values, precisely because neither conservative nor progressive states do consistently well across the range of personal freedoms.

More interesting is how institutions and culture relate to freedom, and whether culture mediates some of the effects of institutions on freedom. State age, particularly as Olson preferred to measure it, is negatively related to economic and overall freedom but positively related to personal freedom. Olson's view was that state age caused interest groups to accumulate, leading to more complex forms of economic regulation. State age therefore should relate strongly to lobbyists or corruption or both, but in fact it does not. State age does relate to left-wing partisanship. We therefore have some preliminary evidence consistent with the view that older states tend to be more left-wing and to have more personal and less economic freedom for that reason, not, as Olson thought, because of an accumulation of interest groups. A plausible alternative explanation for this pattern of correlations is that older states outside the South industrialized earlier, developed stronger labor organizations by the end of the 19th century, and by the middle of the 20th century were strong supporters of the New Deal Democratic Party.

The logged number of words in the constitution does correlate negatively with personal freedom, but we find that this is an artifact of greater constitutional complexity in the South. Excluding the South (as defined by the U.S. Census Bureau), [108] the correlations between constitutional complexity and

---

107. Peverill Squire, "Measuring Legislative Professionalism: The Squire Index Revisited," *State Politics and Policy Quarterly* 7, no. 2 (2007): 211–27.

108. Census Regions and Divisions of the United States, http://www2.census.gov/geo/pdfs/maps-data/maps/reference/us_regdiv.pdf.

TABLE 37

Correlations among State Institutions, Culture, and Policies

	Log Age	Young South	Constitution Words	Professionalism
Log Age	1.00			
Young South	*0.39*	1.00		
Constitution Words	0.09	<u>−0.29</u>	1.00	
Professionalism	0.11	<u>0.27</u>	0.14	1.00
Initiative	<u>−0.25</u>	0.08	<u>0.20</u>	0.02
Lobbyists	0.09	0.09	<u>0.25</u>	**0.61**
Corruption	<u>0.20</u>	−0.02	*0.30*	0.08
Partisanship	<u>0.22</u>	*0.33*	-0.18	*0.49*
Economic Freedom	<u>−0.23</u>	*−0.40*	0.04	**−0.53**
Personal Freedom	-0.16	*0.33*	*−0.38*	0.12
Overall Freedom	<u>−0.29</u>	*−0.32*	-0.08	**−0.52**

Correlation strength: **bold (r≥0.5)**, *italic (0.3≤r<0.5)*, <u>underline (0.2≤r<0.3).</u>

Correlation groups

Institutions-institutions	Institutions-culture	Culture-culture
Institutions-policy	Culture-policy	Policy-policy

Initiative	Lobbyists	Corruption	Partisanship	Economic Freedom	Personal Freedom	Overall Freedom
1.00						
0.06	1.00					
−0.27	0.05	1.00				
−0.22	0.29	0.01	1.00			
0.17	−0.45	−0.19	−0.73	1.00		
−0.02	−0.02	−0.16	0.40	−0.32	1.00	
0.17	−0.48	−0.25	−0.65	0.96	−0.03	1.00

overall, economic, and personal freedom are essentially zero. The correlation between constitutional complexity and corruption outside the South is also almost zero.

Legislative professionalism is strongly negatively correlated with economic and overall freedom. There is an ongoing debate in the literature about whether legislative professionalism causes higher government spending.[109] However, we would note that legislative professionalism is also strongly related to lobbyists per legislator and left-wing partisanship, which also appear to influence freedom. It is implausible to think that legislative professionalism affects public opinion, at the very least. Therefore, we cannot conclude on the basis of this evidence alone that legislative professionalism is harmful for freedom.

Overall freedom is slightly higher in initiative states, but the initiative also correlates slightly negatively with left-wing public opinion and corruption, and so the modest correlation between the initiative and freedom might simply reflect any effect of partisanship and corruption on freedom. We try to disentangle these relationships with multiple regression analysis below.

Some of the strongest relationships we find in Table 37 are that left partisanship, lobbyists, and corruption (this last correlation is less strong than the others) are negatively related to economic and overall freedom.

We begin our multiple regression analysis of freedom with a "baseline" cultural model, in which economic freedom in 2014 depends on left partisanship, lobbyists per legislator, and corruption (Table 38). We focus on economic freedom because theory and our exploratory correlations both suggest that it relates more systematically to institutions than does personal freedom. These are linear, cross-sectional models with robust standard errors on all 50 states. We impute three missing observations on corruption and one missing observation on lobbyists using the Amelia package in R.

Left partisanship and lobbyists are negatively related to economic freedom. The coefficient on "corruption" is not quite statistically significant, but recall that we have already found that corruption relates strongly to cronyist policies specifically. Model (2) adds the state age variable in which Confederate states are zero in 1965. It relates negatively and almost statistically significantly to economic freedom, supporting Olson's hypothesis if not the exact mechanism of his theory (since we are controlling for interest-group influence via lobbyists and corruption). Model (3) then adds constitution length, which is not significant. Model (4) adds legislative professionalism, which is also insignificant. Model (5) adds the ballot initiative, which is again insignificant.

109. Stephanie Owings and Rainald Borck, "Legislative Professionalism and Government Spending: Do Citizen Legislators Really Spend Less?" *Public Finance Review* 28, no. 3 (2000): 210–25; Neil Malhotra, "Disentangling the Relationship between Legislative Professionalism and Government Spending," *Legislative Studies Quarterly* 33, no. 3 (2008): 1–28.

TABLE 38

Regression Models of Culture, Institutions, and Economic Freedom

D.V.: Economic freedom	(1)	(2)	(3)	(4)	(5)
Variable	Coef. (SE)	Coef. (SE)	Coef. (SE)	Coef. (SE)	Coef. (SE)
Partisanship	-0.016 (0.002)	-0.015 (0.003)	-0.015 (0.003)	-0.015 (0.003)	-0.015 (0.003)
Corruption	-0.039 (0.021)	-0.040 (0.021)	-0.040 (0.022)	-0.040 (0.021)	-0.039 (0.022)
Lobbyists	-0.016 (0.007)	-0.016 (0.006)	-0.016 (0.007)	-0.015 (0.008)	-0.017 (0.006)
Young South		-0.083 (0.043)	-0.084 (0.045)	-0.081 (0.044)	-0.085 (0.044)
Constitution words			-0.003 (0.04)		
Professionalism				-0.08 (0.30)	
Initiative					0.01 (0.05)
Intercept	0.12 (0.08)	0.53 (0.23)	0.56 (0.48)	0.53 (0.23)	0.53 (0.23)
F (p)	23.6 (<0.001)	19.7 (<0.001)	15.4 (<0.001)	15.4 (<0.001)	15.4 (<0.001)

To sum up, these results suggest that left partisanship and corruption may depress economic freedom, although it could also be the case that economic freedom suppresses corruption. Some tentative evidence also exists in favor of Mancur Olson's view that state age results in less economic freedom. Since corruption might mediate the relationship between state age and economic freedom, we need to conduct separate analyses of corruption, presented in Table 39.

TABLE 39

Regression Models of Corruption

D.V.: Corruption	(1)	(2)
Variable	**Coef. (SE)**	**Coef. (SE)**
Partisanship	0.009 (0.015)	0.002 (0.017)
Lobbyists	0.026 (0.035)	0.032 (0.034)
Young South		0.54 (0.29)
Southern	0.90 (0.30)	1.26 (0.33)
Intercept	3.1 (0.3)	0.3 (1.5)
$F(p)$	2.94 (0.04)	3.87 (0.01)

Although southern states are more corrupt, controlling for this phenomenon, states with younger age are less corrupt, Model (2) suggests. This relationship is not quite significant at the arbitrary threshold of $p<0.05$. Put together, the models in Tables 38 and 39 suggest that state age may influence economic freedom both directly and indirectly, through corruption. The indirect channel is most consistent with Olson's theory. The direct channel may have something to do with our labor organization hypothesis. Older states industrialized earlier, spawned stronger labor organizations, and therefore moved to the left. However, strong labor organization might affect economic freedom even when it does not affect public opinion, through the collective action of labor unions on specific policies, such as labor regulation. Indeed, log state age ("Young South" measure) correlates with union coverage density in 2009 at a remarkable $r=0.51$. When we control for union density in a regression model of economic freedom, union density is statistically significant, but state age is not.

FREEDOM, MIGRATION, AND GROWTH

America is a land of immigrants. Indeed, immigrants throughout America's history have boarded ships (and eventually planes) in droves to escape tyranny and to breathe the cleaner air of a nation founded on the idea of individual freedom. Sometimes that story is dramatic, as when the Puritans hurriedly left Europe to realize greater religious liberty or when Vietnamese boat people escaped murderous communist oppression to start anew in the New World. Other times, it is less stark, as in the case of a German family fed up with the modern paternalist state and looking for a place to build a business and raise a family or Mexican migrants looking for the better economic opportunities afforded by a freer economy.

Unsurprisingly, given our foreign ancestors, it is also the case that we are a land of internal migrants. According to a Gallup poll, approximately one in four Americans has "moved from one city or area within [the] country to another in the past five years."[110] That factor puts the United States (with countries like New Zealand and Finland) in the top ranks globally for internal mobility (the worldwide average is 8 percent).

But why do those Americans move? They certainly aren't moving one step ahead of oppressive regimes and violence like people fleeing recently from Syria, Venezuela, or Zimbabwe. More likely they move for reasons like economic opportunity and locational amenities, such as better weather or beaches. But freedom might matter too when it comes to internal migration, given the differences across the 50 states we identify in the first chapter of this study. Those differences aren't as severe as those between the United States and the least free countries of the world. But they are meaningful, especially considering that New York is far less free than the average state, while other states also score substantially worse or better than others.

But do Americans value freedom as we define it? One way to try to answer that question is to analyze the relationship between freedom and net interstate migration, that is, the movement of people between states. If, all else being equal, Americans prefer to move to freer states, that would be evidence in favor of the hypothesis that Americans value freedom. In other words, it looks at preferences revealed by behavior rather than mere expressed views. That does not mean that people are responding directly to changes in policy, packing up moving vans, and heading from New York to New Hampshire or the Dakotas. But it could be that they are moving within their region to freer places like Pennsylvania and New Jersey.

We try to answer the question posed in the previous paragraph by examining the statistical correlations between freedom at particular moments and net interstate migration over several subsequent years. Figures 24 to 29

---

110.   Neli Esipova, Anita Pugliese, and Julie Ray, "381 Million Adults Worldwide Migrate within Countries," Gallup, May 15, 2013, http://www.gallup.com/poll/162488/381-million-adults-worldwide-migrate-within-countries.aspx.

plot states' net migration rates from January 1, 2001, to January 1, 2007, and from January 1, 2007, to January 1, 2014, against their overall, economic, and personal freedom scores in 2000 and 2006, respectively. The net migration rate is defined as the number of people moving to a state from other states minus the number of people moving from that state to other states, divided by the initial resident population of the state. The migration data are from the Census Bureau's "components of population change" tables. These figures represent a simple "first cut" at the question. They do not control for any other factors that might drive migration.

Figure 24 shows the relationship between overall freedom and net migration over the first half of the 2001–14 period. It shows a strong relationship between the starting level of freedom and subsequent net migration, suggesting that people are moving to freer states. We can see that from the example of New York, which suffered the second-worst net outmigration of any state, 7.5 percent of its 2001 population, and which is also the least free state. Louisiana is obviously anomalous because Hurricane Katrina drove away hundreds of thousands of people, resulting in a large net outmigration despite an average level of freedom. At the top end, Nevada and Arizona are big outliers in net inmigration, as Americans during this period were flocking to the so-called sand states because of their supposedly desirable climates. [111] Those anomalies illustrate the importance of controlling for potential confounders.

FIGURE 24

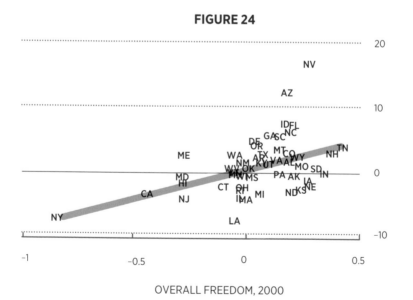

OVERALL FREEDOM, 2000

111. Thomas Davidoff, "Supply Elasticity and the Housing Cycle of the 2000s," *Real Estate Economics* 41, no. 4 (2013): 793–813.

Figure 25 shows the relationship between year-end 2006 freedom and migration over the next seven years. We see less evidence of amenity-driven migration over this period, which includes the financial crisis, housing bust, and Great Recession. However, warm states like the Carolinas, Arizona, Nevada, and Texas still lie above the line of best fit, while cold states like Alaska, New Hampshire, Iowa, and Rhode Island lie below that line. The relationship between freedom and net migration appears, if anything, even stronger in these more recent years than in the first half of the 2000s.

FIGURE 25

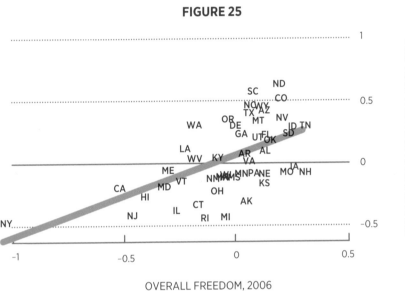

OVERALL FREEDOM, 2006

Figure 26 shows the relationship between economic freedom and net migration in the first half of our period of analysis. Again, a strong relationship exists between economic freedom and inmigration

FIGURE 26

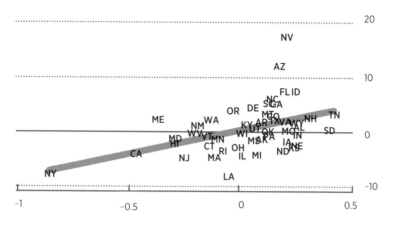

FIGURE 26

NET DOMESTIC MIGRATION, 2001–2007

ECONOMIC FREEDOM, 2000

Figure 27 shows how economic freedom in 2006 relates to subsequent migration. The line of best fit expresses a strong, positive relationship between a state's economic freedom at the beginning of the period and subsequent inmigration. North Dakota lies significantly above the regression line, in part because of its discovery of shale oil and gas. Michigan lies significantly below the regression line, mostly because of the travails of its automobile-manufacturing industry in international markets.

FIGURE 27

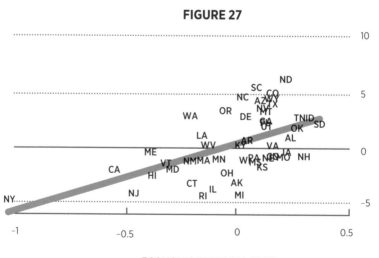

NET DOMESTIC MIGRATION, 2007–2014

ECONOMIC FREEDOM, 2006

Figure 28 moves to personal freedom. Here, we do not find the same relationship between freedom and migration that we found for overall and economic freedom. The line of best fit is essentially flat, implying no relationship between personal freedom and net migration. Recall that personal freedom correlates negatively with economic freedom. If economic freedom is a more important driver of net inmigration than personal freedom, the bivariate relationship between personal freedom and migration expressed here will probably be biased downward.

FIGURE 28

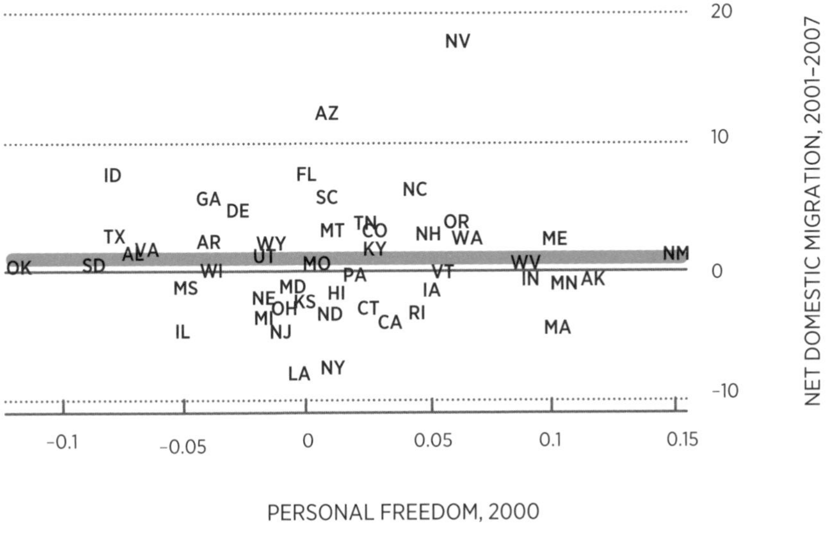

PERSONAL FREEDOM, 2000

Figure 29 shows the relationship between personal freedom at the end of 2006 and subsequent net migration. The line of best fit is again essentially flat, indicating no relationship. However, economic freedom is an important confounder.

FIGURE 29

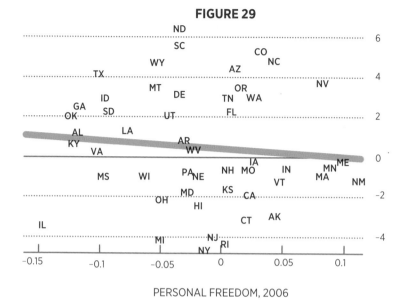

PERSONAL FREEDOM, 2006

NET DOMESTIC MIGRATION, 2007–2014

To deal with confounding variables that affect migration, we turn to multiple regression analysis, which allows us to control for factors such as climate. In previous editions, we have found a positive relationship between each dimension of freedom and migration, although regulatory policy has been related to net migration solely through the channels of cost of living and economic growth. In other words, a lighter regulatory touch may improve the productivity of the economy, but low taxes and personal freedom seem to be amenities that the marginal migrant values for their own sake.

For the first time, we are now able to report separate regression equations for early 2000s migration and late 2000s–early 2010s migration. In the last edition, we merely investigated the correlation between start-of-2001 freedom and net migration over the entire decade of the 2000s. By looking at how later-period freedom (2006 and 2008) relates to migration and growth, we are making a kind of "out-of-sample" prediction from our prior results. In this regard, it is worth noting that, before data collection, Jason Sorens preregistered on Twitter an expectation that personal freedom and taxation (the dominant component of fiscal policy) would be less important for migration in the period of the Great Recession and its aftermath, as Americans have started to migrate less for amenities during this period of economic turbulence.[112]

112.   Jason Sorens, Twitter post, June 12, 2015, 12:22 p.m., https://twitter.com/JasonSorens/status/609440605157105664; Jason Sorens, Twitter post, June 12, 2015, 12:22 p.m., https://twitter.com/JasonSorens/status/609440752121311232; Jason Sorens, Twitter post, June 12, 2015, 12:23 p.m., https://twitter.com/JasonSorens/status/609440996598935552.

We present results from three types of estimations: monadic, matched-neighbors, and dyadic. The monadic regressions simply compare all 50 states with each other. The matched-neighbors regressions subtract the weighted average of neighboring states' values (on migration, freedom, and controls) from each state's value. The weights are the distances between the "centroids" (geographic centers) of each state. The purpose of these regressions is to examine whether freedom has a stronger effect on inmigration when neighboring states differ more on freedom. We expect that a freer state surrounded by less free states will attract more migrants than a freer state surrounded by equally free states, all else equal. Finally, the dyadic models compare state-to-state migration across all state pairs, excluding Alaska and Hawaii. [113] We expect that the bigger the difference in freedom is between any two states, the larger the migration flow will be from the less free of the pair to the freer of the pair, all else equal.

Table 40 presents seven regression equations of net migration over the 2001–7 period. [114] The tables display coefficients and standard errors. A rough rule of thumb for statistical significance is that when the ratio of the coefficient to the standard error is greater than two, the coefficient is statistically significant at the 95 percent confidence level; however, statistical significance is best thought of as a continuum rather than a switch.

---

113. Alaska and Hawaii are excluded because their distance dampens interstate migration to and from these states. However, the results are quite similar when they are included.

114. We tried dropping the outlier case of Louisiana, with only trivial differences in results.

TABLE 40

Monadic Estimates of Freedom and Migration, 2001–2007

Variable	(1) Coef. (SE)	(2) Coef. (SE)	(3) Coef. (SE)	(4) Coef. (SE)	(5) Coef. (SE)	(6) Coef. (SE)	(7) Coef. (SE)
Fiscal freedom	1.32 (0.49)	1.27 (0.50)	1.35 (0.44)	1.30 (0.49)	1.37 (0.51)	1.33 (0.49)	1.41 (0.52)
Regulatory freedom	1.31 (0.51)	0.73 (0.49)	1.20 (0.50)	1.21 (0.51)	1.26 (0.50)	1.48 (0.53)	1.00 (0.50)
Personal freedom	0.66 (0.57)	0.97 (0.56)	0.34 (0.46)	0.65 (0.57)	0.64 (0.57)	0.81 (0.60)	0.52 (0.51)
Cost of living		−1.43 (0.49)					
Accom- modations			1.94 (0.42)				
Capital per worker				−0.38 (0.36)			
Retirees					−0.42 (0.63)		
Violent crime						0.67 (0.62)	
Heating degree days						−0.72 (0.48)	
Precipitation							−0.89 (0.75)
Constant	0.98 (0.58)	0.98 (0.55)	0.98 (0.51)	0.98 (0.58)	0.98 (0.58)	0.98 (0.57)	0.98 (0.57)
R^2	22.4%	29.8%	40.7%	23.1%	23.2%	28.1%	25.9%

Note: All independent variables are standardized to mean zero and standard deviation one. Robust standard errors.

The first equation simply regresses the net migration rate on the three dimensions of freedom. Both fiscal freedom and regulatory freedom are independently, positively, statistically significantly correlated with net inmigration. Personal freedom shows a positive but statistically insignificant correlation. Model (2) adds cost of living in 2000, as measured by Berry, Fording, and Hanson. [115] Cost of living is potentially a bad control, because regulatory policy, especially land-use freedom, can influence migration through the channel of cost of living. Model (3) adds accommodations GDP per capita, which proxies the size of the tourist industry. States with bigger hospitality sectors appear to attract more migrants, presumably because they have more locational amenities. Model (4) controls for capital stock per worker from Garofalo and Yamarik. [116] Model (5) adds the percentage of state population age 65 or older. Model (6) adds the violent crime rate and population-weighted annual heating degree days, a measure of how cold a climate is. (These two are added together because violent crime is higher in warm climates.) Finally Model (7) adds area-weighted statewide average annual precipitation.

Adding each of those controls does not substantially affect the statistical estimates of the correlation between fiscal and regulatory freedom, on the one hand, and net migration, on the other, with one exception. Adding cost of living causes the estimate of the coefficient on regulatory policy to fall substantially, so that it is no longer quite statistically significant. That occurrence suggests that much of the causal effect of regulatory freedom on migration flows through cost of living. States lower on regulatory freedom suffer from higher cost of living, which is the more immediate cause of lower inmigration. Personal freedom does indeed look much less important for migration in 2007–14 than in 2001–7.

Table 41 performs the same set of analyses on the 2007–13 data, with freedom variables measured as of year-end 2006. Again, fiscal freedom and regulatory freedom look like important drivers of interstate migration over this period, with much of the effect of regulatory freedom flowing through cost of living. The relationship between fiscal and regulatory freedom, on the one hand, and migration, on the other, looks robust to the addition of controls other than cost of living.

Table 42 presents the results for the 2001–7 period when we match each state to its neighbors, on the (true) assumption that migration flows between neighboring states are greater than they are between distant states. These matched-neighbor results are somewhat sharper than the monadic results.

115.   William D. Berry, Richard C. Fording, and Russell L. Hanson, "An Annual Cost of Living Index for the American States, 1960–1995," *Journal of Politics* 62, no. 2 (2000): 550–67.

116.   Gasper A. Garofalo and Steven Yamarik, "Regional Growth: Evidence from a New State-by-State Capital Stock Series," *Review of Economics and Statistics* 84, no. 2 (2002): 316–23.

TABLE 41

Monadic Estimates of Freedom and Migration, 2007–2013

Variable	(8) Coef. (SE)	(9) Coef. (SE)	(10) Coef. (SE)	(11) Coef. (SE)	(12) Coef. (SE)	(13) Coef. (SE)	(14) Coef. (SE)
Fiscal freedom	0.78 (0.35)	0.71 (0.33)	0.80 (0.36)	0.80 (0.35)	0.79 (0.36)	0.83 (0.42)	0.79 (0.34)
Regulatory freedom	1.11 (0.40)	0.73 (0.42)	1.09 (0.40)	1.21 (0.44)	1.10 (0.41)	1.12 (0.43)	0.93 (0.41)
Personal freedom	0.23 (0.33)	0.49 (0.34)	0.14 (0.34)	0.30 (0.35)	0.24 (0.33)	0.26 (0.34)	0.08 (0.36)
Cost of living		−0.85 (0.35)					
Accom- modations			0.36 (0.16)				
Capital per worker				0.34 (0.41)			
Retirees					−0.12 (0.41)		
Violent crime						0.25 (0.40)	
Heating degree days						−0.28 (0.35)	
Precipitation							−0.52 (0.34)
Constant	0.50 (0.35)	0.50 (0.34)	0.50 (0.35)	0.50 (0.35)	0.50 (0.35)	0.50 (0.35)	0.50 (0.35)
R^2	31.5%	36.4%	32.9%	32.7%	31.6%	33.4%	34.3%

Note: All independent variables are standardized to mean zero and standard deviation one. Robust standard errors.

They suggest that regulatory freedom drives migration even when cost of living is controlled. As expected, more costly states repel migrants, while states with locational amenities attract them. Models (17) and (18) explain more than two-thirds of all the variance in relative-to-neighbors net migration across all 50 states. The fact that the results sharpen when we match neighboring states to each other implies that the regression model reflects an

TABLE 42

Matched-Neighbors Estimates of Freedom and Migration, 2001–2007

Variable	(15) Coef. (SE)	(16) Coef. (SE)	(17) Coef. (SE)	(18) Coef. (SE)
Fiscal freedom	0.86 (0.45)	1.12 (0.43)	1.17 (0.32)	1.20 (0.32)
Regulatory freedom	2.25 (0.67)	1.88 (0.61)	1.24 (0.47)	1.09 (0.48)
Personal freedom	0.55 (0.40)	0.56 (0.37)	0.26 (0.31)	0.21 (0.32)
Cost of living		-3.1 (0.9)	-3.7 (0.7)	-3.6 (0.7)
Accommodations			2.0 (0.2)	2.0 (0.2)
Capital per worker				-0.41 (0.49)
Constant	-0.25 (0.51)	-0.40 (0.47)	-0.53 (0.39)	-0.57 (0.41)
R^2	44.1%	53.5%	68.6%	69.2%

Note: All independent variables are standardized to mean zero and standard deviation one. Robust standard errors.

underlying causal relationship.

Table 43 presents the matched-neighbors results for the 2007–13 period. All variables have smaller coefficients, due to the fact that absolute rates of net migration were lower during this period compared with the previous period. *R*-squareds are also lower, showing that net migration was simply less predictable during this period, presumably because of idiosyncratic shocks that state economies suffered during the Great Recession. Fiscal freedom is again robustly related to net inmigration. Regulatory freedom seems quite a bit less important for net migration during this period, but there is a great

TABLE 43

Matched-Neighbors Estimates of Freedom and Migration, 2007–2013

Variable	(19) Coef. (SE)	(20) Coef. (SE)	(21) Coef. (SE)	(22) Coef. (SE)
Fiscal freedom	0.73 (0.33)	0.90 (0.32)	0.91 (0.31)	0.89 (0.35)
Regulatory freedom	0.66 (0.43)	0.27 (0.44)	0.17 (0.44)	0.23 (0.62)
Personal freedom	0.29 (0.27)	0.35 (0.24)	0.31 (0.25)	0.34 (0.30)
Cost of living		-1.7 (0.7)	-1.7 (0.6)	-1.8 (0.6)
Accom-modations			0.32 (0.19)	0.33 (0.19)
Capital per worker				0.13 (0.49)
Constant	-0.04 (0.31)	-0.13 (0.31)	-0.15 (0.31)	-0.14 (0.33)
R^2	31.0%	40.5%	41.8%	42.0%

Note: All independent variables are standardized to mean zero and standard deviation one. Robust standard errors.

deal of uncertainty about the estimates on this variable.

Table 44 shows the results of our state-to-state migration estimates. The benefit of using "nondirected dyads," to use the jargon, is that we get many more observations, preventing the regression models from being statistically underpowered. As a result, we are able to include all the control variables that we expect might be related to migration within the same equation. These data come from the Internal Revenue Service and for the same period as the Census Bureau data used previously; the correlation between the two is an extremely tight 0.98. However, the IRS data end on January 1, 2013. Models (23) through (26) cover the 2001–7 period, and Models (27) through (30) cover the 2007–13 period. The dependent variable, net migration rate, is measured for each pair of states and represents the net migration from one state to the other divided by the summed initial populations of both states, times 200. Each observation is weighted by the distance between the two states' centroids, because farther-apart states have less migration between them and therefore display lower residuals (heteroscedasticity).

The additional statistical power helps us see that personal freedom and regulatory freedom are indeed related to net migration, at least in the 2001–7 period. Both variables are strongly statistically significant in Models (24)–(26), and personal freedom is also strongly significant in Models (28)–(30), while regulatory freedom drops out of significance in 2007–13 when cost of living is introduced. The coefficient on fiscal freedom falls in the latter period, consistent with the general observation that amenity-driven migration has become less important since the Great Recession. This phenomenon would also account for the fact that accommodations GDP, heating degree days, and precipitation have become less important drivers of migration, or not important at all, since 2007.

Since the independent variables are all standardized to mean zero and standard deviation one, we can interpret the coefficients on the freedom variables as follows. In 2001–7, a one-standard-deviation increase in fiscal freedom for state i over state j is expected to increase migration from the latter to the former by 0.023 percent of the average of their populations. For instance, a change in Vermont's 2000 fiscal policy to New Hampshire's in the same year (three standard deviations) should increase migration from Vermont to New Hampshire by 0.07 percent of the average of their populations (about 600 people). Over the same period, the same sort of change in regulatory freedom should boost net migration by 0.024 percentage points of population, and the same sort of change in personal freedom should boost net migration by 0.016 percentage points of population. For example, a switch from Illinois's to Indiana's personal freedom in 2000, about two and two-thirds standard deviations, should boost migration over the next six years from Illinois to Indiana by about 0.04 percentage points of the average

TABLE 44

Dyadic Estimates of Freedom and Migration

Variable	(23) Coef. (SE)	(24) Coef. (SE)	(25) Coef. (SE)	(26) Coef. (SE)	(27) Coef. (SE)	(28) Coef. (SE)	(29) Coef. (SE)	(30) Coef. (SE)
Fiscal freedom	0.024 (0.006)	0.026 (0.006)	0.024 (0.006)	0.020 (0.005)	0.013 (0.005)	0.015 (0.004)	0.014 (0.004)	0.018 (0.004)
Regulatory freedom	0.029 (0.006)	0.013 (0.005)	0.014 (0.005)	0.019 (0.006)	0.014 (0.005)	0.001 (0.005)	0.001 (0.005)	0.003 (0.005)
Personal freedom	0.007 (0.005)	0.016 (0.004)	0.013 (0.004)	0.016 (0.004)	0.005 (0.005)	0.013 (0.004)	0.012 (0.004)	0.021 (0.004)
Cost of living		-0.036 (0.005)	-0.037 (0.005)	-0.015 (0.005)		-0.024 (0.005)	-0.025 (0.005)	-0.022 (0.005)
Accom-modations			0.011 (0.004)	0.003 (0.004)			0.003 (0.004)	-0.005 (0.003)
Capital per worker				-0.008 (0.005)				0.012 (0.005)
Retirees				0.005 (0.005)				-0.005 (0.003)
Violent crime				-0.017 (0.006)				-0.019 (0.005)
Heating degree days				-0.044 (0.012)				-0.026 (0.005)
Precip-itation				-0.010 (0.005)				-0.004 (0.003)
Constant	-0.002 (0.006)	-0.002 (0.005)	-0.002 (0.005)	-0.001 (0.005)	0.005 (0.006)	0.005 (0.005)	0.005 (0.005)	0.005 (0.004)
R^2	9.3%	14.0%	15.1%	18.9%	8.4%	13.5%	13.6%	22.3%

Note: All independent variables are standardized to mean zero and standard deviation one. Robust standard errors clustered on destination state.

of their populations.

In 2007–13, the effect of a one-standard-deviation change in 2006 fiscal freedom is 0.018 percentage points of the average of a dyad's populations, while the effect of a one-standard-deviation change in 2006 personal freedom is 0.02 percentage points of the average of a dyad's populations. As already noted, regulatory freedom's direct effect on migration in the later period is trivial, but its indirect effect, through cost of living, is substantial.

Our migration models do not control for state economic growth, which is endogenous (more migration of workers will induce higher economic growth). It is plausible that regulatory freedom, in particular, influences migration almost entirely by affecting the economic climate (cost of living and growth), rather than as a direct amenity. Few workers are likely to study different states' labor laws or tort liability systems before deciding where to live, but it is quite plausible that businesses do so when deciding where to invest.

Therefore, we now turn to analyzing the statistical relationship between economic growth in each state and its economic freedom. The dependent variable in these regression equations is real personal income growth on an annualized basis. For the inflation measure, we use the state-by-state cost-of-living indicator from Berry, Fording, and Hanson in 2000 and 2006 and the Bureau of Economic Analysis (BEA) indicator in 2008 and 2013. Where necessary, we join the two time series through the one year in which they overlap, 2007 (see the f_land_15.xls spreadsheet for details). We run three sets of models, one on the years 2000–2006, another on the years 2006–13, and the third on the years 2008–13, for which we can rely solely on the new BEA time series of real state personal income. To calculate growth rates, we use the annual average personal income figures from the start and the end of each series.

The results are shown in Table 45. For each time period, we regress growth on each dimension of freedom and, consistently with the literature on this topic, dummies for each census region, and then we introduce two controls: cost of living and capital per worker. In 2000–2006 and 2006–13, regulatory freedom is significantly associated with growth. In 2008–13, none of the independent variables are statistically significant, although a joint test that the summed coefficients on fiscal and regulatory freedom are zero rejects the null at greater than 95 percent confidence in every model reported below except Model (32). Since the two variables are highly correlated with each other, this test is necessary to see whether economic freedom in

TABLE 45

Economic Freedom and Real Personal Income Growth Estimates

Variable	(27) Coef. (SE)	(28) Coef. (SE)	(29) Coef. (SE)	(30) Coef. (SE)	(31) Coef. (SE)	(32) Coef. (SE)
Fiscal freedom	-0.03 (0.14)	-0.04 (0.13)	-0.12 (0.15)	-0.11 (0.15)	0.10 (0.10)	0.13 (0.11)
Regulatory freedom	0.50 (0.17)	0.43 (0.19)	0.53 (0.16)	0.66 (0.19)	0.16 (0.12)	0.08 (0.16)
Personal freedom	-0.16 (0.11)	-0.15 (0.10)	-0.07 (0.20)	-0.03 (0.20)	-0.07 (0.12)	-0.08 (0.12)
Cost of living		-0.44 (0.17)		0.31 (0.24)		0.17 (0.10)
Capital per worker		0.09 (0.16)		0.13 (0.12)		-0.28 (0.19)
Northeast	1.3 (0.2)	1.9 (0.4)	3.3 (0.2)	3.0 (0.3)	1.3 (0.2)	1.1 (0.2)
Midwest	0.8 (0.2)	1.0 (0.2)	3.0 (0.6)	3.1 (0.6)	1.3 (0.4)	1.5 (0.4)
South	2.0 (0.2)	1.6 (0.3)	1.2 (0.3)	1.6 (0.4)	1.1 (0.1)	1.3 (0.1)
West	1.6 (0.4)	1.5 (0.3)	2.6 (0.3)	2.3 (0.3)	1.4 (0.2)	1.2 (0.2)
R^2	81.4%	82.7%	83.7%	84.2%	75.1%	77.8%

general is associated with growth, and, it turns out, it is.

In summary, the Great Recession has upended the geographic patterns of economic growth in the United States. In general, however, we do see a relationship between economic freedom and higher income growth, especially when we focus on the regulatory component of economic freedom. The lackluster results on fiscal freedom lend further credence to the earlier observation that fiscal freedom seems to attract migrants as an amenity (through, for instance, lower taxes), but might not actually increase the pro-

CONCLUSIONS

In the first section of the book, we built and justified our index of freedom across the 50 states in the time period 2000–2014. Our index of freedom can be broken down into three dimensions: fiscal freedom, regulatory freedom, and personal freedom. Fiscal and regulatory freedoms together we dub "economic freedom."

It turns out that economic freedom and personal freedom have different origins and effects. Economic freedom is more often found in more conservative states that tend to vote Republican in presidential elections, although there are exceptions, and the relationship was weaker in 2000 than it is now. Personal freedom tends to be higher in more progressive states, by contrast, but this relationship is even noisier and more uncertain than that between ideology and economic freedom.

We then turned to investigating the way freedom correlates with policy ideology. States with more progressive policies score lower on economic freedom, and this relationship is quite strong. States with more civil-libertarian policies score higher on personal freedom, although this relationship admits of more exceptions.

Another reason why freedom tends to prosper in some places and falter in others is institutional design. Much research has been conducted on the effects of institutions on government spending across countries,[117] as well as on institutions and the dynamics of policy change in the American states. [118] Variables of interest include size of the legislature, gubernatorial power, professionalization of the legislature, fiscal decentralization, term limits, and initiative and referendum. In theory, institutions could have consistent effects on individual liberty in one direction or the other, but it is more likely that most institutions affect freedom positively in some areas and negatively in others. For instance, popular initiatives have helped pass strict tax limitation rules, such as Colorado's Taxpayer Bill of Rights, but have also allowed massive spending increases to become law, such as Florida's 2002 initiative requiring that universal prekindergarten be offered throughout the state and a 2000 initiative requiring construction of a high-speed rail system to connect all of Florida's five major cities.

For the first time, we have incorporated estimates of the effect of political institutions on freedom in this study. To be sure, the relatively blunt methods used in this book will be unable to identify some of the subtle effects of particular institutions. For instance, institutions such as the gubernatorial veto that merely slow down the pace of policy change would not affect freedom unconditionally but might preserve it where it already exists. We look at

---

117.   See, for instance, Torsten Persson and Guido Tabellini, *The Economic Effects of Constitutions* (Cambridge, MA: MIT Press, 2003).

118.   See, for instance, Charles R. Shipan and Craig Volden, "Bottom-Up Federalism: The Diffusion of Antismoking Policies from U.S. Cities to States," *American Journal of Political Science* 50, no. 4 (2006): 825–43.

broader-gauge institutional and cultural variables, such as corruption, prevalence of lobbyists, and state age. We find that more corrupt states with more lobbyists have less economic freedom. Older states also tend to have less economic freedom, although most of the reason for it seems to be that such states have stronger labor unions, which push politically for less economic freedom. The ballot initiative, legislative professionalism, and constitutional complexity do not correlate with economic freedom at all.

Although macro phenomena like partisan lean and corruption have a big effect on freedom, we must not discount the role of political entrepreneurs and individual activists at the state and local levels. The late Jerry Kopel, a Colorado legislator and activist, authored the original "sunrise" and "sunset" legislation for occupational licensing agencies and maintained a website where he kept a close watch on licensing regulation. [119] Quite probably because of his indefatigable efforts, Colorado remains today among the highest-rated states in the nation for occupational freedom.

Finally, we examine the consequences of freedom for migration and economic growth. We find strong evidence that states with more freedom attract more residents. We can be especially confident of the relationship between a lighter fiscal impact of government and net inmigration, which was statistically significant in every model we ran, but the best evidence suggests that regulatory freedom and personal freedom also attract residents.

The channel by which regulatory freedom attracts residents is lower cost of living and higher economic growth. Particularly over longer time series, regulatory freedom appears to have the strongest relationship with subsequent income growth of any predictive variable used in the standard literature.

Freedom is not the only determinant of personal satisfaction and fulfillment, but as our analysis of migration patterns shows, it makes a tangible difference for people's decisions about where to live. Moreover, we fully expect people in the freer states to develop and benefit from the kinds of institutions (such as symphonies and museums) and amenities (such as better restaurants and cultural attractions) seen in some of the older cities on the coast, in less free states such as California and New York, as they grow and prosper. Indeed, urban development expert and journalist Joel Kotkin recently made a similar point about the not-so-sexy urban areas that are best situated to recover from the economic downturn:

> Of course, none of the cities in our list competes right now with
> New York, Chicago, or L.A. in terms of art, culture, and urban
> amenities, which tend to get noticed by journalists and casual

---

119. See Jerry Kopel website, http://www.jerrykopel.com/.

travelers. But once upon a time, all those great cities were also seen as cultural backwaters. And in the coming decades, as more people move in and open restaurants, museums, and sports arenas, who's to say Oklahoma City can't be Oz? [120]

These things take time, but the same kind of dynamic freedom enjoyed in Chicago or New York in the 19th century—that led to their rise—might propel places in the middle of the country to be a bit more hip to those with urbane tastes.

Finally, we would stress that the variance in liberty at the state level in the United States is quite small in the global context. Even New York provides a much freer environment for the individual than the majority of countries. There are no Myanmars or North Koreas among the American states. Still, our federal system allows states to pursue different policies in a range of important areas. The policy laboratory of federalism has been compromised by centralization, most recently in health insurance, but is still functioning. Indeed, Colorado, Washington, Alaska, and Oregon have proved how robust this laboratory can be even in the face of federal power when they liberalized their marijuana laws in 2012 and 2014.

Regardless of one's views about freedom as we define it, the information this study provides should prove useful to those looking for a better life. As Americans, especially those who are currently less fortunate, grow richer in future years, quality of life will matter more to residence decisions, while the imperative of higher-paying employment will decline by comparison. For many Americans, living under laws of which they approve is a constituent element of the good life. As a result, we should expect more ideological "sorting" of the kind economist and geographer Charles Tiebout foresaw. [121] High-quality information on state legal and policy environments will matter a great deal to those seeking an environment friendlier to individual liberty.

120. Joel Kotkin, "Welcome to Recoveryland: The Top 10 Places in America Poised for Recovery," November 8, 2010, http://www.joelkotkin.com/content/00320-welcome-recoveryland-top-10-places-america-poised-recovery.

121. Charles Tiebout, "A Pure Theory of Local Expenditures," *Journal of Political Economy* 64, no. 5 (1956): 416–24.

PART 3
FREEDOM STATE BY STATE

The following state profiles contain (a) a chart of each state's personal, economic, and overall freedom rankings over time (because they are ranks, lower numbers are better); (b) some key facts on each state; (c) a descriptive analysis of its freedom situation; and (d) three specific policy recommendations that would increase freedom in each state. We choose policy recommendations that would have the greatest effects on the state's freedom score, consistent with its political environment. For instance, urging New York to pass a right-to-work law would be futile, but eliminating rent control through state legislation might be more feasible. The discussions for each state represent the policy environment as of our data cutoff date, though we have attempted to note some of the most significant policy changes that occurred after that date.

sample spread

KEY TO THE PROFILES

The following profiles contain some basic information about each state, including the state's freedom rankings over time and various institutional, political, demographic, and economic indicators of interest. The next few pages provide a brief description of each element contained in the profiles, keyed to the sample profile opposite. They also supply more information about the variables we have chosen to include.

STATE ID

State Name

State profiles appear in alphabetical order. The District of Columbia and unincorporated organized territories are not included in this index.

State Rankings

Each state's overall rank for 2014 is displayed prominently at the top of the spread, next to the state name. A chart below the state name presents the state's segmented, historical rankings for 2000, 2006, 2008, 2010, and 2012.

DEMOGRAPHICS

Population

Share of Total U.S. Population

Population Ranking

Net Migration Rate

FISCAL FACTORS

State Taxes, Percent of Personal Income

Local Taxes, Percent of Personal Income

Partisan Lean, 2012

INCOME AND WEALTH

Real Per Capita Personal Income

Real Personal Income Growth, CAGR

ANALYSIS

The analysis section of each state profile begins with an introduction and then discusses fiscal, regulatory, and personal freedom issues in the state, in that order.

POLICY RECOMMENDATIONS

There are three policy recommendations for each state, corresponding to the three dimensions of freedom: fiscal policy, regulatory policy, and personal freedom, in that order. We considered three criteria as we decided which policy recommendations to include in this book:

1. Importance. The recommended policy change would result in a significant boost to the state's freedom score.

2. Anomalousness. The policy change would correct a significant deviation of the state's policies from national norms.

3. Feasibility. The policy change would likely prove popular, taking into account the state's ideological orientation and the political visibility of the issue.

ALABAMA

2014 RANK
23rd

Population, 2014
4,849,377

Share of total U.S. population
1.5%

Population ranking	Net migration rate
23rd	**2.0%**

ECONOMIC   **PERSONAL**   **OVERALL**

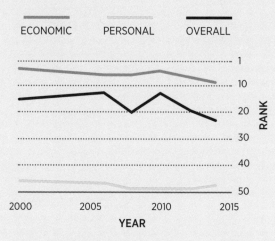

YEAR

State Taxes, Percent of Personal Income, FY 2014
4.7%

Local Taxes, Percent of Personal Income, FY 2012
2.9%

Partisan Lean, 2012
R +12.9

POLICY RECOMMENDATIONS

• **Fiscal:** Encourage the privatization of hospitals and utilities in order to bring government employment down closer to the national average. Private utility monopolies will, however, require careful rate regulation.

• **Regulatory:** Improve the civil liability system by tightening or abolishing punitive damages and abolishing joint and several liability.

• **Personal:** Reduce the incarceration rate with thorough sentencing reform, including abolishing mandatory minimums for nonviolent offenses and lowering maximum sentences for marijuana and other victimless crimes.

Real Per Capita Personal Income, 2013, in 2009 $
$38,794

Real Personal Income Growth, CAGR, 2000–13
1.66%

ANALYSIS

As a socially conservative Deep South state, it is unsurprising that Alabama does much better on economic freedom than on personal freedom. Some of its neighbors do better on economic freedom (Tennessee and Florida), one does about as well (Georgia), and one does much worse (Mississippi).

Alabama has always been one of the lowest-taxed states in the country. Its combined state and local tax collections, excluding motor fuel and severance, were an estimated 7.7 percent of personal income in FY 2013. State-level taxes fell quickly in the early stages of the Great Recession and have not increased much since then. Local taxes crept up a bit over the 2000–2008 period. Alabama has a moderate degree of choice in local government. Municipalities are more important than counties, but counties are still important, and municipalities are not numerous enough to give Alabama even one competing jurisdiction per 100 square miles.

Unlike some other southern states, Alabama spends little on subsidies to business. Its debt burden is also fairly low. However, public employment is high because of publicly owned utilities and hospitals.

On regulatory policy, Alabama does especially well on land-use and labor policies, but it does well below average on its tort system and certain cronyist policies. Local zoning has a light touch, allowing the housing supply to rise elastically with the state's growing population. Alabama enjoys a right-to-work law, no minimum wage, and liberal workers' compensation mandates. Unfortunately, the state passed an E-Verify mandate on employers in 2011–12.

Alabama has made some moves to improve its civil liability system, but it could do further reforms. The standard of evidence for punitive damages remains unreformed. The state has not abolished joint and several liability.

Some cronyist regulations on business and occupation entry are as follows. Like several other southern states, Alabama suffers from strong physicians' and dentists' lobbies that have prevented nurse practitioners and dental hygienists from practicing independently. There is a certificate-of-need requirement for hospital construction. Personal automobile and homeowner's insurance rates require the insurance commissioner's prior approval. Alabama has a long-standing anti-price-gouging law that will create real harm if the state is ever struck by a major natural disaster. The state also bans sales below cost of gasoline and direct-to-consumer wine shipments.

The state is one of the worst in the country on personal freedom, although its ranking is set to rise substantially because of the Supreme Court's *Obergefell* decision, which has the effect of nullifying Alabama's prohibition on all same-sex partnership contracts.

Alabama was long below average for conservative states on gun rights, but in 2013–14 it moved to shall-issue on concealed carry, and permit costs are low. Alcohol regulations have gradually loosened over time, but the state still has some of the highest beer and spirits taxes in the country, along with local blue laws. The state has done nothing to reform its cannabis laws; it is possible to receive life imprisonment for a single marijuana trafficking offense not involving minors or a school zone. Alabama has a much higher incarceration rate than the national average, even adjusting for its violent and property crime rates. However, its police are actually not very vigorous in pursuit of arrests for victimless crimes. The state does much better than average on tobacco freedom because of low taxes and relatively lenient smoking bans on private property. The state is mediocre on educational freedom but did enact a modest private scholarship tax credit law in 2013–14.

ALASKA

2014 RANK

2nd

ECONOMIC   PERSONAL   OVERALL

RANK / YEAR chart (2000–2015)

POLICY RECOMMENDATIONS

• **Fiscal:** Cut spending in the areas of grossest over-spending relative to national averages: education (for which Alaska has the highest spending-to-income ratio in the nation), corrections, administration (especially financial administration and public buildings), and "miscellaneous commercial activities." Use the proceeds to reduce the corporate income tax permanently, helping the economy to diversify away from energy.

• **Regulatory:** Enact a right-to-work law to attract manufacturing investment. This single reform would have raised Alaska from 18th to 12th on regulatory freedom.

• **Personal:** Reform asset forfeiture to require a criminal conviction before forfeiture, and require Department of Justice equitable sharing proceeds to follow the same procedure.

Population, 2014
736,732

Share of total U.S. population
0.2%

Population ranking
48th

Net migration rate
−3.4%

State Taxes, Percent of Personal Income, FY 2014
2.1%

Local Taxes, Percent of Personal Income, FY 2012
4.4%

Partisan Lean, 2012
R +9.6

Real Per Capita Personal Income, 2013, in 2009 $
$44,114

Real Personal Income Growth, CAGR, 2000–13
2.22%

ANALYSIS

Alaska is an unusual state because of its enormous oil and gas reserves and revenues. Its fiscal policy scores fluctuate wildly depending on the global price of oil. With the end of the 2000s' commodity boom, corporate income tax collections plummeted in Alaska, and the state buffered the decline with large withdrawals from its enormous rainy-day fund. Alaska has by far the highest cash-to-liability ratio of any state.[122]

Alaska's enviable net asset position has also made for something of a "resource curse" in the state's expenditures. Over a quarter of the state's employed population works in state or local government. It spends more than the national average on business subsidies. Although local taxes outstrip state taxes, lately by a wide margin, local jurisdictions are so consolidated that there is very little choice among local government options.

Despite its attractive overall fiscal situation, or perhaps because of it, Alaska does poorly on several important regulatory policy indicators. The labor market is far more regulated than one would expect for such a conservative state: no right-to-work law, strict workers' compensation mandates, and a high minimum wage. Many occupations are licensed in Anchorage and Fairbanks, where about half of the state's population lives. Insurance is heavily regulated.

On the other hand, Alaska gives a good bit of practice freedom to nurses and dental hygienists, does not zone out low-cost housing, and has one of the nation's best civil liability systems, an area where the state has improved greatly over the past 14 years.

As one of the country's most libertarian states, Alaska has always done well on personal freedom. Drug arrest rates are quite low, crime-adjusted incarceration is somewhat below the national average, marijuana is legal, homeschooling is unregulated, and gun rights are secure (for instance, concealed carry of handguns does not require a license). However, the state used to have one of the most anti-gay-marriage laws in the nation, forbidding even private partnership contracts for same-sex couples. Judicial action in 2014 overturned those laws. The state's civil asset forfeiture law is also the worst in the country, which probably accounts for why local police do not bother to ask the Department of Justice to "adopt" many cases. The burden of proof is on the owner of the property to prove innocence, property is subject to forfeiture on the basis of mere probable cause, and all of the proceeds go to law enforcement. Sales of all alcohol, even beer, are prohibited in grocery stores. Beer taxes are also among the highest in the country.

---

122. Eileen Norcross, "Ranking the States by Fiscal Condition," Mercatus Research, Mercatus Center at George Mason University, Arlington, VA, July 2015.

ARIZONA

2014 RANK

10th

─── **ECONOMIC**   ┄┄┄ **PERSONAL**   ━━━ **OVERALL**

RANK

1 — 10 — 20 — 30 — 40 — 50

YEAR
2000   2005   2010   2015

POLICY RECOMMENDATIONS

• **Fiscal:** Provide an easy procedure for small groups of neighborhoods to incorporate new municipalities, either out of unincorporated areas or out of existing cities. Keep state aid to localities at a low level to allow local jurisdictions to provide different levels and mixes of public goods according to the desires of their residents.

• **Regulatory:** Provide for full competition in telecommunications and cable, allowing different wireline and wireless companies to attract customers without service mandates, price controls, or local franchising exactions. In 2014, this move would have raised the state from 20th to 16th on regulatory policy.

• **Personal:** Legalize for-profit casinos and card games.

Population, 2014
6,731,484

Share of total U.S. population
2.1%

Population ranking
15th

Net migration rate
15.8%

State Taxes, Percent of Personal Income, FY 2014
4.8%

Local Taxes, Percent of Personal Income, FY 2012
3.9%

Partisan Lean, 2012
R +6.6

Real Per Capita Personal Income, 2013, in 2009 $
$35,537

Real Personal Income Growth, CAGR, 2000–13
2.11%

ANALYSIS

Relative to other states, Arizona has gradually improved on personal freedom and has generally been above average on economic freedom, while losing a little ground there over the 2009–12 period.

Fiscal policy has been more of a strength than regulatory policy. Although local taxes are at or above the national average, state-level taxes are reasonably low. The state depends heavily on sales taxes, permitting generally low individual and business income taxes. Arizona has very little scope for choice among local jurisdictions. Although municipalities are more important than counties, there are only 91 municipalities in the whole state. Given that local taxes are so important in this state, more choice of locality would greatly enhance residents' freedom.

On regulatory policy, Arizona is laudably anti-crony. In most industries, business entry and prices are quite liberalized, although a little backsliding has occurred in the property and casualty insurance market, and occupational licensing has ratcheted up over time. Otherwise, its regulatory environment is a mixed bag. The right-to-work law probably attracts manufacturing businesses, but the state has done little to promote competition in telecommunications and cable. It has a higher-than-federal minimum wage and an E-Verify mandate. Although land-use regulation tightened in the 1990s and early 2000s, a regulatory taking initiative may have curbed its growth a little since 2006.

Arizona's personal freedom improvements are due to growing gun rights ("constitutional carry" passed in 2009–10); a medical marijuana law; school vouchers (passed in 2011–12); declining victimless crime arrests; the abolition of its sodomy law, due to the Supreme Court's decision in *Lawrence v. Texas;* and the judicial legalization of same-sex marriage. On the other side of the ledger, incarceration rates have climbed consistently, and smoking bans have become comprehensive and airtight. (The latter, like the state's minimum wage, is explained in part by the ballot initiative, which really does result in some observable "tyranny of the majority.") Little change has been observed in alcohol freedom, where the state is better than average, or in gambling freedom, where the state is worse than average.

ARKANSAS

2014 RANK
29th

ECONOMIC   PERSONAL   **OVERALL**

RANK

	1
	10
	20
	30
	40
	50

2000   2005   2010   2015

YEAR

POLICY RECOMMENDATIONS

• **Fiscal:** Cut the state sales and use tax, which is high. Let local governments vary property taxes to meet local needs and desires, reducing state aid for education and other purposes.

• **Regulatory:** Roll back occupational licensing. Some occupations that could be deregulated include sanitarians, title abstractors, interpreters, dietitians and nutritionists, pharmacy technicians, veterinary technologists, opticians, athletic trainers, occupational therapist assistants, massage therapists, private detectives, security guards, landscaping contractors, tree trimmers (locally), funeral apprentices, collection agents, 911 dispatchers, tree injectors, construction contractors, security alarm installers, well drillers, mobile home installers, and boiler operators.

• **Personal:** Enact a generous tax credit for contributions to private scholarships for K–12 education.

Population, 2014
2,966,369

Share of total U.S. population
0.9%

Population ranking	Net migration rate
32nd	**2.8%**

State Taxes, Percent of Personal Income, FY 2014
7.4%

Local Taxes, Percent of Personal Income, FY 2012
2.0%

Partisan Lean, 2012
R +13.6

Real Per Capita Personal Income, 2013, in 2009 $
$39,119

Real Personal Income Growth, CAGR, 2000–13
2.32%

ANALYSIS

Throughout our period, Arkansas has been mediocre on economic freedom. Its personal freedom has declined relative to other states in recent years, although this observation does not include same-sex marriage legalization, which occurred because of the Supreme Court decision in 2015 and should raise the state's rank substantially.

Arkansas is highly fiscally centralized. State taxes are way above the national average, and local taxes are way below. Overall, it ends up being about average in tax burden. Debt and subsidies are low, but government employment is high.

Like many other southern states, Arkansas does well on land-use and labor policies and somewhat poorly on cronyist entry and price controls. However, it does better than most other southern states, and indeed the national average, on its civil liability regime. It has also started to deregulate telecommunications and in 2013 enacted statewide video

franchising. The extent of occupational licensing, according to two different measures, is more than a standard deviation worse than the national average. Hospital construction requires a certificate of need, and there is an anti-price-gouging law and also a general law against "unfair pricing" or sales below cost.

Arkansas does better than most of its neighbors on criminal justice policies. Victimless crime arrests are below average, and the crime-adjusted incarceration rate is not much above average. On the other hand, the state does a bit worse than one might expect on gun rights, with heavy training requirements and significant limitations on the right to carry concealed. Marijuana laws are unreformed. In personal freedom categories other than these and the aforementioned marriage laws, Arkansas deviates little from the average. School choice particularly looks like an opportunity for improvement, given the state's fiscal centralization (so there's not much choice among public schools), its generally conservative ideological orientation, and its minority student populations.

CALIFORNIA

2014 RANK
49th

ECONOMIC   PERSONAL   OVERALL

RANK: 1, 10, 20, 30, 40, 50

YEAR: 2000, 2005, 2010, 2015

Note: Economic and overall rankings tied.

POLICY RECOMMENDATIONS

• **Fiscal:** Cut spending in the areas of general administration, housing and community development, and employee retirement, where it exceeds the national average, and use the proceeds to reduce indebtedness.

• **Regulatory:** Eliminate the California Coastal Commission's authority to regulate private land use. Instead, give it the authority to overturn local zoning rules that undermine sound environmental objectives, such as housing density.

• **Personal:** Expand legal gambling. California's political culture is unlikely to have many qualms about gaming, but legalizing nontribal casinos would require a constitutional amendment. If California's gambling regime rose, consistently with that culture, to a standard deviation better than the national average, it would rise from 16th to 9th on personal freedom.

Population, 2014
38,802,500

Share of total U.S. population
12.2%

Population ranking
1st

Net migration rate
−4.9%

State Taxes, Percent of Personal Income, FY 2014
6.9%

Local Taxes, Percent of Personal Income, FY 2012
3.9%

Partisan Lean, 2012
D +9.4

Real Per Capita Personal Income, 2013, in 2009 $
$40,236

Real Personal Income Growth, CAGR, 2000–13
1.06%

ANALYSIS

Although it has long been significantly freer on personal issues than the national average, California has also long been one of the lowest-scoring states on economic freedom.

Despite Proposition 13, California is one of the highest-taxed states in the country. Excluding severance and motor fuel taxes, California's combined state and local tax collections were 10.8 percent of personal income. Moreover, because of the infamous Serrano decision on school funding, California is a fiscally centralized state. Local taxes are about average nationally, while state taxes are well above average. Government debt is high, at 22.8 percent of personal income. The state subsidizes business at a high rate (0.16 percent of the state economy). However, government employment is lower than the national average.

Regulatory policy is even more of a problem for the state than fiscal policy. California is one of the worst states on land-use freedom. Some cities have rent control, new housing supply is tightly restricted in the coastal areas, and eminent domain reform has been nugatory. Labor law is anti-employment, with no right-to-work law, high minimum wages, strict workers' comp mandates, mandated short-term disability insurance, and a stricter-than-federal anti-discrimination law. Occupational

licensing is extensive and strict, especially in construction trades. It is tied for worst in nursing practice freedom. The state's mandatory cancer labeling law (Proposition 65) has significant economic costs. [123] It is one of the worst states for consumer freedom of choice in homeowner's and automobile insurance. On the plus side, there is no certificate-of-need law for new hospitals, some moves have occurred to deregulate cable and telecommunications, and the civil liability regime has improved gradually over the past 14 years.

California is a classic left-wing state on social issues. Gun rights are among the weakest in the country and have been weakened consistently over time. It was one of the first states to adopt a smoking ban on private property, but other states have since leapfrogged California in their restrictiveness, and tobacco taxes are actually a bit lower than average. Similarly, California led in cannabis liberalization in 2000, but it has not further relaxed its laws at all since then. Alcohol is not as strictly regulated as in most other states. Private school choice programs are nonexistent, though there is some public school choice, and homeschooling is moderately regulated. Incarceration and drug arrest rates used to be higher than average but have fallen over time, especially since 2010. The state adopted same-sex partnerships and then civil unions fairly early but received same-sex marriage only recently.

---

123. David R. Henderson, "Proposition 65: When Government Cries Wolf," *Econlog*, April 14, 2013, http://econlog.econlib.org /archives/2013/04/proposition_65_1.html.

COLORADO

2014 RANK
11th

Population, 2014
5,355,866

Share of total U.S. population
1.7%

Population ranking	Net migration rate
22nd	**7.9%**

ECONOMIC   PERSONAL   OVERALL

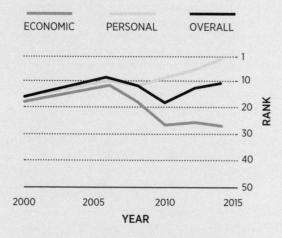

YEAR

State Taxes, Percent
of Personal Income, FY 2014
4.2%

Local Taxes, Percent
of Personal Income, FY 2012
4.7%

Partisan Lean, 2012
D +0.4

Real Per Capita Personal
Income, 2013, in 2009 $
$42,786

Real Personal Income
Growth, CAGR, 2000–13
1.65%

POLICY RECOMMENDATIONS

• **Fiscal:** Trim spending on local parks, a category that excludes conservation lands. The state spends almost twice the national average (as a share of the economy). Also trim spending on unemployment compensation and on business subsidies, which are a little above the national average. Reduce taxes in these areas.

• **Regulatory:** Abolish remaining entry restrictions, such as on moving companies, and price controls.

• **Personal:** Require all equitable sharing revenues from the Department of Justice to follow state-level procedures for civil asset forfeiture.

ANALYSIS

Colorado has long been one of America's freer states, but its economic and personal freedom trajectories have diverged relative to the rest of the country since 2007.

Colorado's overall tax burden is a little lower than the national average, but state-level taxes have crept upward since FY 2009. Local tax revenues, meanwhile, peaked in FY 2009 and fell back slightly to FY 2012. Although fiscal decentralization is high when measured as the ratio of local to state taxes, there isn't much choice of local government, given the importance of counties and the paucity of incorporated cities. Subsidies are about average, and debt is a little higher than average. State and local employment is lower than average but has risen by quite a bit since 2000, now amounting to 12.4 percent of private employment.

Colorado does generally well on regulatory policy—it is one of the top states on our freedom from cronyism index. It earns its score on the latter through its relatively open occupational licensing system, including broad scope of practice for health care professionals and lack of a certificate-of-need law for hospitals. However, it does require household goods movers to get certificates of public convenience and necessity, bans Tesla's direct sales model, prohibits price increases for pharma-ceuticals during emergencies, and proscribes all "unfair" pricing in gasoline specifically and in other industries. Its legal regime for torts is much better than average. In 2013–14, it deregulated telecommunications somewhat, though it still lacks statewide video franchising. It is a little below average on labor-market freedom, with no right-to-work law and a minimum wage. It has remained freer for new housing construction than most other states with significant amenities driving demand. However, its renewable portfolio standard for electricity is much stricter than the national average and probably results in higher rates.

Colorado started out personally freer than the average state in 2000 and is now among the personally freest states. It has led the way with recreational cannabis legalization, which occurred in stages from 2012 to 2014. Legal gambling has gradually expanded over the past 14 years. Gun rights are generally secure, despite an insignificant decline in 2013–14, but the qualifications for carry licensure are fairly strict. The state asset forfeiture law is good, though local agencies frequently circumvent it with equitable sharing. Crime-adjusted incarceration rates are above the national average, but drug arrest rates are low and declining. The state enacted civil unions in 2013 and then was judicially granted same-sex marriage in 2014. Educational freedom is somewhat below average, as there are no private school choice programs.

CONNECTICUT

2014 RANK
45th

ECONOMIC   PERSONAL   OVERALL

RANK: 1, 10, 20, 30, 40, 50

YEAR: 2000, 2005, 2010, 2015

POLICY RECOMMENDATIONS

• **Fiscal:** Cut individual income taxes, which are much higher than average. Housing and "miscellaneous" government spending categories are higher than the national average and could likely be trimmed.

• **Regulatory:** Enact statewide restrictions on eminent domain and the ability of local communities to impose building limits, minimum lot sizes, and other mechanisms of racial and income exclusion.

• **Personal:** Reduce the incarceration rate by reducing maximum sentences and eliminating mandatory minimums for nonviolent crimes.[124]

Population, 2014
3,596,677

Share of total U.S. population
1.1%

Population ranking
29th

Net migration rate
−5.0%

State Taxes, Percent of Personal Income, FY 2014
6.8%

Local Taxes, Percent of Personal Income, FY 2012
4.5%

Partisan Lean, 2012
D +6.8

Real Per Capita Personal Income, 2013, in 2009 $
$52,126

Real Personal Income Growth, CAGR, 2000–13
1.67%

124.   See Terrance Adams, "Crimes with Mandatory Minimum Prison Sentences: Updated and Revised," Office of Legislative Research, Connecticut General Assembly, Hartford, February 5, 2013, https://www.cga.ct.gov/2013/rpt/2013-R-0103.htm.

ANALYSIS

Connecticut has become one of the least economically free states in the Union, even as it enjoys more than the average level of personal freedom.

In past editions, we credited Connecticut with a "remnant streak of Yankee fiscal conservatism," but the state's politics have become increasingly tax and spend. Although residents of Connecticut enjoy broad scope of choice among local governments, state government tax collections are about 50 percent greater than local tax collections, making the choice of local government less important. After a big decline in state-level taxation from FY 2000 to FY 2009, it has grown again to its former level. Debt now hovers around 20 percent of personal income, a few percentage points above its 2000–2006 level.

Connecticut also does poorly in most areas of regulatory policy. Exclusionary zoning is common. Renewable portfolio standards are tight, keeping electricity rates high. The state has a minimum wage but lacks a right-to-work law. Connecticut was once a leader in occupational openness, but the state grew dramatically more closed between 2000 and 2012. However, in 2013–14, the state legalized independent nurse practitioner practice with prescription authority, a significant achievement. Price regulation in the property and casualty market has become more interventionist over time. The civil liability system is mediocre.

On personal freedom, Connecticut is about what one would expect for a left-of-center New England state. Guns are regulated strictly, but a medical cannabis law was enacted in 2011–12, and the alcohol blue laws were finally repealed. The state has long hosted popular casinos. It has no private school choice programs, but there is interdistrict public school choice. Cigarette taxes are sky-high ($2.90 a pack in 2006 dollars), and smoking bans, except for private workplaces, are tight. The state's asset forfeiture law and practice are better than average. Crime-adjusted incarceration rates are higher than the national average and much higher than those of other New England states, but victimless crime arrest rates are much lower than the national average. The state legalized same-sex marriage in 2007–8.

DELAWARE

2014 RANK
31st

ECONOMIC   PERSONAL   OVERALL

RANK
1
10
20
30
40
50

2000   2005   2010   2015

YEAR

POLICY RECOMMENDATIONS

• **Fiscal:** Reduce state-level taxes and education spending. Delaware is one of the freest-spending states in the country on education. Allow local governments to pick up more of the school spending out of their own fiscal resources.

• **Regulatory:** Liberalize insurance laws by moving to a "use and file" system for property and casualty rates and life insurance forms, and join the IIPRC. These changes would vault Delaware from 33rd to 28th place on regulatory policy, just below Texas.

• **Personal:** Enact a tax credit program for parents' educational expenses and contributions to scholarship funds. This change would have moved Delaware from 31st to 25th on personal freedom.

Population, 2014
935,614

Share of total U.S. population
0.3%

Population ranking
45th

Net migration rate
7.6%

State Taxes, Percent of Personal Income, FY 2014
6.9%

Local Taxes, Percent of Personal Income, FY 2012
2.1%

Partisan Lean, 2012
D +7.7

Real Per Capita Personal Income, 2013, in 2009 $
$41,202

Real Personal Income Growth, CAGR, 2000–13
1.43%

ANALYSIS

Delaware has lost ground even relative to the rest of the country on economic freedom since 2010. Part of the reason is that it had one of the most free-market health insurance systems before the enactment of the Patient Protection and Affordable Care Act (PPACA), and so it suffered disproportionately because of the federal law. Moreover, we find in this edition of the index that its much-touted advantage on corporate law is significantly overstated.

On fiscal policy, Delaware is about average. The overall tax burden, at about 9.2 percent of personal income, is average, but the state is highly fiscally centralized. With 1.6 competing jurisdictions per 100 square miles, Delawareans would stand to benefit were the state to allow more tax space for local governments. Subsidies and debt are a bit higher than average, but public employment is a bit lower than average.

Delaware is below average on most regulatory policy categories. Labor law is fairly anti-employment, with a new minimum wage and no right-to-work law. Land-use regulation ratcheted up significantly in the 2000–2010 period, as have renewable portfolio standards for utilities. Occupational freedom is mediocre. The state's insurance commissioner treats property and casualty insurance rates under "prior approval" contrary to statute, according to the Insurance Information Institute.[125] Delaware remains one of a handful of states not to have joined the Interstate Insurance Product Regulation Compact (IIPRC). Even the state's vaunted liability system has actually deteriorated to just below average, we find. The state has enacted no tort reforms, and the size of the legal sector has grown, whether measured in number of lawyers or share of GDP.

Delaware is close to the national average in most personal freedom categories. In 2013, the state legislature legalized same-sex marriage, after having legalized civil unions in 2011. In 2011–12, the state's medical cannabis law was expanded. Alcohol taxes, already a bit lower than average, have eroded over time because of inflation. The state is mediocre on gun rights; the biggest problem area is the may-issue regime for concealed-carry licensing. Gambling is more restricted than the national average, although the state has legalized online gambling for its own residents; in the future, this move may yield significant new business. Delaware has no private school choice programs, but homeschooling is easy. Smoking bans are comprehensive, but cigarette taxes are only modestly higher than average. The state's civil asset forfeiture law is tied for worst in the country, with few protections for innocent owners.

---

125. See the "Metadata" tab of the n_reg_15.xls spreadsheet.

FLORIDA

2014 RANK

8th

ECONOMIC — PERSONAL — **OVERALL**

RANK

1	
10	
20	
30	
40	
50	

2000   2005   2010   2015

YEAR

POLICY RECOMMENDATIONS

• **Fiscal:** Trim spending on sanitation and sewerage, public parks, and police and fire protection, which are all significantly higher as a share of income than the national average. Use the proceeds to cut general and utility sales taxes.

• **Regulatory:** Abolish the Citizens Property Insurance Corporation, and remove all price controls on private property insurance.

• **Personal:** Enact a medical marijuana law.

Population, 2014
19,893,297

Share of total U.S. population
6.2%

Population ranking
3rd

Net migration rate
10.0%

State Taxes, Percent of Personal Income, FY 2014
3.9%

Local Taxes, Percent of Personal Income, FY 2012
4.0%

Partisan Lean, 2012
R +1.4

Real Per Capita Personal Income, 2013, in 2009 $
$39,159

Real Personal Income Growth, CAGR, 2000–13
1.33%

ANALYSIS

Lacking an individual income tax and featuring a hot climate, Florida has long enjoyed substantial migration of well-off retirees. Its personal freedom has lagged well behind, however.

Florida's state-level tax collections are more than a standard deviation below the national average, while its local tax collections are about average. Florida's fiscal decentralization does not offer homeowners a great deal of choice, however, because the state has only about half an effective competing jurisdiction per 100 square miles of private land. Government subsidies and debt are average, while government employment is much below average, falling from 11.1 percent of private employment in 2010 to 9.9 percent in 2014.

Florida's regulatory policy is slightly freer than the national average. Despite the temptations posed by high housing demand, homeowners have been unable to enact exclusionary zoning on anything like the levels of California or New Hampshire. Our two measures of local zoning give a split judgment on just how restrictive Florida is. Land-use regulation appears to be a major political issue, but the courts have tools to restrain local governments, as the state has a particularly strong regulatory takings law. Florida has gone further than just about any other state to tighten criteria for eminent domain. Labor law is also above average because of a right-to-work law, but the state has a minimum wage. Cable and telecommunications are partially deregulated. The civil liability system is better than average and has improved significantly since 2000. On the other side of the ledger, the state is far below average on occupational freedom, and the homeowner's insurance market is the most regulated and dysfunctional in the country.

On personal freedom, Florida now appears well below average, but as shown in Appendix Table B17, the state can expect to enjoy a substantial boost from the Supreme Court's nationalization of same-sex marriage. Before that decision, Florida did not recognize any kind of same-sex partnership and banned private contracts amounting to marriage with a super-DOMA. Florida is also one of the states that had a sodomy law before *Lawrence v. Texas*. Florida's crime-adjusted incarceration rate has risen over time and is now above average, even as its arrest rates for victimless crimes have fallen substantially. Florida is one of the top states for educational freedom, although homeschool regulations remain substantial. The cannabis regime is fairly harsh, while alcohol is lightly regulated. Gun rights are mediocre, as the state has waiting periods for some weapons, local dealer licensing, stricter-than-federal minimum age for possession, and virtually no open carry.

GEORGIA

2014 RANK
22nd

Population, 2014
10,097,343

Share of total U.S. population
3.2%

Population ranking	Net migration rate
8th	**7.3%**

ECONOMIC   PERSONAL   OVERALL

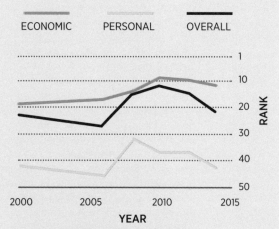

RANK

YEAR

State Taxes, Percent
of Personal Income, FY 2014
4.5%

Local Taxes, Percent
of Personal Income, FY 2012
4.3%

Partisan Lean, 2012
R +5.9

Real Per Capita Personal
Income, 2013, in 2009 $
$38,415

Real Personal Income
Growth, CAGR, 2000–13
1.52%

POLICY RECOMMENDATIONS

• **Fiscal:** Phase out state-level business subsidies and prohibit them at the local level. Even without any dynamic benefits to the economy, this action would have been sufficient in 2014 to raise Georgia from 4th to 12th on fiscal policy, just ahead of Pennsylvania.

• **Regulatory:** Liberalize health care professions: permit independent nurse practitioner practice with prescription authority, join the Nurse Licensure Compact, allow dental hygienists to clean teeth independently of dentist supervision, and allow physician assistants to prescribe on all schedules. These moves in 2014 would have raised Georgia to 12th on regulatory policy, ahead of South Carolina.

• **Personal:** Reform civil asset forfeiture by putting the burden of proof on the government, requiring evidence beyond a reasonable doubt that the property was the product of criminal activity, sending forfeiture proceeds to the general fund, and requiring all equitable sharing revenues to meet state standards.

ANALYSIS

Georgia has been one of the fastest-growing southern states, perhaps due in part to one of the best regulatory environments in the region. Lately, its fiscal situation has been improving as well.

At 4.5 percent of personal income, state tax collections are significantly below the national average, while local taxes—4.3 percent of income—are slightly above. Like most southern states, Georgia has less than one effective competing local government per 100 square miles, which reduces the benefit from its fiscal decentralization. Georgia also keeps subsidies to business a bit lower than the national average and debt substantially lower. Government employment used to be about the national average, but Georgia has brought it down from 13.2 percent of private employment in 2010 to 12.0 percent in 2014.

Like other conservative southern states, Georgia does well on labor and land-use policy. It has a right-to-work law, no minimum wage, relaxed workers' comp regulations, and moderate zoning. It has partially deregulated telecommunications and enacted statewide video franchising. Unlike some other states in its neighborhood, however, Georgia also enjoys a relatively good civil liability system, which has also shown some improvement between 2008 and 2014. In 2007–8, the state relaxed the approval process for automobile insurance rates. The one regulatory policy area where Georgia does poorly is occupational freedom. The extent of licensing is a bit broader than the national average, and health care professions face generally tight scope-of-practice rules.

On personal freedom, Georgia is about what one would expect from a conservative southern state. Its incarceration rates are very high, even adjusted for crime rates, although victimless crime arrests have fallen. It has not reformed civil asset forfeiture sufficiently, and it also participates much more than average in federal equitable sharing. The burden of proof falls on innocent owners, all proceeds go to law enforcement, and some actions require only probable cause to show that the property is subject to forfeiture. It is one of the worst states for cannabis or gambling. On the other hand, it is one of the best states for educational freedom, scores well on gun rights, and regulates tobacco use lightly compared with most other states. At the end of 2014, it was also one of the worst states for marriage freedom, which means it stands to rise significantly post-*Obergefell*.

HAWAII

2014 RANK
48th

ECONOMIC   PERSONAL   OVERALL

RANK

YEAR

POLICY RECOMMENDATIONS

• **Fiscal:** Cut spending on sanitation and sewerage, parks and recreation, public buildings, health and hospitals, and "miscellaneous" areas where local government looks quite inefficient and the state spends far more than the national average. Also cut local taxes.

• **Regulatory:** Relax the state's extreme land-use regulations. Allow residential uses on land deemed "agricultural," and eliminate either state or county review, which are duplicative.

• **Personal:** Adopt a shall-issue concealed-carry license rather than continue to waste taxpayers' money on the futile appeal of a current court ruling. Federal courts are almost certain to strike down the state's de facto ban on carrying firearms in public.

Population, 2014
1,419,561

Share of total U.S. population
0.4%

Population
ranking
40th

Net migration
rate
−3.3%

State Taxes, Percent
of Personal Income, FY 2014
9.0%

Local Taxes, Percent
of Personal Income, FY 2012
3.0%

Partisan Lean, 2012
D +19.9

Real Per Capita Personal
Income, 2013, in 2009 $
$36,267

Real Personal Income
Growth, CAGR, 2000–13
2.36%

ANALYSIS

Hawaii has long had one of the lowest levels of economic freedom in the country, but it now also has fallen behind on personal freedom, despite the enactment of same-sex marriage in 2013. Even with its huge locational rents, Hawaii has experienced net outflow of residents to the rest of the United States since at least the beginning of the past decade.

Hawaii's fiscal policy is decidedly tax and spend. State-level taxes rose from an already-high 7.8 percent of personal income in FY 2009 to 9.3 percent in FY 2013. Local government also taxes at a very high level given how little it has to do. Local taxes were 3.0 percent of personal income in FY 2012, only slightly below the national average, even though there are no local schools (education is a state government responsibility). Government subsidies and debt are much higher than the national average. Government employment is at about the national average.

Hawaii does badly in almost every area of regulatory policy, but its two worst categories are land-use and labor-market freedom. It has among the strictest restrictions on residential building in the country. Eminent domain abuse is unchecked by law. The state has a minimum wage, but it was fairly modest in 2014 ($7.75 per hour), though it is scheduled to rise to $10.10 per hour at the end of 2017. It has no right-to-work law, strict workers' comp mandates, a short-term disability insurance mandate, and a stricter-than-federal anti-discrimination law. Hawaii is also one of the most "cronyist" states, with occupational entry much more regulated than the national average according to multiple sources, very little scope-of-practice freedom for second-line health care professionals, a hospital certificate-of-need requirement, strict insurance regulations, a price-gouging law, and a general "unfair sales" law (you are not allowed to sell at prices that are "too low"). However, we do show a sustained and substantial improvement in the quality of Hawaii's civil liability system, which rose from about average in 2000 to well above average by 2014. That result came about because of increasing scores in the Chamber of Commerce survey of businesses and shrinkage in the size of the legal sector relative to the economy, whether measured by number of lawyers or legal services share of GDP.

Hawaii does better than the national average on incarceration rates, but we see a doubling of the drug enforcement rate from the 2000–2010 average to the post-2010 average. Other victimless crime arrests have also increased. Tobacco freedom is among the lowest in the country, with extremely high cigarette taxes and draconian smoking bans on private property. The state has virtually no legal gambling, other than home social games. Hawaii has a long-standing and permissive medical cannabis law, but it has made no further moves to liberalize cannabis in the past decade. Alcohol freedom is better than average, especially with grocery store sales of wine and spirits and no state involvement in distribution, but beer taxes are high, and there is a "happy hour" ban. Gun rights are among the lowest in the country. It is virtually impossible to get a concealed-carry license, all Class III weapons are banned, registration and purchase permitting of firearms are comprehensive, dealers are licensed, "assault weapons" are banned, large-capacity magazines are banned, and so on.

IDAHO

2014 RANK
7th

Population, 2014
1,634,464

Share of total U.S. population
0.5%

Population ranking	Net migration rate
39th	**9.4%**

ECONOMIC   PERSONAL   OVERALL

RANK

	1
	10
	20
	30
	40
	50

2000   2005   2010   2015

YEAR

State Taxes, Percent of Personal Income, FY 2014
5.6%

Local Taxes, Percent of Personal Income, FY 2012
2.7%

Partisan Lean, 2012
R +18.3

POLICY RECOMMENDATIONS

• **Fiscal:** Comprehensively decentralize power by making it easy for new municipalities to incorporate and secede from existing ones, shifting responsibilities from counties to municipalities, freeing up local property tax–varying power, and reducing state aid to schools so that localities rely on their own tax base. The last move will also allow the state to cut taxes, particularly the general sales tax, which will give localities more tax room.

• **Regulatory:** Make workers' compensation participation voluntary for employers, as in Texas.

• **Personal:** Eliminate or reduce mandatory minimums for nonviolent offenses to reduce the incarceration rate. Allow currently imprisoned offenders to petition for release under the new guidelines.

Real Per Capita Personal Income, 2013, in 2009 $
$36,340

Real Personal Income Growth, CAGR, 2000–13
2.38%

ANALYSIS

Idaho is one of the most economically and socially conservative states in the country. As a result, it is perhaps unsurprising that it enjoys one of the very highest levels of economic freedom and one of the very lowest levels of personal freedom. Nevertheless, the state continues to enjoy substantial inmigration, primarily from the less-free West Coast.

Idaho's fiscal policy has been improving over time, but it remains a weak spot in certain respects. State-level tax collections as a share of income have fallen from 6.8 percent in FY 2000 to 5.7 percent in FY 2013 and are a projected 5.6 percent for FY 2015. That is now about the national average. Local taxes are below the national average, at 2.7 percent of income. Local governments are territorially large: there is only about one effective competing jurisdiction per 200 square miles of private land. Government debt and subsidies are well below the national average, but government employment is only about average.

Idaho does well across the board on regulatory policy. It is one of the best states for occupational freedom, but in 2011, the state began to license more occupations. It is one of the very best states for insurance freedom. There is no hospital certificate-of-need requirement, and direct auto sales were legalized in 2013–14. However, the state does have a general sales-below-cost law. The state's civil liability system is one of the best, and it also scores well above average on labor law,

although workers' compensation mandates are strict. Despite its huge influx of new residents over the past two decades, Idaho held the line on land-use controls for a long time. We do see evidence that new building restrictions have started to come into force since 2006, however. Idaho has done little to curb eminent domain abuse. Since 2012, the state also forbids employers from prohibiting weapons on their property (parking lots)—a trivial part of the index but a symbolically significant restriction on property rights. Statewide video franchising was enacted in 2012.

Idaho is the worst state outside the Deep South on criminal justice policy. Crime-adjusted incarceration rates are nearly two standard deviations above the national average and have been increasing over time. Victimless crime arrests are about average, showing that the state's real problem is sentencing. It is also much less freer than average for alcohol, cannabis, and gambling. The only personal freedom on which it is much freer than average is tobacco: cigarette taxes are not high, and there is not a smoking ban for bars. Homeschooling and private schooling are almost unregulated, but the state has no private school choice programs. Gun rights are better than average, but the state does have a weak law on self-defense in public and a stricter-than-federal minimum age to possess firearms. The expense of a concealed-carry license, including training, is about the national average.

ILLINOIS

2014 RANK
44th

ECONOMIC   PERSONAL   **OVERALL**

RANK

YEAR	
2000	2005 2010 2015

1
10
20
30
40
50

POLICY RECOMMENDATIONS

• **Fiscal:** Enact strict, *ex post* balanced budget requirements in the constitution to reduce state debt and improve the state's poor credit rating.

• **Regulatory:** Reform the civil liability system by capping punitive damages, setting the standard for punitive damages at "beyond a reasonable doubt," and abolishing joint and several liability.

• **Personal:** Continue to reduce drug arrests to reasonable levels. One way to do that would be to make possession of small amounts of cannabis and psychedelics a civil violation rather than a crime.

Population, 2014
12,880,580

Share of total U.S. population
4.0%

Population ranking	Net migration rate
5th	**−7.5%**

State Taxes, Percent of Personal Income, FY 2014
6.0%

Local Taxes, Percent of Personal Income, FY 2012
5.2%

Partisan Lean, 2012
D +4.7

Real Per Capita Personal Income, 2013, in 2009 $
$43,364

Real Personal Income Growth, CAGR, 2000–13
1.05%

ANALYSIS

Illinois used to be a relatively decent state for economic freedom, but it has recently lost economic vitality, even as its well-publicized woes with employee retirement spending have driven taxes and debt higher. However, in the past four years, the state posted one of the most dramatic improvements in personal freedom we have ever seen.

Illinois's state-level taxes have risen from 4.9 percent of personal income in FY 2009, slightly lower than the national average, to a projected 6.0 percent of personal income in FY 2015, with the biggest increase coming in 2011–12. Local taxes have also crept up over time and are now well above the national average, at 5.2 percent of income. However, residents have good choice among local jurisdictions, with almost two effective competing governments per 100 square miles. Government subsidies are much higher than the national average, at 0.15 percent of income, but they have come down a bit over time. Government debt has risen from 17.1 percent of income in FY 2000 to 24.3 percent today, well above the national average. Government employment remains significantly below the national average, at 11.4 percent of private employment.

Illinois has historically done well on land-use and insurance freedom, but much less well on civil liability, labor policy, and occupational freedom. We show few changes on regulatory policy over the past decade, other than liberalization of telecommunications and cable. The state has consistently had a minimum wage, the bindingness of which varies by year, depending on inflation and when it was last updated. Renewable portfolio standards have been gradually tightened, raising electricity rates. Direct auto sales for Tesla were legalized in 2013–14. As of 2013, the state remains on the list of "judicial hell-holes."[126]

Illinois was long our bête noire on personal freedom, but that has dramatically changed with federal court decisions that have overturned some extreme restrictions on gun rights, the legalization of same-sex marriage and medical marijuana, and the new availability of driver's licenses without Social Security numbers (especially important for illegal immigrants). It is now comfortably in the middle of the pack. Illinois's new concealed-carry law, begrudgingly enacted by the legislature, is technically shall-issue but remains one of the country's strictest. The state still has local "assault weapon" and large-capacity magazine bans, waiting periods for gun purchases, background checks for private sales, permitting of buyers for some weapons, local registration of some firearms, mandatory locking devices, and so on. Alcohol freedom is better than average, with no state role in distribution and wine and spirits available in grocery stores. However, there are local blue laws. Formerly one of the most restrictive states for cannabis, Illinois now has a medical marijuana law. Despite a handheld cell phone ban, travel freedom grew in 2013–14 because of the driver's license bill. Legal gambling is expansive. Educational freedom is reasonably good, as virtually no restrictions are placed on homeschools or private schools, and there is a small tax deduction law for parents' educational expenses. Smoking bans are comprehensive, and cigarette taxes are high. Civil asset forfeiture is open to abuse. Drug arrest rates are still extremely high but have come down since 2006.

126. Judicial Hellholes program website, ATR Foundation, http://www.judicialhellholes.org/archives/.

INDIANA

2014 RANK
4th

ECONOMIC PERSONAL OVERALL

RANK

YEAR

2000 2005 2010 2015

1
10
20
30
40
50

POLICY RECOMMENDATIONS

• **Fiscal:** Reduce debt and sales and income taxes by cutting spending on public welfare, libraries, and housing and community development, areas where Indiana spends more than average.

• **Regulatory:** Allow independent nurse practitioner practice with full prescription authority, join the Nurse Licensure Compact, provide for a nursing consultation exception for interstate practice, and legalize independent dental hygienist practice. Combined, these reforms would have moved Indiana into a clear third-place finish on overall freedom in 2014.

• **Personal:** Legalize happy hours, direct wine shipments, and Sunday alcohol sales. Combined, these reforms would have raised Indiana from sixth to fourth on personal freedom in 2014.

Population, 2014
6,596,855

Share of total U.S. population
2.1%

Population ranking
16th

Net migration rate
−0.9%

State Taxes, Percent of Personal Income, FY 2014
6.1%

Local Taxes, Percent of Personal Income, FY 2012
3.4%

Partisan Lean, 2012
R +7.5

Real Per Capita Personal Income, 2013, in 2009 $
$39,397

Real Personal Income Growth, CAGR, 2000–13
1.51%

ANALYSIS

Indiana has quietly built a record as one of America's freest states and the freest state in the Great Lakes region. Although it has still experienced small net outmigration to the rest of the country over the past 15 years, its record in that department has been better than that of any other of the eight Great Lakes states, and its economic growth has been better than the national average since 2006.

Although Indiana's fiscal policy deteriorated quite a bit between FY 2000 and FY 2009, it has made a good recovery since then. Local taxes fell from 4.1 percent of income in FY 2009 to 3.4 percent in FY 2012, even as state taxes have remained essentially steady. Government debt also fell over that period. Government subsidies and employment remain a little smaller than the national average.

Although the PPACA disproportionately harmed the state because of its previously fairly free-market health insurance policies, Indiana has continued to improve those elements of regulatory policy that it can. Land-use freedom is high by any measure. The state passed right-to-work legislation in 2011–12, and it is a model state for telecom deregulation. Occupational freedom is exten-

sive, though not for second-line health care professions. There is no hospital certificate-of-need requirement. Insurance freedom is above average, and the state has recently allowed direct Tesla sales. The civil liability system has shown steady improvement over the past decade and a half.

Indiana has more personal freedom than most other conservative states. It was forced to legalize same-sex marriage in 2014 but never had an oppressive super-DOMA. Gun rights are fairly secure, especially for concealed carry, but the state has a stricter-than-federal minimum age for possession, dealer licensing, and a ban on short-barreled shotguns. Victimless crime arrest rates are fairly low, but the incarceration rate is a bit higher than average, adjusted for crime rates. Educational freedom is excellent, and the state posted major gains in 2011–12 with a new statewide voucher law and a limited scholarship tax credit law. The state's civil asset forfeiture law is fairly good, though it is often circumvented through equitable sharing. Legal gambling is extensive and growing. Smoking bans have not gone quite as far as in other states. Cannabis freedom is virtually nonexistent, and alcohol freedom is only a bit better than average, as the state bans offsite, direct-to-consumer wine shipments and off-premises Sunday sales.

IOWA

2014 RANK
9th

Population, 2014
3,107,126

Share of total U.S. population
1.0%

Population ranking
30th

Net migration rate
−1.8%

ECONOMIC   PERSONAL   OVERALL

RANK

1
10
20
30
40
50

2000   2005   2010   2015

YEAR

State Taxes, Percent of Personal Income, FY 2014
5.5%

Local Taxes, Percent of Personal Income, FY 2012
4.2%

Partisan Lean, 2012
D +0.9

POLICY RECOMMENDATIONS

• **Fiscal:** Trim spending on areas where the state spends more than the national average—education, hospitals, highways, and public welfare—and use the savings to trim property, sales, income, and motor vehicle license taxes.

• **Regulatory:** Repeal the certificate-of-need (CON) requirement for new hospital construction. In 2014, this action would have raised Iowa from fifth to third on regulatory policy.

• **Personal:** End teacher licensing for private schools, and make curriculum requirements general rather than detailed.

Real Per Capita Personal Income, 2013, in 2009 $
$46,247

Real Personal Income Growth, CAGR, 2000–13
2.68%

ANALYSIS

Iowa has long stood out above other center-left states on economic freedom. The state benefited from this policy regime, federal farm subsidies, and the 2002–8 global commodity boom to post impressive growth in the past decade and a half. However, there is some indication that its competitive policy advantages are starting to fade.

State and local taxes are pretty close to average in Iowa, with the latter being slightly above. Iowans also have some degree of choice in local government, with about one different government per 100 square miles. Subsidies and debt are quite low. Government employment is about average: 13.6 percent of private employment in 2014.

Iowa stands out more on regulatory policy. Land-use freedom is ample, though the state hasn't done as much as some others about eminent domain for private gain. It is a right-to-work state without a minimum wage, and workers' compensation mandated coverages were liberalized slightly in 2007–8. Telecommunications and cable have long been partially deregulated. Occupational freedom is about average and has fallen over time because of the licensing of new occupations. Insurance freedom fell with a switch to "file and use" in 2007–8. The civil liability system is rated well above average and has generally improved.

Iowa has had same-sex marriage since 2009, due to a court decision. Incarceration and victimless crime arrest rates are a little lower than average. Educational freedom is high, because the state has a long-standing tax credit scholarship program as well as inter-district public school choice. Homeschooling was significantly liberalized in 2013–14. However, private schools are tightly regulated, with mandatory teacher licensure and detailed curriculum control. Gambling freedom is high, and the industry has generally grown over time. Cannabis freedom is sharply limited; a single marijuana offense not involving minors can carry up to 50 years of prison time. For a rural state, Iowa does not do very well on gun freedoms, though it improved in 2009–10. Class III weapons are banned, even though their ownership is tightly regulated federally. Purchasing handguns requires a permit and waiting period, and open carry requires a license. Alcohol freedom is mediocre because of state involvement in wholesaling and high distilled spirits taxes.

KANSAS

2014 RANK
16th

ECONOMIC   PERSONAL   OVERALL

RANK vs. YEAR chart (2000–2015), RANK axis 1 to 50

POLICY RECOMMENDATIONS

• **Fiscal:** Cut spending on health and hospitals and public buildings, areas where the state spends far more than the national average. Cuts could be made in part through privatizations. Reduce government employment closer to the national average.

• **Regulatory:** Legalize independent nurse practitioner practice with full prescription authority, join the Nurse Licensure Compact, and enact a nursing consultation exception for interstate practice. In 2014, these moves would have raised Kansas to second on regulatory policy.

• **Personal:** End state approval, registration, teacher licensing, and curriculum requirements for all private schools.

Population, 2014
2,904,021

Share of total U.S. population
0.9%

Population ranking
34th

Net migration rate
−4.0%

State Taxes, Percent of Personal Income, FY 2014
5.0%

Local Taxes, Percent of Personal Income, FY 2012
4.1%

Partisan Lean, 2012
R +13.3

Real Per Capita Personal Income, 2013, in 2009 $
$45,619

Real Personal Income Growth, CAGR, 2000–13
2.42%

ANALYSIS

In 2013–14, Kansas reversed a long-standing trend toward less freedom. Time will tell whether the reversal will hold.

Kansas has made national news with its fiscal policy in 2013–14. The state's tax cuts were large, but we show that their projected outcome brings Kansas's state-level tax burden only slightly below the national average (5.0 percent of income), while its local tax burden (4.1 percent of income) is a little above the national average. Kansans have little choice among local governments: only one jurisdiction for every 200 square miles across the state. The state spends much less than average on business subsidies, but government employment is much higher than average (15.0 percent of private employment). Government debt peaked at 24 percent of income in 2008 and is now down to about 21 percent.

Like other states between the Rockies and the Mississippi, Kansas tends to do well on regulatory policy. Land-use freedom is high, though the state has enacted stricter-than-normal renewable portfolio standards, presumably as a sop to the wind industry. It has a right-to-work law and no state-level minimum wage. The civil liability system is much better than average. In 2011–12 a telecom deregulation bill passed. Occupational freedom is traditionally high, except for nurses, but has fallen noticeably in recent years. The state has no hospital certificate-of-need law. It has a price-gouging law, as well as a Depression-era law licensing moving companies.

On personal freedom, Kansas benefits from having been forced to legalize same-sex marriage, a move that also overturned the state's oppressive super-DOMA. Kansas has been better than most other conservative states on criminal justice, but the incarceration rate has crept up over time, as have victimless crime arrest rates. Marijuana sentencing policies are actually milder than in most states, but Kansas has made no move to remove criminal penalties altogether. The state has very little legal gambling. In 2013–14, permitless open carry was legalized, although our index does not take into account the permitless concealed-carry bill that was enacted in 2015. Educational freedom improved in 2013–14 with a new, albeit modest tax credit scholarship law. However, nonsectarian private schools are tightly regulated: they must get state approval and must hire only licensed teachers. Smoking bans are comprehensive, but cigarette taxes are relatively low. Alcohol is much less regulated than it was in the days when Kansas banned bars, but wine or spirits are still not sold in grocery stores, and local blue laws are still on the books. The state takes in way more than the average state in civil asset forfeiture equitable sharing funds.

KENTUCKY

2014 RANK
41st

ECONOMIC   PERSONAL   OVERALL

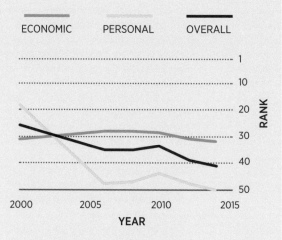

RANK

YEAR

POLICY RECOMMENDATIONS

- **Fiscal:** To reduce debt, tighten the rules for municipal bond issuance and cut spending, particularly on grants to local school districts, employee compensation (repeal the prevailing wage law), and retirement.

- **Regulatory:** Enact a right-to-work law, preferably one of the kind discussed in the "Labor-Market Freedom" section of this book, which does not violate freedom of association.

- **Personal:** Reform sentencing for nonviolent offenders with an eye toward reducing the incarceration rate to the national average. In 2014, this change would have raised Kentucky from 50th to 45th on personal freedom.

Population, 2014
4,413,457

Share of total U.S. population
1.4%

Population ranking
26th

Net migration rate
1.9%

State Taxes, Percent of Personal Income, FY 2014
5.9%

Local Taxes, Percent of Personal Income, FY 2012
2.9%

Partisan Lean, 2012
R +13.2

Real Per Capita Personal Income, 2013, in 2009 $
$37,916

Real Personal Income Growth, CAGR, 2000–13
1.35%

ANALYSIS

Like its neighbor West Virginia, Kentucky has been one of the more regulated states in the country on both the economic and personal freedom dimensions. Unlike West Virginia, however, Kentucky so far shows little sign of improvement.

Although local taxes are low in Kentucky (2.9 percent of income), state taxes are high (5.9 percent). That means the state is very fiscally centralized. Government debt is also extremely high, at about 27.0 percent of personal income. Government employment is slightly higher than average, and subsidies are slightly lower than average.

Land-use freedom is ample in Kentucky, although eminent domain for private gain remains mostly unreformed. The state lacks either a minimum wage or a right-to-work law. The state has done more than most other low-income states to maintain reasonable standards for lawsuits, although punitive damages have not been reformed. Insurance and occupational freedoms are mediocre, and the state has a hospital CON law. Nurse practitioners' limited freedom of independent practice was revoked in 2011–12. However, a court did strike down the state's anti-competitive regulations on moving companies in 2013–14. Some telecom deregulation has taken place, but there is still local cable franchising. Health insurance mandated

coverages grew tremendously in the years to 2010, but it remains to be seen what effect they will have on the small-group market going forward.

As of the end of 2014, Kentucky still had a super-DOMA in force, and so the *Obergefell* decision should increase the state's personal freedom substantially (see Appendix Table B17). Incarceration rates and victimless crime arrest rates have gone in opposite directions: the former, already very high, have risen further, even as the latter have fallen. Drug arrests are still a bit above average, but nowhere near the heights of 2006–8, when arrests amounted to about 15 percent of the monthly reported drug-using population. Law enforcement uses the Department of Justice's forfeiture revenues from equitable sharing with abandon—more than one standard deviation above the national mean. Tobacco freedoms and gun rights seem quite secure, however. Educational and alcohol freedom scores are mediocre, while cannabis and gambling freedoms are extremely limited. With alcohol, the state has local blue laws, very high beer and wine taxes, a total ban on direct wine shipment, and no wine or spirits in grocery stores. With education, there are no private school choice programs, and the state recently expanded mandatory schooling to 12 years. Kentucky also looks to be one of the lowest states on travel freedom, though that is a small part of the index.

LOUISIANA

2014 RANK
34th

ECONOMIC   PERSONAL   **OVERALL**

RANK

1
10
20
30
40
50

2000   2005   2010   2015

YEAR

POLICY RECOMMENDATIONS

• **Fiscal:** Cut spending in areas well above the national average: employee retirement, miscellaneous commercial activities, water transportation (the state spends six times as much as a share of personal income as Texas and more than twice as much as Mississippi), sanitation and sewerage, parks and recreation, libraries, housing and community development, health and hospitals, corrections, and general administration. Use the proceeds to cut the sales tax, one of the nation's highest.

• **Regulatory:** Abolish judicial elections and enact punitive damages reforms.

• **Personal:** Eliminate mandatory minimum sentences for victimless offenses, such as offenses involving manufacture or sale of drugs to consenting adults.

Population, 2014
4,649,676

Share of total U.S. population
1.5%

Population ranking
25th

Net migration rate
−7.0%

State Taxes, Percent of Personal Income, FY 2014
4.2%

Local Taxes, Percent of Personal Income, FY 2012
4.4%

Partisan Lean, 2012
R +10.4

Real Per Capita Personal Income, 2013, in 2009 $
$42,144

Real Personal Income Growth, CAGR, 2000–13
2.23%

ANALYSIS

Louisiana has long been one of the least economically free states in the South, but that is starting to change. It has improved significantly since 2008.

State-level taxes are now just a projected 4.2 percent of personal income, a significant decline from a peak of 6.2 percent in FY 2007. Meanwhile, local taxes have remained steady at about 4.4 percent of income. Louisianans don't have much local government, with only about one competing jurisdiction per 200 square miles of territory. Government debt is about average and has fallen slightly over time. Government employment has fallen significantly, from 17.0 percent of private employment in 2000 to 13.6 percent today. Government subsidies spiked in 2008 but have fallen since then toward national norms.

Louisiana is one of the top states for both land-use and labor-market freedom. Zoning is light. The state has a right-to-work law and no minimum wage. A telecom deregulation bill was enacted in 2013–14, and the state has long had statewide video franchising. On the other hand, occupational freedom is notoriously bad in Louisiana (it is the only state to license florists—out of a concern for public health and safety, no doubt). Nurses and dental hygienists have very little freedom of practice, and there is a hospital certificate-of-need law. Moving companies have to get a "certificate of public convenience and necessity" to open. The state has both an "unfair" pricing ban and a "price-gouging" ban. Needless to say, it is one of the most "cronyist" states. Louisiana's court system has long been terrible no matter how you measure it (enacted tort reforms, survey ratings, size of

the legal sector), but some slight improvements have been made since 2008.

On personal freedom, Louisiana has stayed still, while the rest of the country has surged forward. However, the *Obergefell* decision will help Louisiana rise substantially on marriage freedom (see Appendix Table B17). Crime-adjusted incarceration rates are extremely high and have gotten worse, rising from 1.2 to 2.1 standard deviations above the national mean between 2000 and 2012. Drug arrest rates are also quite high but have come down in recent years. Louisiana is one of the worst states for cannabis consumers and producers. The maximum penalty for a single offense not involving minors is 80 years; even low-level cultivation carries a five-year mandatory minimum. The asset forfeiture law was strengthened slightly in 2007–8, but the state remains about average on its asset forfeiture regime. It remains a fairly good state for tobacco freedom, but smoking bans in bars were passed for the first time in 2013–14. Louisiana is also a standout on educational freedom, with public school choice, a limited voucher law, and an expansive tax credit scholarship program. However, private school teachers have to be licensed. Gambling freedom is extensive, and the industry has grown over time. Alcohol freedom is high, with moderately taxed wine and spirits widely available, although the state still interferes with direct wine shipping. Gun rights are about average, as the state makes it almost impossible to get a Class III weapon, some firearm owners have to be registered, concealed carry is weighed down with limitations, the permit cost for concealed carry is high, and the age for possession is stricter than the federal minimum.

MAINE

2014 RANK

42nd

Population, 2014
1,330,089

Share of total U.S. population
0.4%

Population ranking	Net migration rate
41st	**2.1%**

ECONOMIC   PERSONAL   OVERALL

RANK

YEAR

2000   2005   2010   2015

1
10
20
30
40
50

State Taxes, Percent of Personal Income, FY 2014
6.3%

Local Taxes, Percent of Personal Income, FY 2012
4.5%

Partisan Lean, 2012
D +6.0

POLICY RECOMMENDATIONS

• **Fiscal:** Cut spending on public welfare and housing and community development. Maine is the most free-spending state on public welfare in the country, going even beyond Alaska and Vermont, and it also spends more than average on housing and community development. Also cut individual and corporate income taxes.

• **Regulatory:** Roll back exclusionary zoning, perhaps by allowing state veto of local zoning ordinances that limit housing supply.

• **Personal:** Sell off the state liquor stores, and replace the markup with a transparent ad valorem tax, as Washington has done. Maine will never be able to compete with New Hampshire prices anyway; perhaps it can compete on convenience.

Real Per Capita Personal Income, 2013, in 2009 $
$39,056

Real Personal Income Growth, CAGR, 2000–13
2.09%

ANALYSIS

Maine has long been one of the freest states in the country personally and one of the least free economically—the opposite of Alabama. Since 2009, however, the state has gradually improved on economic freedom.

Maine's taxes have long been high but have come down a bit in recent years. State taxes fell from 7.1 percent of personal income in FY 2007 to a projected 6.2 percent today. Local taxes have remained basically steady over that period. Mainers have slightly less choice of local government than other New Englanders, but more than most Americans: about 1.5 jurisdictions per 100 square miles. Government debt is reasonably low, at 15.7 percent of income, and government employment is down to 12.2 percent of private employment (from a peak of 12.9 percent in 2010). Subsidies are about average and have risen slightly over time.

Maine is one of the most regulated states for land use in the country. Indeed, we show that exclusionary zoning leaped upward in Maine between 2000 and 2006 and has risen further since then. Maine has the most extreme renewable portfolio standard in the country, by our measure. It has a fairly modest minimum wage and no right-to-work law. In 2011–12, a telecom deregulation bill was passed. Different measures of occupational freedoms give a conflicting picture of that policy, but there is no doubt that Maine allows more scope of practice to second-line health professions than just about any other state. Freedom from abusive lawsuits is above average in Maine and has improved steadily over time. The state enacted an anti-science labeling law for genetically modified organisms in 2013–14 that will take effect only if other states sign on. It also has a price-gouging law and a general law against sales below cost. So remember not to price your goods either higher or lower than the state legislature deems acceptable.

Maine is a progressive state with ample gun and cannabis rights, same-sex marriage since 2012 (legalized by ballot initiative), very low incarceration rates, and a better-than-average civil asset forfeiture law. It is, in brief, a very civil libertarian state. However, tobacco consumers will face extraordinarily high taxes ($1.70 a pack in 2006 dollars) and have been evicted from commercial private property by penalty of law. Educational freedom is also low. The state regulates private schools to the hilt: teacher licensing, detailed curriculum control, and state approval. However, some towns can "tuition out" to private schools, a form of voucher law that has been on the books for decades. Limited public school choice was enacted in 2011–12. We also show gambling freedom increasing over time, as the legal industry has expanded. Alcohol freedom is below average, due to state monopolization of wine and spirits retailing.

MARYLAND

2014 RANK
46th

ECONOMIC   PERSONAL   OVERALL

RANK

- 1
- 10
- 20
- 30
- 40
- 50

2000   2005   2010   2015

YEAR

POLICY RECOMMENDATIONS

- **Fiscal:** End all business subsidies and cut taxes equivalently. Doing so would be enough to raise Maryland from 34th to 24th on fiscal policy, in the company of Colorado and South Carolina, all else being equal.

- **Regulatory:** End rent control. This move would have raised Maryland from 49th to 45th on regulatory policy in 2014.

- **Personal:** Enact a shall-issue license for public firearms carry before being forced to do so by a federal court.

Population, 2014
5,976,407

Share of total U.S. population
1.9%

Population ranking
19th

Net migration rate
−2.4%

State Taxes, Percent of Personal Income, FY 2014
5.5%

Local Taxes, Percent of Personal Income, FY 2012
4.2%

Partisan Lean, 2012
D +11.2

Real Per Capita Personal Income, 2013, in 2009 $
$45,280

Real Personal Income Growth, CAGR, 2000–13
0.98%

ANALYSIS

Maryland is always one of the least free states in the country, although it encounters nowhere near the difficulty facing New York, California, or Illinois, and it enjoys locational rents from its proximity to Washington, D.C. Moreover, we show Maryland's personal freedom rank gradually increasing over time.

Maryland's overall tax burden is about average: the state-level component a little below and the local component a little above, making for a favorable degree of fiscal decentralization. However, Marylanders have little choice in local government, with only one competing jurisdiction per 200 square miles. Also, state-level taxes have risen over time, from 4.6 percent of personal income in FY 2009 to a projected 5.5 percent in FY 2015. Although it is less indebted than other states and also features lower government employment, Maryland spends more than average on subsidies to business.

Maryland does poorly on the most important component of regulatory policy, land-use freedom. Zoning restrictions are extensive, eminent domain abuse is mostly unchecked, and some local rent control exists. The state enacted a new minimum wage in 2013–14, though it is still pretty modest, and has no right-to-work law. As of 2010, Maryland had some of the most extensive mandated benefits for small-group plans in the country, but time will tell whether they have carried over to the post-PPACA world. Cable and telecommunications have not been deregulated. Occupational freedom is extremely low, for health professions and for others. By one measure (index of statutory mentions of regulatory keywords), Maryland has the most licensed occupations in the country. It also has a hospital certificate-of-need law and both general and gasoline-focused anti-sales-below-cost laws. Its tort system is only about average.

Maryland is an average state on criminal justice, the most important category of personal freedom. Crime-adjusted incarceration rates are a bit below the national average, but drug arrest rates are well above, though they have fallen from the heights of the mid-2000s. The state's asset forfeiture law is stronger than average. Smoking bans are comprehensive, and cigarette taxes are very high, encouraging smuggling ($1.70 a pack in 2006 dollars). Educational freedom is among the lowest in the country. Homeschools and private schools are tightly regulated, the latter more so (mandatory state approval and teacher licensing). The state raised the years of compulsory schooling from 11 to 12 in 2013–14. Maryland raised its travel freedom score by allowing illegal immigrants to get driver's licenses in 2013–14. It also raised its cannabis freedom score substantially by enacting a "real" medical marijuana law and decriminalizing small-scale possession. Maryland has always been one of the best states for alcohol freedom because of privatization and low taxes; however, beer taxes were hiked substantially in 2011–14. The state has sharply limited firearms freedom. It does allow Class III weapons other than machine guns, but it also mandates locking devices, registers handgun owners, requires licensing with safety training for handgun purchasers, licenses dealers, bans possession for those under 21, bans certain types of guns and magazines, and makes it extremely difficult to get permission to carry in public.

MASSACHUSETTS

2014 RANK
33rd

Population, 2014
6,745,408

Share of total U.S. population
2.1%

Population ranking	Net migration rate
14th	**−4.8%**

State Taxes, Percent of Personal Income, FY 2014
6.1%

Local Taxes, Percent of Personal Income, FY 2012
3.9%

Partisan Lean, 2012
D +13.9

Real Per Capita Personal Income, 2013, in 2009 $
$49,744

Real Personal Income Growth, CAGR, 2000–13
2.01%

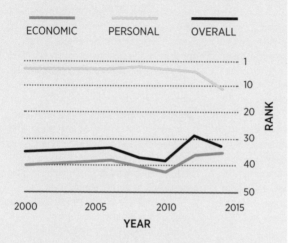

ECONOMIC   PERSONAL   OVERALL

RANK

YEAR

POLICY RECOMMENDATIONS

• **Fiscal:** Abolish government subsidies to business and cut taxes accordingly. This move would raise Massachusetts from 39th to 23rd on fiscal policy, all else equal.

• **Regulatory:** Repeal outdated and cronyist regulations, such as the price-gouging law, the sales-below-cost laws, moving company licensure, and the CON law for hospitals.

• **Personal:** Reform civil asset forfeiture to require a criminal conviction before forfeiture, and ban equitable sharing that does not comply with this standard. In 2014, this move would have raised Massachusetts from 11th to 7th on personal freedom, ahead of New Hampshire and Alaska.

ANALYSIS

Massachusetts has long had a better economic policy regime than one would expect given its strongly left-of-center electorate, and one of the best records on personal freedom, particularly criminal justice.

On fiscal policy, the nickname "Taxachusetts" is a bit of a misnomer. Massachusetts's overall tax burden is about average, although individual income taxes are among the highest in the country. Massachusetts residents have ample choice of local government, more than four every 100 square miles. Government subsidies are extremely high, about two standard deviations above the mean, and have risen over time. Government debt is also high, at about 24.0 percent of personal income, but has fallen 5 percentage points since FY 2009. Government employment is among the lowest in the country, at 10.2 percent of the private workforce.

On the most important category of regulatory policy, land-use regulation, Massachusetts is below average, although our two indicators of zoning stringency give somewhat conflicting judgments. Renewable portfolio standards have grown rather high. Eminent domain for private gain is completely unrestrained. The state has consistently had a higher-than-federal minimum wage, though not one of the highest in the country. Workers' compensation coverage mandates are extreme, though employers have great freedom of choice in funding them. The state passed a telecom deregulation bill in 2013–14. The extent of occupational licensing is lower than average in Massachusetts, though nurses enjoy little freedom from the state. Personal automobile insurance remains tightly regulated, and the state has a CON law for hospitals, as well as an anti-price-gouging law, licensure of moving companies, and both general and gasoline-focused sales-below-cost laws. The civil liability system is subpar but has improved over time, though not because of any particular statutory or institutional reforms.

Massachusetts has long locked up fewer of its residents than the vast majority of other states. It also arrests fewer people for drugs and other victimless crimes than most other places. Moreover, it scores highly for cannabis freedom, with a comparatively liberal medical marijuana law enacted in 2011–12. However, its asset forfeiture law is tied for worst in the country, putting the burden of proof on innocent owners, giving all the proceeds to law enforcement, and requiring only probable cause for showing the property is subject to forfeiture. The Second Amendment is virtually a dead letter in Massachusetts: the state tries to make guns as expensive as possible (locking mandates, dealer licensing, license to purchase any gun, with safety training) and nearly prohibits carry in public. It is the third-worst state for tobacco freedom, with comprehensive smoking bans and punishingly high cigarette taxes ($3.51 a pack after having been raised again in 2013–14). Educational freedom is low. Homeschooling parents have to jump through many hoops and must meet detailed curriculum guidelines. Private schools are subject to government approval. Massachusetts's casino plans have not yet fully become operational (with only one open as of the end of 2015), but once they do, expect the state's gambling freedom score to rise. The state's alcohol freedom score improved in 2013–14, due to the repeal of the direct wine shipping ban, but wine in grocery stores remains subject to mind-numbingly complex rules undoubtedly designed for some obscure political purpose.

MICHIGAN

2014 RANK
24th

ECONOMIC   PERSONAL   OVERALL

RANK
1
10
20
30
40
50

2000   2005   2010   2015

YEAR

POLICY RECOMMENDATIONS

• **Fiscal:** Repeal Proposal A, cutting the state sales tax and state school aid and giving localities the freedom to determine school budgets once again.

• **Regulatory:** Eliminate the parties' role in nominating judicial candidates, and enact tort reforms (such as abolishing punitive damages) to improve the tort system.

• **Personal:** Enact a liberal tax credit scholarship program for private education.

Population, 2014
9,909,877

Share of total U.S. population
3.1%

Population ranking
10th

Net migration rate
−6.9%

State Taxes, Percent of Personal Income, FY 2014
5.8%

Local Taxes, Percent of Personal Income, FY 2012
3.3%

Partisan Lean, 2012
D +3.1

Real Per Capita Personal Income, 2013, in 2009 $
$38,666

Real Personal Income Growth, CAGR, 2000–13
0.46%

ANALYSIS

Michigan has been hit hard by global economic conditions despite its relatively decent economic policies. Unfortunately, Great Lakes states cannot afford merely "decent" policies; they have to be outstanding to overcome the headwinds they face in global markets and to compete with neighboring states such as Indiana.

Michigan's local tax burden is relatively low, probably because of a school finance centralization accomplished by ballot initiative in the 1990s. The state tax burden has historically been higher than the national average, but it fell substantially in the early 2000s. It fell further with a tax cut in 2013–14, to a projected 5.8 percent of personal income in FY 2015. Government debt has also fallen somewhat since 2008 and is now about average. Government employment fell from 13.2 percent of the private workforce in 2010 to 11.5 percent today. Government subsidies are slightly lower than average. Michiganders do have reasonable freedom of choice among local governments, with about one per 100 square miles, but the centralization of school finance has made this choice less significant.

Michigan has little zoning restriction, but it has ratcheted up renewable portfolio standards since 2010. It also has a relatively high minimum wage for the local economy. A right-to-work law was enacted in 2012. Freedom from abusive lawsuits has been worse than average in Michigan since 2000,

but it has improved some since 2008, though not because of any statutory or institutional change. Occupational freedom is about average but has declined in the past four years, due to new occupations' being licensed. Michigan has had deregulated telecommunications and cable since 2006. The state had among the fewest mandated health insurance benefits for small-group plans in 2010.

On personal freedom, Michigan is hurt by the fact that it had a super-DOMA banning same-sex partnerships of all kinds in 2014. It will rise in the future (see Appendix Table B17). On criminal justice policy, Michigan arrests somewhat fewer than average for victimless crimes, but it has a fairly high incarceration rate. Those rates have been stable over time. The asset forfeiture law is better than average, but it is frequently circumvented. Smoking bans are comprehensive, and cigarette taxes are high. Educational freedom is low. Although homeschools are scarcely regulated, private schools face many barriers. The state has no private school choice programs, and compulsory schooling has extended to 12 years since 2009. Michigan does score a bit above average for gambling freedom, an area that grew in 2011–12. Travel freedom also grew a bit when the state repealed its motorcycle helmet law in 2013–14. The state scores better than average on cannabis freedom because it has had a reasonably broad medical marijuana law since 2008. Alcohol and firearms freedoms are only about average.

MINNESOTA

2014 RANK

38th

ECONOMIC   PERSONAL   **OVERALL**

RANK

1
10
20
30
40
50

2000   2005   2010   2015

YEAR

POLICY RECOMMENDATIONS

• **Fiscal:** Trim spending on public welfare and parks and recreation, on which Minnesota spends much more than average, and reduce taxes on individual income and selective sales (excluding alcohol, tobacco, and utilities), which are above national norms.

• **Regulatory:** Deregulate telecommunications and cable entry and pricing.

• **Personal:** Liberalize off-premises alcohol sales by repealing blue laws and allowing wine and spirits in grocery stores. These changes would have raised Minnesota above Alaska on personal freedom.

Population, 2014
5,457,173

Share of total U.S. population
1.7%

Population ranking
21st

Net migration rate
−1.5%

State Taxes, Percent of Personal Income, FY 2014
8.2%

Local Taxes, Percent of Personal Income, FY 2012
3.0%

Partisan Lean, 2012
D +1.7

Real Per Capita Personal Income, 2013, in 2009 $
$45,385

Real Personal Income Growth, CAGR, 2000–13
2.03%

ANALYSIS

Minnesota is a classic "blue state" in that it scores well above average on personal freedom and below average on economic freedom. Its economic performance has been similar to Wisconsin's but well behind Iowa's and both Dakotas'.

Minnesota is fiscally centralized, with low local taxes (3.0 percent of income) and high state taxes (projected 8.1 percent of income). Overall, the tax burden is high. Debt is about average, while public employment and subsidies are somewhat below average.

On the most important category in regulatory policy, land-use and environmental freedom, Minnesota is about average. However, both have declined recently with strict renewable portfolio standards. On labor policy, the state is below average, lacking a right-to-work law and passing a modest minimum wage in 2013–14. Workers' comp funding was liberalized slightly in 2011–12. Minnesota has never tried to deregulate telecommunications or cable. Occupational freedom is middling, but the state did pass an extensive nurse practitioner freedom-of-practice law in 2013–14. The state lacks a hospital certificate-of-need law and various other cronyist policies (it abolished moving company licensing in 2011–12), but it does have sales-below-cost laws for gasoline and retailers generally. Its court system is highly rated and has improved over time.

Minnesota rates slightly below average on most categories of personal freedom but makes up for it with good criminal justice policies and same-sex marriage (enacted 2013). The incarceration rate is well below the national average but has risen over time (in 2000, it was three standard deviations lower than average!). The drug arrest rate is lower than average, while arrest rates for other victimless crimes are higher than average, but falling. The state's asset forfeiture law was reformed in 2013–14, but without getting a handle on equitable sharing, its impact will be limited. Minnesota enacted a strictly limited medical marijuana program in 2014. Tobacco freedom took a big hit in 2013–14 with a hike in the cigarette tax (to $2.41 a pack in 2006 dollars). Educational freedom is above average, despite some private school and homeschool regulation, because of interdistrict public school choice, a modest tax credit/deduction law, and compulsory schooling of only nine years. Alcohol freedom and gun rights are both subpar.

MISSISSIPPI

2014 RANK
36th

ECONOMIC   PERSONAL   OVERALL

RANK

1
10
20
30
40
50

2000   2005   2010   2015

YEAR

POLICY RECOMMENDATIONS

• **Fiscal:** Cut spending on health and hospitals, where Mississippi is the second most liberal-spending state, and also on education, public welfare, and government employment, where the state spends well more than the national average, as a share of the economy. Reduce state taxes, especially on sales and business income.

• **Regulatory:** Liberalize insurance by moving to a "no-file" system like Wyoming's.

• **Personal:** Reduce incarceration by abolishing mandatory minimums for nonviolent offenses and allowing prisoners to petition for clemency under the new rules.

Population, 2014
2,994,079

Share of total U.S. population
0.9%

Population ranking
31st

Net migration rate
−2.2%

State Taxes, Percent of Personal Income, FY 2014
6.7%

Local Taxes, Percent of Personal Income, FY 2012
2.8%

Partisan Lean, 2012
R +7.5

Real Per Capita Personal Income, 2013, in 2009 $
$36,441

Real Personal Income Growth, CAGR, 2000–13
1.70%

ANALYSIS

Mississippi is a typical Deep South state in that its economic freedom far outstrips its personal freedom. However, its economic policies are worse than those of all its neighbors, having been bested recently by Louisiana.

Mississippians' overall tax burden is about average nationally, but state taxes are above average, while local taxes are low. This fiscal centralization goes along with a lack of choice among local government (less than 0.4 per 100 square miles). Debt and subsidies are lower than average, but government employment is far higher than average. State and local employment is 17.7 percent of private-sector employment.

Like most southern states, Mississippi does well on land-use and labor-market freedom. In 2011–12, it also finally enacted a limited eminent domain reform. It has no minimum wage and a right-to-work law. However, it does have an E-Verify mandate. In 2011–12, a telecom deregulation bill was passed, but the state lacks statewide cable franchising. Occupational licensing is less extensive than average but increased dramatically in 2011–12. Nurses and dental hygienists enjoy little practice freedom. The state strictly regulates insurance rates, hospital construction, and pricing during disasters. Its civil liability system used to be much worse than average, but it is now actually better than average. The state reformed punitive damages and abolished joint and several liability in 2002 and 2004.

Mississippi's criminal justice policies are notoriously awful. The state imprisons its population at a rate of two and a half standard deviations above the national average, even adjusting for its high crime rate. Drug arrest rates are very high but have actually fallen since 2008. Other victimless crime arrest rates are below average. The state asset forfeiture law is mediocre, but it doesn't matter anyway because local law enforcement enthusiastically pursues adoptions from the Department of Justice. Cannabis law is draconian: a single marijuana offense not involving minors can receive life imprisonment, and low-level cultivation carries mandatory minimums. The "decriminalization law" is a ruse because local governments may criminalize possession, and the mostly harmless psychedelic Salvia divinorum is also banned. Gun laws are slightly above average. A stricter-than-federal minimum age for possession was put in place in 2009–10. Permitless open carry was reinstated in 2013–14, but concealed carry faces many restrictions, even though it is shall-issue. Alcohol freedom is below average. The state monopolizes liquor stores, wine direct shipping is banned, and wine and spirits are unavailable in grocery stores. Legal gambling is more open than in the average state. Educational freedom is about average. A very limited voucher law was enacted in 2011–12, but public school choice was repealed about the same time. Tobacco freedom is above average, as smoking bans leave plenty of exceptions, and cigarette taxes are not too high. The state banned same-sex marriage at year-end 2014 but should rise because of the *Obergefell* decision.

MISSOURI

2014 RANK

18th

Population, 2014
6,063,589

Share of total U.S. population
1.9%

Population ranking	Net migration rate
18th	**0.0%**

ECONOMIC   **PERSONAL**   **OVERALL**

RANK: 1, 10, 20, 30, 40, 50

YEAR: 2000, 2005, 2010, 2015

State Taxes, Percent of Personal Income, FY 2014
4.2%

Local Taxes, Percent of Personal Income, FY 2012
4.1%

Partisan Lean, 2012
R +7.1

POLICY RECOMMENDATIONS

• **Fiscal:** Adopt a gubernatorial item reduction veto, which is associated with lower spending over the long run.

• **Regulatory:** Enact a right-to-work law, preferably in a form similar to that suggested in the "Labor-Market Freedom" section of this book, which would not infringe on freedom of association. In 2014, this move would have raised Missouri eight places on the regulatory policy ranking.

• **Personal:** Expand gun rights in a manner more consistent with the state's conservative ideology. Allow nonresident licenses, permit guns on all private property with permission, allow possession and carry at age 18, expand the right of self-defense in public, and legalize Class III weapons.

Real Per Capita Personal Income, 2013, in 2009 $
$42,501

Real Personal Income Growth, CAGR, 2000–13
2.07%

ANALYSIS

Missouri is one of the country's freer states, but in recent years it has run the risk of falling back into the middle of the pack.

Missouri's local taxes are about average (4.0 percent of personal income), but state taxes are well below average (4.2 percent of income), making for reasonably high fiscal decentralization. In addition, Missourians have some choice in local government, with more than one effective competing jurisdiction per 100 square miles. We show that state taxes have fallen since FY 2007. Subsidies, debt, and government employment are all below average.

We see a little evidence of backsliding on regulatory policy. Missouri has adopted renewable portfolio standards, which remain pretty lax, but may add a small amount to electric bills. The state adopted a minimum wage in 2011–12 and lacks a right-to-work law. Occupational licensing increased a touch in 2011–12. The civil liability system remains below average. Still, the state does well in most regulatory categories and even improved on some policies, such as direct auto sales and repealing mover licensing.

Insurance rate-setting freedom is fairly high. Cable and telecommunications are somewhat liberalized. Local zoning is quite loose, and eminent domain requirements were tightened slightly in 2013–14, though they remain substandard.

Missouri has a fairly strict approach to criminal justice, involving long sentences and high arrest rates for drugs, but it is far less aggressive than a state like Mississippi. It does share with that state the dubious distinction of being willing to lock a person up for a lifetime for selling marijuana to a consenting adult. The state's asset forfeiture law is better than most, but it is frequently circumvented through equitable sharing. Same-sex marriage was banned in 2014, but the state will improve in future editions because of the *Obergefell* decision. Missouri is a good state for gambling, alcohol, and tobacco freedoms. Gun rights are slightly better than average. Open carry is locally regulated, and concealed carry is hedged with restrictions, and the license is costly to obtain. The state also has a stricter-than-federal minimum age for possession and a duty to retreat from attackers in public. Most Class III weapons are effectively banned.

MONTANA

2014 RANK

17th

ECONOMIC   PERSONAL   OVERALL

RANK

1
10
20
30
40
50

2000   2005   2010   2015

YEAR

POLICY RECOMMENDATIONS

• **Fiscal:** Decentralize program responsibility and taxation authority from counties to municipalities, and make it easy for neighborhoods to incorporate. Having even one effective competing government per 100 square miles would have raised Montana's overall freedom rank two places in 2014.

• **Regulatory:** Enact a right-to-work law, similar to those of the surrounding states, that does not violate freedom of association, like the one proposed in the "Labor-Market Freedom" section of this book.

• **Personal:** Abolish all mandatory minimum sentences for victimless crimes, and reduce maximum sentences significantly.

Population, 2014
1,023,579

Share of total U.S. population
0.3%

Population ranking
44th

Net migration rate
6.3%

State Taxes, Percent of Personal Income, FY 2014
5.0%

Local Taxes, Percent of Personal Income, FY 2012
3.1%

Partisan Lean, 2012
R +9.7

Real Per Capita Personal Income, 2013, in 2009 $
$38,895

Real Personal Income Growth, CAGR, 2000–13
2.51%

ANALYSIS

Big Sky Country just might be better for freedom right now than it has ever been, which is not saying as much as one might expect. Personal freedom has generally been below the national average in Montana, but it spiked in 2013–14 because of same-sex marriage, while economic freedom remains a bit above the national average.

Montana's tax burden is well below the national average. State taxes have held steady over the past several years at about 5.0 percent of personal income. Local taxes spiked in FY 2009 but have settled down since to about 3.1 percent of income. Montanans have virtually no choice in local government, as counties control half of local taxes. Montana's debt burden has fallen from 20.3 percent of income in FY 2007 to 13.3 percent now. Subsidies are low, and government employment is slightly higher than average. Overall, Montana has posted consistent gains on fiscal policy over the time period we analyze.

Despite significant inmigration, Montana still does not have onerous building regulations. Eminent domain reform has not gone far. The state's renewable portfolio standards are among the toughest in the country, raising the cost of electricity. The state has a fairly high minimum wage for its median wage level. Overall, it is one of the least free states when it comes to the labor market. Montana has gone from one of the least regulated states for occupational licensing in 2000 to one of the more regulated today. However, nurse practitioners, dental hygienists, and physician assistants enjoy a moderate amount of practice freedom. Insurance

freedom is middling, as the state imposes some restrictions on rating criteria but has gone to "file and use" for most lines. It joined the IIPRC in 2013–14. On lawsuit freedom, it is slightly above average (less vulnerable to abusive suits).

Montana is one of the best states for gun rights, although it has fairly extensive limits on where one may carry within cities, and the effective cost of a carry license increased in 2011–12. Montana also does well on gambling, where it has an unusual, competitive model for video terminals that does not involve casinos. On criminal justice, Montana is about average. Drug arrest rates are more than one standard deviation below the national average, but the incarceration rate is above average, when adjusted for crime rates. The state is schizophrenic on cannabis, with a reasonably liberal medical marijuana program (scaled back slightly in 2011–12) but also the possibility of a life sentence for a single cannabis offense not involving minors and a one-year mandatory minimum for any level of cultivation. The civil asset forfeiture law is among the worst for property rights in the country. The burden of proof is on innocent owners, all the proceeds go to law enforcement, and the burden of proof for showing a property is forfeitable is mere probable cause. Tobacco and alcohol freedoms are subpar, with draconian smoking bans, higher-than-average cigarette taxes, and a state monopoly on liquor stores. Educational freedom is mediocre, with fairly light regulation of private schools and homeschools but no choice programs. The state was forced to legalize same-sex marriage in 2014, and its oppressive super-DOMA was therefore overturned.

NEBRASKA

2014 RANK
25th

ECONOMIC ----- PERSONAL ----- OVERALL

Population, 2014
1,881,503

Share of total U.S. population
0.6%

Population ranking
37th

Net migration rate
−2.6%

RANK / YEAR
- 1
- 10
- 20
- 30
- 40
- 50

2000 2005 2010 2015

POLICY RECOMMENDATIONS

• **Fiscal:** Cut spending on public utilities, which is far higher than average. This could be accomplished through privatizations. Trim utilities sales and income taxes.

• **Regulatory:** Repeal the CON requirement for hospital construction. In 2014, this move would have raised Nebraska to a virtual tie with Iowa for fifth place in regulatory freedom.

• **Personal:** Prohibit equitable sharing with the Department of Justice on locally initiated cases.

State Taxes, Percent of Personal Income, FY 2014
5.0%

Local Taxes, Percent of Personal Income, FY 2012
4.5%

Partisan Lean, 2012
R +13.3

Real Per Capita Personal Income, 2013, in 2009 $
$48,600

Real Personal Income Growth, CAGR, 2000–13
3.09%

ANALYSIS

Like other Great Plains states, Nebraska has usually had very good regulatory policy. It benefited from the commodity boom, federal farm subsidies, and its own policy regime during the 2000s and early 2010s, posting one of the highest growth rates in the country. However, it has started to lag its neighbors in recent years.

Nebraska is relatively fiscally decentralized, with somewhat lower-than-average state tax revenues (about 5.0 percent of personal income, a drop from 5.6 percent in FY 2007) and higher-than-average local tax revenues (4.5 percent of income). However, Nebraskans have little choice of local governments, limiting the benefits of this approach; it has only 0.50 effective competing jurisdictions per 100 square miles. Subsidies are well below average, while debt and government employment are close to average. Nebraska is more or less an average state on fiscal policy.

Nebraska does very well on the most important regulatory policy category, land-use and environmental freedom. However, it has not done much to check eminent domain for private gain. On labor policy it is above average because of a right-to-work law and flexible workers' comp funding rules, but it enacted a minimum wage in 2013–14. We show a huge jump in mandated benefits for small-group health insurance between 2008 and 2010, now worth about 51 percent of premiums, but time will tell whether these mandates carry over to the post-PPACA regime. Nebraska does a little better than average in keeping occupational licensing in check, although nurses still lack a great deal of practice freedom. The state has long had one of the best civil liability systems in the country. It also has a certificate-of-need law for hospital construction.

Nebraska's 2014 personal freedom score is hurt by the fact that it had a comprehensive ban on same-sex partnerships (super-DOMA) at the time. It should rise in the next edition, due to the *Obergefell* decision (see Appendix Table B17). Nebraska is only middling on criminal justice policy. Incarceration rates have generally been low, but they have increased over time. Drug and victimless crime arrest rates, by contrast, have been high, but they have come down over time. Meanwhile, the state's asset forfeiture law is relatively restrictive of policing for profit, but as a consequence, law enforcement frequently circumvents state law by having the Department of Justice "adopt" local cases. Equitable sharing revenues have been more than one standard deviation higher than average since at least 2006. Educational, gambling, travel, and cannabis freedoms are all below average. However, Nebraska is solidly above average on alcohol policy and a bit above average on gun rights and tobacco freedom. Like other states with the ballot initiative, the nonsmoking majority of Nebraska has foisted on private business owners fully comprehensive smoking bans, but tobacco taxes are below average. Most of Nebraska's lower scores on firearms policies come from special provisions for Omaha or a general lack of preemption. Homeschoolers are not tightly regulated apart from detailed annual reporting requirements, but nonsectarian private schools are subject to mandatory approval and teacher licensing. The state has no private school choice programs.

NEVADA

2014 RANK

12th

Population, 2014

2,839,099

Share of total U.S. population

0.9%

Population ranking	Net migration rate
35th	**19.9%**

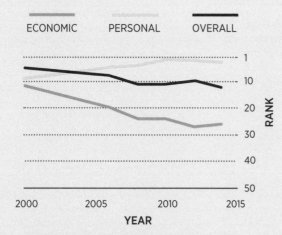

ECONOMIC   PERSONAL   OVERALL

RANK — 1, 10, 20, 30, 40, 50

YEAR — 2000, 2005, 2010, 2015

State Taxes, Percent of Personal Income, FY 2014

5.9%

Local Taxes, Percent of Personal Income, FY 2012

3.6%

Partisan Lean, 2012

D +1.0

Real Per Capita Personal Income, 2013, in 2009 $

$37,269

Real Personal Income Growth, CAGR, 2000–13

2.16%

POLICY RECOMMENDATIONS

• **Fiscal:** Cut air transportation, employment security administration, public buildings, and parks and recreation. Use the proceeds to trim sales and "other" taxes. Nevada spends far more than the national average on police, but that may be warranted given the nature of its social and economic model.

• **Regulatory:** Deregulate occupations such as epidemiologists, environmental health specialists, title plant personnel, interior designers, sign language interpreters, clinical laboratory technologists, pharmacy technicians, veterinary technologists, opticians, athletic trainers, massage therapists, security guards, landscaping contractors, child-care workers, bill and account collectors, well drillers, alarm installers, taxi drivers, and crane operators.

• **Personal:** Abolish private school teacher licensing, state approval of private schools, and detailed curriculum requirements.

ANALYSIS

Unsurprisingly, Nevada is consistently one of the top states for personal freedom. However, Nevada's economic freedom has suffered as the state's ideological orientation has shifted from center-right to center-left. From 2006 to 2013, the state posted one of the lowest rates of personal income growth in the country, just 0.8 percent annually. Only Florida, Maryland, Delaware, and Virginia were worse.

Nevada's fiscal policy has worsened over time, a fact that might have something to do with a 2003 Nevada Supreme Court decision setting aside part of the state constitution, which required a supermajority for tax increases.[127] State-level taxes have risen from a low of 4.9 percent of personal income in FY 2009 (and 5.5 percent in FY 2000) to about 5.9 percent today, while local taxes rose from 3.4 percent in FY 2000 to 3.6 percent in FY 2012. Nevadans have virtually no choice of local governments, given the importance of territorially vast counties. Subsidies are a little below average, government employment is well below average, and government debt is well above average and rising. From 22.0 percent of income in FY 2000, state and local debt now stands at over 26 percent of income.

As one of the "sand states" attracting huge net inmigration in the 1990s and early 2000s, Nevada has retained an admirable degree of land-use freedom. However, renewable portfolio standards are quite high and rising, affecting the cost of electricity. Nevada does have a right-to-work law but also a modest minimum wage. Cable and telecommunications have been liberalized. Occupational freedom declined dramatically between 2000 and 2006 because of the expansion of licensing, but in 2013–14, nurse practitioners gained the right of independent practice with full prescription authority. Insurance freedom is low because of prior approval of rates and forms, but Nevada joined the IIPRC in 2011–12.

The state has a hospital certificate-of-need requirement. The court system is a little better than average but has not improved over time, unlike many other states.

Nevada is number one for gambling freedom (no surprise), and it is the only state with legal prostitution (local option). In 2014, it moved from civil unions to same-sex marriage. However, on criminal justice policy, Nevada is more of a mixed bag. Nondrug victimless crime arrest rates are quite high but have fallen over time, and it is possible that they are overstated because of Nevada's high tourist population. The incarceration rate is about average for its crime prevalence. The civil asset forfeiture regime is mediocre. Gun rights are extensive and have generally gained over time. The state also has a long-standing medical cannabis law that was expanded slightly in 2013–14. However, it is also possible to get life imprisonment for a single marijuana offense not involving minors, and even low-level cultivation has a one-year mandatory minimum. Nevada is one of the top states for alcohol freedom, with fully private wholesaling and retailing, low taxes, no blue laws, legal direct wine shipping, and wine and spirits in grocery stores. In 2013–14, the state enacted a law giving illegal immigrants access to driver's licenses, which outweighs its 2011–12 move to ban handheld cell phone use in increasing overall travel freedom. As of our data cutoff, Nevada was one of the worst states for educational freedom. Private schools are tightly regulated, facing mandatory state approval, mandatory teacher licensing, and detailed private school curriculum control. However, our index does not take account of the educational savings account plan passed in 2015, which in 2014 would have raised its educational freedom score to average. Even tobacco is not as tightly controlled as one would expect from a state with the ballot initiative. Nevadans may still light up in bars with permission of the owner.

---

127. Michael J. New, "Judicial Nonsense in Nevada," Cato Institute, August 8, 2003, http://www.cato.org/publications/commentary/judicial-nonsense-nevada.

NEW HAMPSHIRE

2014 RANK

1st

Population, 2014
1,326,813

Share of total U.S. population
0.4%

Population ranking	Net migration rate
42nd	**2.2%**

State Taxes, Percent of Personal Income, FY 2014
2.8%

Local Taxes, Percent of Personal Income, FY 2012
4.8%

Partisan Lean, 2012
D +0.7

Real Per Capita Personal Income, 2013, in 2009 $
$44,942

Real Personal Income Growth, CAGR, 2000–13
1.91%

ECONOMIC   PERSONAL   OVERALL

RANK

YEAR

POLICY RECOMMENDATIONS

• **Fiscal:** To go yet further in fiscal decentralization, amend the constitution to give the legislature the right to define an adequate education, then reduce the statewide property tax and state aid to local school districts.

• **Regulatory:** Review local zoning ordinances, and strike down those that increase the price of new housing beyond that needed to pay for the cost of new infrastructure.

• **Personal:** Reform asset forfeiture to require a criminal conviction and to end equitable sharing that circumvents state law.

ANALYSIS

New Hampshire is overall the freest state in the Union, combining relatively high scores on both personal and economic freedom. In the more distant past, it was one of the leading states on economic freedom. It fell well back of the lead in 2007–8, but since then has clawed its way halfway back from where it had sunk. The three states of northern New England still pose a stark contrast in economic policies and, for most of the late 20th and early 21st centuries, economic outcomes.

New Hampshire's government taxes less than any other state but Alaska. We show a decline in state taxes as a share of personal income from 3.7 percent in FY 2000 to a projected 2.8 percent today. Meanwhile, local taxes have risen from 3.9 percent of income in FY 2000 to 4.8 percent in FY 2012. New Hampshire is therefore a highly fiscally decentralized state. Granite Staters have quite a wide choice in local government, with two and a half competing jurisdictions every 100 square miles. Government subsidies, debt, and employment are all lower than average, and in all those categories we see improvements between 2010 and 2014.

New Hampshire's regulatory outlook is not so sunny. Its primary sin is exclusionary zoning. It is generally agreed that the Granite State is one of the four worst states in the country for residential building restrictions. Part of the problem might be the absence of a regulatory taking law. However, the eminent domain law is strong. On labor-market freedom, New Hampshire is below average primarily because of the absence of a right-to-work law and of any exceptions to the workers' compensation mandate, and it has no state-level minimum wage. A telecom deregulation bill was passed in 2011–12, but the state has not yet adopted statewide video franchising. New Hampshire is above average on occupa-

tional freedom solely because the health professions enjoy broad scope of practice; the extent of licensing grew significantly during the 2000s, and the state is now below average on most indicators of licensing extent. Insurance freedom is generally better than average, except for some rate classification prohibitions. The hospital certificate-of-need law was abolished in 2011–12, but only effective in 2016, so we code it as still being in force. Otherwise, the state has steered laudably clear of entry and price regulation. The civil liability system is far above the national average; punitive damages were abolished long ago.

New Hampshire is personally relatively free. Incarceration rates and drug arrest rates are low. Nondrug victimless crime arrest rates are only about average, however. The state was one of the first to enact same-sex civil unions and then marriage through the legislative process. However, the civil asset forfeiture law is below average, and equitable sharing revenues are above average. Tobacco freedom is below average, as taxes are fairly high, and smoking bans are extensive. A liberal tax credit scholarship law was enacted in 2011–12, raising the state above average on educational freedom, even though there is no public school choice, compulsory schooling lasts 12 years, and private schools require state approval. Because the state has only charitable gambling, it scores below average in the gambling freedom category. Cannabis freedom is only about average. The state adopted a limited medical cannabis law in 2013–14, but the governor has dragged her feet on implementing it. Alcohol freedom is about average; the state monopolizes liquor retail and wine wholesale, but the effective tax rate is extremely low. Grocery stores carry wine but not spirits. It is one of the best states in the country for gun rights, especially when it comes to lack of restrictions on open and concealed carry.

NEW JERSEY

2014 RANK
47th

Population, 2014
8,938,175

Share of total U.S. population
2.8%

Population ranking	Net migration rate
11th	**−7.8%**

ECONOMIC   PERSONAL   OVERALL

RANK

1
10
20
30
40
50

2000   2005   2010   2015

YEAR

State Taxes, Percent
of Personal Income, FY 2014
5.7%

Local Taxes, Percent
of Personal Income, FY 2012
5.5%

Partisan Lean, 2012
D +7.2

POLICY RECOMMENDATIONS

• **Fiscal:** Cut spending on parking lots; New Jersey spends almost three times as much as New York. It also spends more than average in the "miscellaneous" category and on employee retirement. Income, utilities, and property taxes are abnormally high and could be cut.

• **Regulatory:** End rent control. This move would have raised New Jersey four places on regulatory policy.

• **Personal:** Decriminalize low-level cannabis possession, and make high-level possession a misdemeanor. These reforms would have raised New Jersey two places on personal freedom.

Real Per Capita Personal
Income, 2013, in 2009 $
$45,113

Real Personal Income
Growth, CAGR, 2000–13
1.03%

ANALYSIS

About 50 years ago, New Jersey was considered a tax haven. It grew wealthy under that regime, but over the past two decades it has competed with California for the position as the second-worst state for economic freedom. As long as it is better than New York, it will probably continue to get tax refugees from that state, but more New Yorkers now move to Florida than to New Jersey.

New Jersey's state-level taxes are slightly higher than average (5.7 percent of income), while local taxes are much higher than average (5.5 percent). New Jerseyans have more choice of local government than any other state, with 6.2 effective competing jurisdictions per 100 square miles. Government subsidies and debt are above average, but state and local employment is a little below average. We show a small improvement in each of those three areas between 2010 and 2014.

Land-use freedom is quite limited in New Jersey. The state lets cities adopt rent control, and local zoning rules are often highly exclusionary, even though the state has been losing population for years. Renewable portfolio standards are among the highest in the country, raising electricity rates. In 2013–14, the state adopted a minimum wage. Labor-market freedom was already bad because of strict workers' compensation rules, mandated short-term disability insurance, mandated family leave, no right-to-work law, and a stricter-than-federal anti-discrimination law. Occupational freedom is, perhaps surprisingly for such a corrupt state, close to average. However, in 2013–14, nurse practitioner freedom of independent practice was abolished. Insurance regulation is fairly strict, and there is a price-gouging law, which Governor Christie deployed after Hurricane Sandy to devastating effect.[128] The civil liability system is somewhat better than average.

New Jersey has improved over time on personal freedom and is now better than average. Incarceration and victimless crime arrest rates, drug and nondrug, have all fallen since 2000. Asset forfeiture, however, has not been reformed much. New Jersey is a bad state for tobacco freedom, travel freedom, and gun rights, but it is a good state for gambling and same-sex marriage. The picture on educational freedom is mixed. Homeschools and private schools are barely regulated, but there are no public or private school choice programs. Cannabis freedom is similarly mixed. The state has a limited medical cannabis law, but otherwise it has done nothing to reduce penalties. Alcohol freedom is a bit above average, but the state interferes here too. Direct wine shipment is tightly regulated, and the rules on when a grocery store may sell wine are complicated—perhaps to create a "tollbooth" where state politicians can extract rents.

---

128. Matthew Yglesias, "Miles-Long Gasoline Lines in New Jersey Show the Case for 'Price Gouging,'" Slate, November 1, 2012, http://www.slate.com/blogs/moneybox/2012/11/01/gas_lines_in_new_jersey_the_state_needs_more_price_gouging .html.

NEW MEXICO

2014 RANK
30th

ECONOMIC   PERSONAL   OVERALL

RANK

1
10
20
30
40
50

2000   2005   2010   2015

YEAR

POLICY RECOMMENDATIONS

• **Fiscal:** Trim spending on air transportation, corrections, education, general administration, public buildings, health and hospitals, public welfare, and employee retirement, which are all much higher than the national average, as a share of income. Cut the gross receipts tax.

• **Regulatory:** Roll back occupational licenses, such as those for teacher assistants, ambulance drivers, mobile home installers, pipe layers, boilermakers, and dental assistants.

• **Personal:** Enact a generous private scholarship tax credit program.

Population, 2014
2,085,572

Share of total U.S. population
0.7%

Population ranking
36th

Net migration rate
−0.2%

State Taxes, Percent of Personal Income, FY 2014
5.7%

Local Taxes, Percent of Personal Income, FY 2012
3.3%

Partisan Lean, 2012
D +2.0

Real Per Capita Personal Income, 2013, in 2009 $
$35,293

Real Personal Income Growth, CAGR, 2000–13
2.00%

ANALYSIS

New Mexico has long had far more personal than economic freedom, but it has started to do a little better on economic freedom as well, despite its move from being a "purple" state to a "blue" one.

New Mexico's overall tax burden is slightly below the national average. We show significant declines in state-level taxes over time, from 7.4 percent of personal income in FY 2000 to a projected 5.7 percent today. Local taxes have risen, but not as much, from 2.6 percent of income in FY 2000 to 3.3 percent in FY 2012. That growing fiscal decentralization does little for choice in government, however, with less than one competing jurisdiction per 100 square miles of private land. Government debt ballooned during the Great Recession but has started to come down again. Government employment is far higher than the national average. In 2014, state and local workers were 18.7 percent of private workers. Subsidies are about average.

New Mexico looks relatively good on land-use freedom. However, the state has implemented comparatively strict renewable portfolio standards. New Mexico has long had a minimum wage, but it is not extremely high. Health insurance mandated benefits were quite high as of 2010. In 2013–14, the state passed a telecom deregulation bill but has not implemented statewide video franchising. The extent of occupational licensing skyrocketed between 2000 and 2006 but has been almost steady since. Nurses enjoy broad scope-of-practice freedom. Insurance freedom has been fairly high since reforms were enacted in 2009–10. New Mexico has no CON law for hospital construction. Otherwise, cronyist regulation is limited, besides licensing for moving companies. The civil liability system is much worse than average, and the state has done little to address the problem.

New Mexico's criminal justice policies stand out from the pack. Victimless crime arrest rates, drug and nondrug, are low, as are incarceration rates—but they have risen over time. The state's asset forfeiture law is one of the best in the country, but the state has done little to address equitable sharing. A bill to abolish civil asset forfeiture and use only criminal forfeiture passed in 2015. Gambling, cannabis, alcohol, firearms, and travel freedoms are all strong suits for New Mexico, although the state isn't a leader in any of those areas. In 2013–14, physician-assisted suicide was legalized, but that is a tiny part of our index. Same-sex marriage was legalized in 2013. Tobacco and educational freedoms are weak spots.

NEW YORK

2014 RANK
50th

▬▬ ECONOMIC   ▬▬ PERSONAL   ▬▬ **OVERALL**

Population, 2014
19,746,227

Share of total U.S. population
6.2%

Population ranking	Net migration rate
4th	**−11.2%**

State Taxes, Percent of Personal Income, FY 2014
6.8%

Local Taxes, Percent of Personal Income, FY 2012
7.8%

Partisan Lean, 2012
D +12.5

Real Per Capita Personal Income, 2013, in 2009 $
$44,047

Real Personal Income Growth, CAGR, 2000–13
1.19%

Note: Economic and Overall ranking tied

POLICY RECOMMENDATIONS

• **Fiscal:** Cut spending on hospitals, housing, libraries, public welfare, sanitation and sewerage, public transit, employee retirement, and "miscellaneous"; cut all taxes, and pay down debt.

• **Regulatory:** Abolish rent control. This move could have raised New York to 47th, just behind Connecticut, on regulatory policy.

• **Personal:** Slash tobacco taxes, which are so high as to be almost tantamount to prohibition.

ANALYSIS

New York is again the least free state in the country. Its huge, glaring weakness is fiscal policy. If New York were to adopt a fiscal regime closer to that of California, New Jersey, or Connecticut, its overall economic freedom score would be close to theirs. As it is, New York looks set to remain the least free state for many years to come.

New York's local tax burden is twice that of the average state: 7.8 percent of income in FY 2012. However, New Yorkers have ample choice in local government: 4.1 competing jurisdictions per 100 square miles of private land. The state tax burden, at a projected 6.7 percent of income in FY 2015, is also higher than the national average. The government spends almost four times what the average state does on subsidies to business. Debt is the highest in the country at 31.9 percent of income. Government employment, however, is slightly lower than average and has come down since 2010.

New York is also the worst state on regulatory policy, although here it is at least within striking distance of number 49. Land-use freedom is very low, primarily because of the economically devastating rent control law in New York City. Local zoning is actually fairly moderate compared with surrounding states not named "Pennsylvania." Renewable portfolio standards are high. The state enacted a minimum wage in 2013–14 and also has a short-term disability insurance mandate. Cable and telecommunications are unreformed. Occupational freedom is a bit subpar, but nurse practitioners did gain some independence in 2013–14. Insurance freedom is a mixed bag (the state has stayed out of the IIPRC), but property and casualty insurers gained some freedom to set rates in 2013–14. The civil liability system looks poor, but we may underrate it slightly because of the state's large legal sector.

New York's criminal justice policies are reasonably decent. Although drug arrests are about average, nondrug victimless crime arrest rates are quite low. Incarceration rates are below average. Local law enforcement enthusiastically participates in equitable sharing, even though the state law imposes only modest limits in the first place. New York finally legalized same-sex marriage in 2011. Tobacco freedom is the worst in the country because of smoking bans and stratospheric taxes ($3.70 a pack in 2006 dollars in 2014). New York is perhaps the worst state for homeschoolers, and it has no private school choice programs. All fireworks are completely banned, as are mixed martial arts competitions. There is little gambling. Cannabis freedom is now slightly above average, as the state enacted a limited medical law in 2013–14. Alcohol freedom is a bit above average, but grocery stores can't sell wine. Gun rights are hedged about with all kinds of restrictions, but it is barely possible to get a concealed-carry license in some parts of the state.

NORTH CAROLINA

2014 RANK
19th

——— ECONOMIC ——— PERSONAL **——— OVERALL**

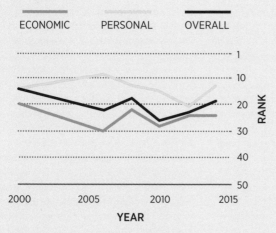

YEAR

POLICY RECOMMENDATIONS

• **Fiscal:** Cut spending on hospitals, possibly through privatization, which is very high by national standards. Individual income taxes could stand to be trimmed further.

• **Regulatory:** Eliminate all rate regulations on property and casualty insurance. These reforms would have raised North Carolina five places on regulatory policy.

• **Personal:** Eliminate the state monopoly on distilled spirits.

Population, 2014
9,943,964

Share of total U.S. population
3.1%

Population ranking
9th

Net migration rate
10.0%

State Taxes, Percent of Personal Income, FY 2014
5.4%

Local Taxes, Percent of Personal Income, FY 2012
3.2%

Partisan Lean, 2012
R +3.0

Real Per Capita Personal Income, 2013, in 2009 $
$39,341

Real Personal Income Growth, CAGR, 2000–13
1.90%

ANALYSIS

North Carolina is a rapidly growing southern state with a reasonably good economic freedom profile and an even better record on personal freedom, especially when compared with its neighbors.

We show improvement on most fiscal policies in the 2010–14 period. State taxes fell from 5.8 percent of personal income to a projected 5.4 percent. Local taxes also fell between FY 2011 and FY 2012, to 3.2 percent. Subsidies increased slightly but are still below average, while debt and government employment fell. Government employment is a bit above the national average at 14.3 percent of the private workforce, possibly due to the prevalence of public hospitals.

Despite large inmigration, North Carolina has disdained controls on the housing supply. Labor law is good, with no minimum wage, a right-to-work law, and relatively relaxed workers' compensation rules. Cable and telecommunications have been liberalized. Occupational freedom is a weak spot, especially for the health professions. A sunrise review requirement for occupational licensing proposals was scrapped in 2011–12. North Carolina is one of the worst states for insur-ance freedom. It has a large residual market for personal automobile insurance, prior approval for homeowner's insurance rates, prior approval for life insurance forms, and rate classification prohibitions. It also has a price-gouging law and a minimum-markup law for gasoline. Its civil liability system is worse than average.

North Carolina has one of the best criminal justice regimes in the South. Incarceration and victimless crime arrest rates are all below average. There is no state-level civil asset forfeiture at all, but local law enforcement frequently does an end-run around the law through the Department of Justice's equitable sharing program. In most personal freedom categories, North Carolina is actually below average, but it enjoys its high ranking in 2014 because of its criminal justice policies, having been forced to legalize same-sex marriage, and having passed a statewide voucher program in 2014. Gun rights are more restricted than in many other southern states, with carry licenses somewhat costly to obtain and hedged with limitations. Plus, buying a pistol requires a permit, there is local dealer licensing, and most Class III weapons are difficult to obtain (sound suppressors were legalized in 2013–14).

NORTH DAKOTA

2014 RANK

13th

ECONOMIC   PERSONAL   OVERALL

RANK

2000   2005   2010   2015

YEAR

POLICY RECOMMENDATIONS

• **Fiscal:** Enhance fiscal decentralization and choice among local governments with different policies by cutting state taxes and aid to local schools and allowing local towns to vary property tax to meet school-funding needs. The state tax in greatest need of cutting is the sales tax.

• **Regulatory:** Allow employers to purchase workers' compensation insurance from any willing seller, or to self-fund, and allow the smallest businesses to opt out entirely.

• **Personal:** Eliminate teacher licensing, mandatory state approval, and detailed curriculum requirements for private schools, and reduce the notification and record-keeping burdens on homeschooling families.

Population, 2014
739,482

Share of total U.S. population
0.2%

Population ranking
47th

Net migration rate
3.9%

State Taxes, Percent of Personal Income, FY 2014
6.5%

Local Taxes, Percent of Personal Income, FY 2012
2.8%

Partisan Lean, 2012
R +12.3

Real Per Capita Personal Income, 2013, in 2009 $
$54,261

Real Personal Income Growth, CAGR, 2000–13
5.01%

ANALYSIS

The shale gas boom presages a big increase in North Dakota's fiscal policy scores, but that increase has not fully materialized yet, as the state is building up its rainy-day fund. Amazingly, mineral severance taxes brought in as much to state coffers in fiscal year 2012 as all taxes do to both state and local government in the average state, measured as a percentage of personal income.

North Dakota's measured tax burden actually increased between FY 2011 and FY 2013, as state taxes, excluding mineral severance, rose from 5.6 percent of personal income to 6.6 percent, while local taxes fell from 3.0 percent to 2.8 percent of income. North Dakota looks fiscally quite centralized, which is unfortunate because North Dakotans do have substantial choice of local government: 1.9 per 100 square miles. Government debt and employment have declined substantially in recent years, while subsidies have declined but slightly.

Most Great Plains states have good regulatory policies, and North Dakota is no exception. Land use is lightly regulated, and the state has one of the strongest limits on eminent domain abuse in the country. The state has a right-to-work law and no state-level minimum wage. However, North Dakota has a monopoly state fund for workers' compensation insurance. We show a big increase in health insurance mandated benefits between 2008 and 2010, but time will tell whether those mandates carry over to post-PPACA

small-group plans. Our sources give a split judgment on the extent of occupational licensing in North Dakota, but nurses and physician assistants enjoy ample freedom of practice. The state moved from prior approval to "use and file" for automobile and homeowner's insurance in 2013–14, a significant improvement. There is no CON law for hospitals, but there is a general "unfair sales" act. The civil liability system is one of the best in the country.

North Dakota's criminal justice policies have improved over time, as the state has brought down its incarceration rate. However, nondrug victimless crime arrest rates are extremely high. The state still had a super-DOMA taking away gay citizens' freedom of contract but will rise because of the *Obergefell* decision (see Appendix Table B17). The state's civil asset forfeiture law is among the worst in the country, but local law enforcement rarely participates in equitable sharing. Smoking bans were intensified in 2011–12, but tobacco taxes are below average. With just a few exceptions, gun rights are strong in North Dakota, but we show that training requirements for carry licenses were increased in 2011–12. Alcohol freedom is generally good, but wine and spirits are available in grocery stores only when put into a separate enclosure. There has been no cannabis liberalization. Educational freedom is a big problem area for North Dakota. Private schools and homeschools are both more harshly regulated than anywhere else in the country. The state has no private school choice.

OHIO

2014 RANK

35th

—— ECONOMIC ········· PERSONAL ▬▬ OVERALL

RANK

YEAR

POLICY RECOMMENDATIONS

- **Fiscal:** Trim spending on employment security administration, public welfare, and employee retirement, areas where Ohio spends more than the average state. Cut state taxes, particularly on individual income.

- **Regulatory:** Look at Indiana as a model "Rust Belt" state with regard to regulatory policy, and reform Ohio's regulatory system according to that model. For instance, consider liberalizing the workers' comp system and rolling back occupational licensing. Adopt a right-to-work law in line with Indiana and Michigan.

- **Personal:** Abolish mandatory minimum sentences for nonviolent offenses with an eye toward reducing the incarceration rate to a level more consistent with its crime rate.

Population, 2014
11,594,163

Share of total U.S. population
3.6%

Population ranking	Net migration rate
7th	**−4.3%**

State Taxes, Percent of Personal Income, FY 2014
5.0%

Local Taxes, Percent of Personal Income, FY 2012
4.6%

Partisan Lean, 2012
R +0.5

Real Per Capita Personal Income, 2013, in 2009 $
$42,747

Real Personal Income Growth, CAGR, 2000–13
1.60%

ANALYSIS

Relative to other states, Ohio has improved just slightly on economic freedom since 2008, but its policy regime is worse than other Great Lakes states that have been reforming, such as Indiana, Michigan, and Wisconsin.

Ohio is a little more fiscally decentralized than the average state. Local taxes add up to about 4.6 percent of personal income, while state taxes sit at a projected 5.0 percent of income in FY 2015. The discovery of shale gas has allowed Ohio to raise severance taxes and essentially shift some of its tax burden to consumers of natural gas throughout North America. Government subsidies are a bit higher than average in Ohio, while state and local debt and employment are lower than average.

On the most important regulatory policy category, land-use and environmental freedom, Ohio does well. Zoning has a light touch, and renewable portfolio standards exist but are very low. Labor-market freedom is a problem area for Ohio. The state has a minimum wage, no right-to-work law, and strict workers' compensation coverage and funding rules. Cable and telecommunications have been liberalized. The average of different measures suggests that in Ohio, the extent of occupational licensing is greater than average. Nursing scope of practice is the most restricted in the country. The state has a hospital CON law, but price regulation in most markets is limited. The civil liability system is worse than average, but a punitive damages cap enacted in 2005 has changed perceptions somewhat.

Ohio has a higher-than-average, crime-adjusted incarceration rate, and it has risen over time. Meanwhile, victimless crime arrest rates are lower than average and have fallen over time. The state's asset forfeiture law and practice are both subpar. Apart from decriminalization of small-scale possession, cannabis remains highly restricted. Gun rights are a bit better than average. The state is about average on gambling. Educational freedom is above average, due mostly to a statewide voucher program, but private schools and homeschools are sharply regulated. Draconian smoking bans have been in place for a decade. The state had a super-DOMA banning contracted gay relationships at the end of 2014, and so the Supreme Court's *Obergefell* decision should result in an increase in the state's personal freedom (see Appendix Table B17).

OKLAHOMA

2014 RANK

3rd

Population, 2014
3,878,051

Share of total U.S. population
1.2%

Population ranking	Net migration rate
28th	**2.2%**

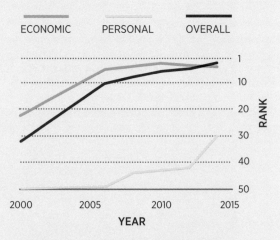

ECONOMIC   PERSONAL   OVERALL

RANK

YEAR

State Taxes, Percent
of Personal Income, FY 2014
4.6%

Local Taxes, Percent
of Personal Income, FY 2012
2.9%

Partisan Lean, 2012
R +18.1

POLICY RECOMMENDATIONS

• **Fiscal:** Reduce the government payroll, and cut spending in areas well out of line with national averages, public welfare and highway spending. The proceeds could be applied to shaving the sales tax.

• **Regulatory:** Legalize nurse practitioner independent practice with full prescription authority, join the Nurse Licensure Compact, and pass a nursing consultation exception for interstate practice. These reforms would have raised Oklahoma two places on regulatory policy.

• **Personal:** Legalize Sunday alcohol sales, happy hours, direct wine shipments, and wine and spirits in grocery stores. Combined, these reforms would have raised Oklahoma five places on personal freedom.

Real Per Capita Personal
Income, 2013, in 2009 $
$43,428

Real Personal Income
Growth, CAGR, 2000–13
2.54%

ANALYSIS

As noted earlier in this book, Oklahoma is the most improved state for the 2000–2014 period. Moreover, although the Sooner State's personal freedom lags its economic freedom, it has made significant progress on both dimensions.

Oklahoma is one of the lowest-taxed states in America. However, it is also fiscally centralized. Local taxation is about 2.9 percent of personal income, while state taxation is 4.6 percent of personal income. Government subsidies are lower than average but have risen a touch over time, to 0.06 percent of personal income. State and local debt is much lower than average (11.4 percent of income), and government employment is much higher than average (15.2 percent of private employment). Oklahoma has managed to cut its debt even as its tax receipts fell significantly as a share of the economy.

Land-use regulation is light in Oklahoma, although the state has not restrained eminent domain for private gain. Labor law is excellent, with a right-to-work law, no state-level minimum wage, a federally consistent anti-discrimination law, and lighter workers' compensation mandates than most states. Occupational licensing has grown over time, but not as much as in most other states. However, nurses' practice freedom remains fairly restricted. Insurance freedom is high, and rating classification prohibitions were eliminated in 2013–14. The state does have both general and gasoline-focused sales-below-cost prohibitions. The court system is relatively good, due to tort reforms in the 1990s and early 2000s.

Oklahoma's incarceration rate, adjusted for the crime rate, is more than a standard deviation higher than the national average, but it has not been changing much recently. Meanwhile, victimless crime arrest rates have been declining since 2006. Civil asset forfeiture reform has not gone far. It is still possible to get sentenced to life in prison for a single cannabis offense not involving minors. And a two-year mandatory minimum exists for even small-scale cultivation. For a state without a government liquor monopoly, Oklahoma does poorly on alcohol freedom. It has statewide blue laws, a happy hour ban, a total ban on direct wine shipment, and a ban on wine and spirits in grocery stores. Gambling expanded significantly in 2011–12. Educational freedom has grown recently with a very limited voucher law in 2010 and a modest tax benefit for contributions to private scholarship funds enacted in 2011–12. Homeschools and private schools are virtually unregulated. Tobacco freedom is relatively good, although new smoking restrictions in bars surfaced in 2013–14. The state was forced to legalize same-sex marriage, suspending its super-DOMA, in 2014.

OREGON

2014 RANK
37th

ECONOMIC   PERSONAL   OVERALL

RANK

1
10
20
30
40
50

2000   2005   2010   2015

YEAR

POLICY RECOMMENDATIONS

- **Fiscal:** Cut employee retirement, health and hospitals, and public welfare down to levels consistent with national norms. Cut individual income and property taxes.

- **Regulatory:** Eliminate occupational licensing for massage therapists, funeral attendants, pest control workers, agricultural graders and sorters, and other occupations.

- **Personal:** Legalize commercial casinos, preferably through a competitive model.

Population, 2014
3,970,239

Share of total U.S. population
1.2%

Population ranking
27th

Net migration rate
6.9%

State Taxes, Percent of Personal Income, FY 2014
5.5%

Local Taxes, Percent of Personal Income, FY 2012
4.1%

Partisan Lean, 2012
D +4.0

Real Per Capita Personal Income, 2013, in 2009 $
$37,648

Real Personal Income Growth, CAGR, 2000–13
1.36%

ANALYSIS

Oregon has generally had higher freedom than its neighbors to the north and south—and reaped the benefits. However, since 2000, its economic growth rate has barely surpassed California's and failed to match Washington's, in part because of cost-of-living growth.

Oregon's state taxes collapsed during the Great Recession but bounced back quickly. Taxes were raised in 2013–14 and are now a projected 5.6 percent of personal income. Local taxes have been more or less steady over that time and are now about 4.1 percent of income. Oregonians have little choice of local government, with just 0.45 effective competing jurisdictions per 100 square miles of private land. Government subsidies and debt are higher than average, but state and local employment is lower. From a better-than-average fiscal policy in FY 2000, Oregon now looks subpar in this dimension.

Land use has been a controversial issue in Oregon, and the Beaver State is indeed more regulated in this department than most other states, but we do not show any further tightening since the 1990s. However, the state ratcheted up its renewable portfolio standard in 2013–14. Oregon's labor policy is generally anti-employment, with one of the highest minimum wages in the country relative to the median wage, no right-to-work law,

and comprehensive workers' compensation mandates. Several independent measures show that Oregon licenses far more occupations than most other states. However, health professions' practice freedom is moderate. Insurance freedom has grown over the past four years with an end to rating classification prohibitions and the joining of the IIPRC. The civil liability system looks a bit better than the national average.

Oregon's criminal justice policy does not quite match the state's live-and-let-live reputation. Incarceration rates are a bit higher than average, but victimless crime arrest rates have come down substantially over the past several years to a roughly average level. Although recreational cannabis legalization passed in a November 2014 ballot initiative, it does not yet show up in our index. However, the state already had a fairly expansive medical cannabis law and decriminalization of small amounts. Civil asset forfeiture is fairly restricted, and law enforcement does not often circumvent state law through equitable sharing. Gun rights are better than one might expect from a left-of-center state, but during the late 2000s open- and concealed-carry rules were tightened. Illegal immigrants can now get driver's licenses. Smoking bans are comprehensive and airtight. Oregon has little legal gambling other than social games and Indian casinos. Same-sex marriage was legalized in 2014.

PENNSYLVANIA

2014 RANK
26th

Population, 2014
12,787,209

Share of total U.S. population
4.0%

Population ranking	Net migration rate
6th	**−1.0%**

State Taxes, Percent of Personal Income, FY 2014
5.1%

Local Taxes, Percent of Personal Income, FY 2012
4.2%

Partisan Lean, 2012
D +0.9

Real Per Capita Personal Income, 2013, in 2009 $
$43,715

Real Personal Income Growth, CAGR, 2000–13
1.84%

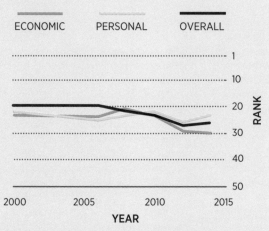

ECONOMIC PERSONAL OVERALL

RANK — 1, 10, 20, 30, 40, 50

YEAR — 2000, 2005, 2010, 2015

POLICY RECOMMENDATIONS

• **Fiscal:** Reduce spending, especially on public welfare and employee retirement benefits, which are high by national standards. Reduce numerous minor taxes that are relatively high by national standards.

• **Regulatory:** Improve the civil liability system by abolishing punitive damages and joint and several liability, and by ending partisan elections to the Supreme Court.

• **Personal:** Privatize and break up the state liquor monopoly.

ANALYSIS

The Keystone State is freer than all its neighbors, but it is a little below the national average, especially on economic policy.

Pennsylvania's tax burden is about average, but the state is a bit more fiscally decentralized than average, with local governments making up a larger share of the total tax take. The tax burden has declined slightly since 2000. Pennsylvanians have ample choice of local government, with more than 4.9 effective competing jurisdictions per 100 square miles. State and local debt and subsidies are higher than average, but public employment is much lower than average (10 percent of the private workforce).

Pennsylvania has drifted down on regulatory policy over time. It does reasonably well on land-use freedom, especially for a northeastern state, a fact that economist William Fischel attributes to the Pennsylvania Supreme Court's willingness to strike down minimum lot sizes and other zoning regulations that have exclusionary intent.[129] Pennsylvania is not as bad as most other northeastern states on labor-market regulation, but it lacks a right-to-work law. By most measures, occupational licensing is not very extensive in Pennsylvania, but there was a big jump upward in 2009–10. Nurses enjoy little practice freedom. Insurance freedom is extremely low, with "prior approval" of rates and forms and rating classification prohibitions. The civil liability system is much worse than the national average. The state has partisan judicial elections and has made none of the tort reforms we track.

Pennsylvania's criminal justice policy has worsened over time, at least as measured by crime-adjusted incarceration rates. Nonviolent victimless crime arrests are down since 2006, however. Civil asset forfeiture is mostly unreformed. Pennsylvania has lagged other center-left states in implementing medical cannabis and same-sex marriage, although the latter was imposed by judicial ruling in 2014. Gun rights are much better respected than in other progressive states, with carry licenses affordable and not terribly restricted, all Class III weapons legal, and a right to defend oneself in public, legally recognized in 2009–10. Since legalizing casinos in 2007–8, Pennsylvania has risen to become one of the best states in the country for gambling liberty. On the other hand, Pennsylvania is one of the worst states for alcohol freedom. A notoriously inefficient state bureaucracy monopolizes wine and spirits. Wine markups are especially high, direct wine shipments are banned, and even beer is prohibited in grocery stores. On education, Pennsylvania has a long-standing, liberal tax credit scholarship program, but private schools and homeschools are tightly regulated. Smoking bans have gone far but are not total.

---

129. William A. Fischel, *The Homevoter Hypothesis: How Home Values Influence Local Government Taxation, School Finance, and Land-Use Policies* (Cambridge, MA: Harvard University Press, 2001), p. 282.

RHODE ISLAND

2014 RANK

43rd

—— ECONOMIC ········ PERSONAL ━━ OVERALL

RANK

1
10
20
30
40
50

2000   2005   2010   2015

YEAR

POLICY RECOMMENDATIONS

• **Fiscal:** Cut state and local governments' abnormally high spending on public buildings, housing, public welfare, and employee retirement. The savings could be applied to reductions in selective sales and individual income taxes.

• **Regulatory:** Reform land-use regulations, perhaps through an Arizona-style regulatory taking compensation requirement combined with eminent domain reform.

• **Personal:** Legalize cultivation, sale, and possession of recreational cannabis.

Population, 2014
1,055,173

Share of total U.S. population
0.3%

Population ranking
43rd

Net migration rate
−6.3%

State Taxes, Percent of Personal Income, FY 2014
5.4%

Local Taxes, Percent of Personal Income, FY 2012
5.0%

Partisan Lean, 2012
D +11.9

Real Per Capita Personal Income, 2013, in 2009 $
$44,670

Real Personal Income Growth, CAGR, 2000–13
2.36%

ANALYSIS

Rhode Island is a fairly typical "deep blue" state in that it is much better on personal than economic liberties. The Ocean State compares favorably with its western neighbor but unfavorably to its neighbor to the north and east.

Rhode Island's fiscal policy is slightly subpar. Government subsidies and debt and local taxes are high, while state taxes are about the national average, and taxes were cut in 2013–14. With four effective competing jurisdictions per 100 square miles, Rhode Island affords its residents quite a bit of choice among localities. Government employment is well below the national average. This pattern is fairly typical for urban, coastal states, probably reflecting the higher cost per unit of labor than in the Midwest.

Rhode Island's regulatory policy has deteriorated somewhat over the past decade and a half, even ignoring the effects of the federal health law. Land-use freedom is low because of exclusionary zoning and eminent domain abuse, and indications are that it has worsened since the early 2000s. Renewable portfolio standards are high. Labor policy is also anti-employment, with a high minimum wage, no right-to-work law, a short-term disability insurance mandate, and, since 2013–14, a paid family leave mandate. We show a massive increase in health insurance mandated benefits in 2009–10, up to a premium additional cost for all benefits of plus

54.8 percent. Cable and telecommunications have, however, been liberalized. Occupational licensing is about average, but in 2013–14, nurse practitioner freedom of practice was expanded. A price-gouging law was enacted in 2011–12, and the state has long had a general ban on "unfair(ly low) prices." Freedom from abusive lawsuits is a bit below average.

Rhode Island has one of the best criminal justice systems in the country. Incarceration rates are well below average, as are drug and nondrug victimless crime arrest rates. Unfortunately, the state has not sufficiently reformed civil asset forfeiture, and, although a big equitable sharing payout somewhat skews Rhode Island's scores on that variable, evidence suggests that local law enforcement participated eagerly in the program even before that payout. The state has a fairly extensive medical cannabis law and decriminalized low-level possession of cannabis in 2011–12. However, it is still possible to get life imprisonment for a single marijuana offense not involving minors. Rhode Island has a little legal gambling, but the state is well behind Connecticut here. A tax credit scholarship law and repeal of private school teacher licensing passed in 2011–12, bringing the state's educational freedom above average. Same-sex marriage was legalized in 2013. Tobacco freedom is one of the lowest in the country, due to sky-high cigarette taxes (over $3 a pack) and comprehensive smoking bans. Gun laws are extremely restrictive and have become more so over time.

SOUTH CAROLINA

2014 RANK
15th

ECONOMIC — PERSONAL — **OVERALL**

Population, 2014
4,832,482

Share of total U.S. population
1.5%

Population ranking	Net migration rate
24th	**10.4%**

State Taxes, Percent of Personal Income, FY 2014
4.7%

Local Taxes, Percent of Personal Income, FY 2012
3.8%

Partisan Lean, 2012
R +7.0

Real Per Capita Personal Income, 2013, in 2009 $
$36,940

Real Personal Income Growth, CAGR, 2000–13
1.93%

[Chart: RANK vs YEAR, 2000–2015, scale 1 to 50]

POLICY RECOMMENDATIONS

• **Fiscal:** Prune state employment, and cut spending on health and hospitals, which is far above national norms. Cut the sales tax.

• **Regulatory:** Abolish the price-gouging law and all sales-below-cost/minimum-markup/unfair-sales laws. These reforms would have raised the state two places on economic freedom in 2014.

• **Personal:** Revise the state's asset forfeiture laws to make it more difficult for the government to seize assets, and reduce the government's incentive to do so by lowering the percentage of proceeds that go to law enforcement. Ban equitable sharing with the Department of Justice so that the federal government does not ignore state law.

ANALYSIS

South Carolina has traditionally done better on economic than personal freedom, but the legalization of same-sex marriage, among other policy trends, has, at least for the moment, turned that pattern upside down.

As one of the states more dependent on the federal government, the Palmetto State gets by with high government employment and a relatively low tax burden. Local taxes are average, but state taxes, at a projected 4.7 percent of personal income in FY 2015, are below the national average for 2000–2014 of 5.6 percent. South Carolina enjoyed big tax cuts in the mid- to late 2000s, according to our measure. Subsidies are below average, and debt—at 23.8 percent of income—is well above.

South Carolina's regulatory policy has improved noticeably over time. Much of that is due to tort reform and an improving civil liability system. Land-use freedom is extensive, and eminent domain reform has gone far. Labor law is generally good with no state-level minimum wage and a right-to-work law, but the state did enact an E-Verify mandate in 2007–8. Health insurance mandates are lower than average. Cable and telecommunications have been liberalized. The extent of occupational licensing is about average, but nurses enjoy only a little practice freedom. Insurance freedom is a bit subpar, and the state regulates prices for gasoline, for general retailers, and in emergencies.

South Carolina's criminal justice policies are not much like the Deep South. Incarceration and victimless crime arrest rates are more or less average. Asset forfeiture abuse has not been curbed. Cannabis penalties are somewhat harsh but not as draconian as in some other states. Gun rights are reasonably broad, but probably below the level enjoyed in, say, Pennsylvania. Open carry is illegal in most places, dealers are licensed, and the age for possession is stricter than the federal minimum. Educational freedom is mediocre. Private schools and homeschools are tightly, even harshly, regulated, and only a modest tax benefit exists for school choice program. Tobacco freedom is above average, as smoking bans on private property contain exceptions, and cigarette taxes are low. The state was forced to legalize same-sex marriage in 2014, overturning its super-DOMA banning private contracts for gay couples. Beer taxes are remarkably high.

SOUTH DAKOTA

2014 RANK
5th

ECONOMIC   PERSONAL   OVERALL

RANK

1

10

20

30

40

50

2000   2005   2010   2015

YEAR

POLICY RECOMMENDATIONS

• **Fiscal:** Trim spending on employment security administration, natural resources, and parks and recreation, areas far above national averages. Eliminate the business income tax.

• **Regulatory:** Amend the constitution to require a supermajority (say, 60 percent) to pass any new regulatory infringement on the rights of private citizens through the initiative process.

• **Personal:** Reduce the arrest rate for victimless crimes by prioritizing police resources toward solving violent and property crimes.

Population, 2014
853,175

Share of total U.S. population
0.3%

Population ranking
46th

Net migration rate
2.5%

State Taxes, Percent of Personal Income, FY 2014
3.5%

Local Taxes, Percent of Personal Income, FY 2012
3.7%

Partisan Lean, 2012
R +11.5

Real Per Capita Personal Income, 2013, in 2009 $
$48,989

Real Personal Income Growth, CAGR, 2000–13
3.89%

ANALYSIS

South Dakota is a quintessential "deep red" state with a vast gulf between its economic and personal freedom. The state has been growing like gangbusters for at least 20 years, but lawmakers might also consider whether man can live by money alone.

South Dakota's fiscal policy is excellent. It has one of the lowest tax burdens in the country, and both state and local tax burdens have fallen over time. It is also relatively fiscally decentralized, and South Dakotans do have some choice among local jurisdictions (1.2 effective ones per 100 square miles). State and local subsidies and debt are well below national averages, while public employment is just below the national average, at 13.1 percent of private employment. We register a fairly significant reduction in debt since FY 2009.

South Dakota's regulatory policy is also well above average, but it has not improved much, even discounting the PPACA, since 2000. Land-use freedom is extensive, and housing supply is elastic. Labor law is generally good because of right-to-work and other provisions, but a very high (for the local market) minimum wage was enacted by ballot initiative in 2013–14. Telecommunications have been liberalized, but statewide video franchising has not been enacted. Multiple indicators suggest the extent of occupational licensing is a bit below the national average, even as it has increased with time (like every-

where). Nursing practice freedom is, however, subpar. Insurance freedom is mediocre, as the state has held out against the IIPRC and has enacted a rate classification prohibition. However, South Dakota is mercifully free of a variety of other cronyist entry and price regulations, including a CON law. The state's civil liability system is above average and has improved slightly over time.

South Dakota's criminal justice policies surely qualify as draconian. For its crime rate, it imprisons far more than it should. Drug and other victimless crime arrest rates are all above national norms, however measured. Asset forfeiture is virtually unreformed, though local law enforcement does not participate much in equitable sharing. The cannabis law is harsher than in most states, though not the harshest. The state takes DNA samples from nonviolent misdemeanant suspects without any judicial process. Some legal gambling takes place. Private school and homeschool regulations are not as burdensome as those of the neighbor to the north, but without any school choice programs its educational liberty is below average. Smoking bans are extreme, and tobacco taxes are relatively high. As of 2014, the state had not yet been forced to legalize same-sex marriage, and it had a super-DOMA. In future years, the state should improve (see Appendix Table B17). South Dakota is one of the best states in the country for gun rights. Alcohol freedom is also fairly extensive, but direct wine shipments are banned.

TENNESSEE

2014 RANK
6th

ECONOMIC   PERSONAL   OVERALL

RANK

2000   2005   2010   2015

YEAR

POLICY RECOMMENDATIONS

• **Fiscal:** Separate spending and tax committees in the legislature, a reform shown to correspond to lower spending over time. Sales taxes are high and could be cut.

• **Regulatory:** Repeal the price-gouging law and all minimum-markup laws. This reform could have raised Tennessee above South Carolina on regulatory policy.

• **Personal:** Prioritize violent and property crimes in policing and deprioritize drug arrests. Even an average drug enforcement rate in Tennessee would have raised the state four places on personal freedom.

Population, 2014
6,549,352

Share of total U.S. population
2.1%

Population ranking
17th

Net migration rate
6.0%

State Taxes, Percent of Personal Income, FY 2014
4.0%

Local Taxes, Percent of Personal Income, FY 2012
3.2%

Partisan Lean, 2012
R +12.1

Real Per Capita Personal Income, 2013, in 2009 $
$40,738

Real Personal Income Growth, CAGR, 2000–13
1.63%

ANALYSIS

Tennessee has long been one of the economically freest states, largely due to its fiscal policies, but it also used to be one of the personally freest states in the South. No longer is that true.

The Volunteer State lacks an income tax, and both state and local tax collections fall below the national average. We show state-level taxes falling from 5.0 percent of personal income in FY 2007 to a projected 4.0 percent this year. Local taxes have also fallen a bit since 2006, from about 3.5 to 3.2 percent of income. State and local debt is low, at 14.5 percent of income, and so is government employment, at 11.5 percent of income. Subsidies are about average.

Tennessee's land-use regulations are flexible, and it has a regulatory takings law. However, eminent domain reform has not gone far. Tennessee is the number two state for labor-market freedom, with a right-to-work law, no minimum wage, relaxed workers' comp rules, no E-Verify mandate, and federally consistent anti-discrimination law. Cable and telecommunications have been liberalized. We show a significant decline in health insurance mandates between 2008 and 2010. On the downside, the extent of occupational licensure looks rather high, though different indicators give different pictures. Nurse practitioners lost whatever independent scope of practice they had in 2009–10, but dental hygienists gained some in 2013–14. The state marginally loosened insurance rate regulation in 2009–10. There are general and gasoline-specific minimum-markup laws, as well as an anti-price-gouging law. The civil liability system improved to above average with reforms in 2011 to punitive damages.

Tennessee's criminal justice policies have deteriorated over time. The crime-adjusted incarceration rate is still slightly below the national average but has risen since 2000. Drug arrest rates are now well above the national average. Asset forfeiture is mostly unreformed. Cannabis laws are strict. Tennessee is one of the best states for gun rights, but the rules for open carry are fairly strict. Alcohol freedom is below average because of the blue laws and very high beer taxes, which were raised in 2013–14 to $1.06 a gallon in 2008 dollars. The state has little gambling. Educational freedom is low: private school choice programs are nonexistent, and private schools and homeschools face significant regulatory burdens. Tobacco freedom is a bit better than average. As of 2014, the state had no legal recognition of same-sex partnerships but at least lacked a super-DOMA banning even private contracts.

TEXAS

2014 RANK
28th

─── ECONOMIC ⋯⋯ PERSONAL ━━━ OVERALL

RANK: 1, 10, 20, 30, 40, 50

YEAR: 2000, 2005, 2010, 2015

POLICY RECOMMENDATIONS

• **Fiscal:** Tighten the rules for municipal annexation and make municipal secession easy, to provide Texans with more choice in local government. Raise requirements for local debt issuance.

• **Regulatory:** Improve the liability system by eliminating partisan judicial elections and capping punitive damages.

• **Personal:** Enact a general educational savings account plan similar to the one enacted in Nevada in 2015.[130]

Population, 2014
26,956,958

Share of total U.S. population
8.5%

Population ranking
2nd

Net migration rate
6.7%

State Taxes, Percent of Personal Income, FY 2014
3.6%

Local Taxes, Percent of Personal Income, FY 2012
4.5%

Partisan Lean, 2012
R 9.7

Real Per Capita Personal Income, 2013, in 2009 $
$42,305

Real Personal Income Growth, CAGR, 2000–13
2.24%

130.   On this, see Kent Grusendorf and Nate Sherer, "How ESAs Can Keep Texas the Land of the Free and Home of the Brave," policy brief, Texas Public Policy Foundation, Austin, January 2016, http://www.texaspolicy.com/library/doclib/PB-How-ESAs-Can-Keep-Texas-the-Land-of-the-Free-and-Home-of-the-Brave.pdf.

ANALYSIS

Texas is one of the economically freest and personally least free states in the country. Its economic freedom is likely one reason it has been such a job-producing and population-attracting machine. However, its economic policies may get a bit more attention than deserved because of the state's size. Yes, the Lone Star State draws a bunch of business from California and other highly regulated locales in an absolute sense and is a jobs juggernaut. But its economic growth rate over the past decade and a half still lags states like the Dakotas, Utah, and Wyoming that have also benefited from the energy revolution.

Texas's fiscal policy is very good. It is a fiscally decentralized state, with local taxes at about 4.5 percent of personal income, above the national average, and state taxes at about 3.6 percent of income, well below the national average. However, Texans don't have much choice of local government, with only 0.36 jurisdictions per 100 square miles. State and local debt is above average (with the biggest problem being local debt burdens), at 23.1 percent of income, but it has come down slightly since FY 2011. Government subsidies are below average. Public employment has fallen significantly below average, at 11.8 percent of private employment.

Texas's land-use freedom keeps housing prices down. It also has a regulatory taking compensation law, but it only applies to state government. The renewable portfolio standard has not been raised in years. Texas is our top state for labor-market freedom. Workers' compensation coverage is optional for employers; most employees are covered, but not all. The state has a right-to-work law, no minimum wage, and a federally consistent anti-discrimination law. Cable and telecommunications have been liberalized. However, health insurance mandates were quite high as of 2010, the last available date. The extent of occupational licensing is high, but the state recently enacted a sunrise review requirement for new licensure proposals. Time will tell whether it is at all effective. Nurse practitioners enjoy no freedom of independent practice at all. Texas has few cronyist entry and price regulations, but it does have a price-gouging law, and Tesla's direct sales model is still illegal. The civil liability system used to be terrible, but now it is merely below average. The state abolished joint and several liability in 2003, but it could do more to cap punitive damages and end parties' role in judicial elections.

Personal freedom is relatively low in Texas, but it should rise with the *Obergefell* decision, setting aside Texas's super-DOMA (see Appendix Table B17). Criminal justice policies are generally aggressive—though Texas has emerged as a leading voice in the national reform movement. Even controlling for crime rates, the incarceration rate is far above the national average and has not improved since 2000. Drug arrest rates have fallen over time but are still above average for the user base. Nondrug victimless crime arrest rates have also fallen over time and are now below the national average. Asset forfeiture is mostly unreformed, and law enforcement frequently participates in equitable sharing. Cannabis laws are harsh. A single offense not involving minors can carry a life sentence. Even cultivating a tiny amount carries a mandatory minimum of six months. In 2013–14, the state banned the mostly harmless psychedelic *Salvia divinorum*. Travel freedom is low. The state takes a fingerprint for driver's licenses and does not regulate automated license plate readers at all. It has little legal gambling. Private school choice programs are nonexistent, but at least private schools and homeschools are basically unregulated. Tobacco freedom is moderate, as smoking bans have not gone as far as in other states. Gun rights are moderately above average and should improve a bit in the next edition with the new open-carry law. Alcohol freedom is above average, with taxes low. Texas has virtually no campaign finance regulations.

UTAH

2014 RANK
20th

Population, 2014
2,942,902

Share of total U.S. population
0.9%

Population ranking	Net migration rate
33rd	**2.5%**

State Taxes, Percent of Personal Income, FY 2014
5.2%

Local Taxes, Percent of Personal Income, FY 2012
3.8%

Partisan Lean, 2012
R +26.3

Real Per Capita Personal Income, 2013, in 2009 $
$35,141

Real Personal Income Growth, CAGR, 2000–13
2.86%

―― ECONOMIC   ―― PERSONAL   ▬▬ OVERALL

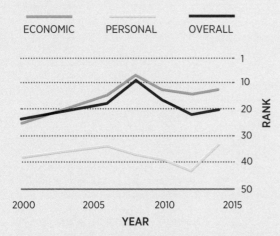

RANK

YEAR

POLICY RECOMMENDATIONS

- **Fiscal:** End business subsidies and apply the proceeds to reducing debt.

- **Regulatory:** Eliminate occupational licensing for taxi drivers and chauffeurs, funeral attendants, occupational therapist assistants, recreational therapists, interpreters and translators, and other occupations. Enact mandatory sunrise review for new licensing proposals, involving an independent committee comprising consumers and professional economists.

- **Personal:** Restore the civil asset forfeiture law that Utahans originally enacted in 2000.

ANALYSIS

Utah's economic policies are good and have generally improved over time, despite some backsliding in the 2009–12 years. Personal freedoms are a mixed bag, consistent with the state's religious and ideological background. The Beehive State is growing rapidly.

Utah's tax burden is a bit below average. We show a dramatic drop in state revenues with the onset of the Great Recession, which were never replaced. In fact, further tax cuts were made in FY 2014. Local taxes, meanwhile, have remained generally steady at right about the national average rate of 3.8 percent of personal income. Government subsidies, debt, and employment are all about average.

Utah does very well on regulatory policy overall. On land-use freedom, it is a little better than average, but it appears to be tightening zoning rules over time. Eminent domain reform was watered down in 2007–8. Labor law is solid. The state has a right-to-work law but no minimum wage. Health insurance mandates were well below the national average in the last available year of 2010. As everywhere, occupational licensing has increased over time, but sources differ on whether it is more or less extensive than else-

where. Nursing freedom is generally good, but freedom for dental hygienists is not. Insurance freedom is among the best in the country, with "use and file" for most property and casualty lines, long-standing membership in the IIPRC, and "file and use" for new life insurance policies. The state has a price-gouging law and a sales-below-cost law for gasoline, but its general sales-below-cost law was repealed in 2007–8. Its civil liability system is better than average.

On personal freedom, Utah unsurprisingly does well on gun rights, travel freedom, and educational liberty, but quite poorly on alcohol, cannabis, gambling, and tobacco. It was also very bad on marriage, but it was forced to legalize same-sex marriage in 2014, a move that also overturned its super-DOMA prohibiting gay partnership contracts. Utah actually does generally well on criminal justice policy. Its crime-adjusted incarceration rate is below the national average, although it has crept up over time. Victimless crime arrest rates used to be way above average but have come down to national norms. The state had an excellent asset forfeiture law, but it has been successively weakened, most recently in 2013–14. Utah has recently moved to require fingerprints from drivers when they get their licenses.

VERMONT

2014 RANK
40th

ECONOMIC   PERSONAL   OVERALL

RANK

	1
	10
	20
	30
	40
	50

2000   2005   2010   2015

YEAR

POLICY RECOMMENDATIONS

• **Fiscal:** Undo the past two decades of centralization with a constitutional amendment limiting state government responsibility for education. Return property tax-varying power and school budgeting power fully to towns, and reduce state aid to a low level. Use the proceeds to cut income taxes.

• **Regulatory:** Cap punitive damages and abolish joint and several liability.

• **Personal:** Legalize recreational cannabis sale, cultivation, and possession.

Population, 2014
626,562

Share of total U.S. population
0.2%

Population ranking	Net migration rate
49th	**−1.0%**

State Taxes, Percent of Personal Income, FY 2014
9.5%

Local Taxes, Percent of Personal Income, FY 2012
1.7%

Partisan Lean, 2012
D +15.4

Real Per Capita Personal Income, 2013, in 2009 $
$42,337

Real Personal Income Growth, CAGR, 2000–13
2.43%

ANALYSIS

Vermont's economic policies are generally much worse than its social policies, but Vermont businesses have carved out a niche for themselves that has afforded the state reasonable economic growth over the past decade and a half. Time will tell whether this performance can be sustained; we expect not, unless the state reforms its fiscal regime.

Vermont is one of the highest-tax states in the country. It also looks extremely fiscally centralized, with state government taking 9.5 percent of personal income and local government taking just 1.7 percent. However, this statistic is overstated, since Vermont counts the property tax as a state tax, even though towns have some discretion over the rate at which it is set locally. Vermonters would benefit from more fiscal decentralization, though, as they have 3.5 effective competing jurisdictions per 100 square miles. Government subsidies have usually been above average but have recently fallen to average (0.1 percent of income). Government debt is a bit below average and public employment a bit above.

Vermont does not do very well on land-use freedom, but it actually does better than neighbors New Hampshire and Massachusetts. As a result, land is more affordable than in those states. The state has done little to restrain eminent domain for private gain. The minimum wage for the local economy is very high, and it has been rising since 2010. We show a big jump in health insurance mandates between 2008 and 2010, the last available year. The state legislature authorized single-payer health insurance, but the executive branch declined to implement the law, and so we do not code this law in our index. Cable and telecommunications have been liberalized. Occupational freedom is better than the national average. For instance, it is the only state not to license landscape architects. Vermont has sunrise review for new licensing proposals, and it is one of the few states with such a requirement to have taken it seriously, as evidenced by the review reports posted online.[131] Nurse practitioners gained full independent prac-

tice authority in 2011–12. Insurance freedom is excellent, with a "use and file" system for most property and casualty lines, longstanding membership in the IIPRC, and no rating classification prohibitions. In general, Vermont is one of the least "cronyist" states. However, it has a hospital certificate-of-need law and in 2013–14 enacted an anti-science and anti-consumer labeling law for genetically modified organisms. Its civil liability system is mediocre; the state has passed no tort reforms.

Vermont is our number one state for gun rights. The only policies it could improve are in allowing carry in more locations, providing an optional carry license for reciprocity with other states, specifying no duty to retreat, and legalizing silencers. It is one of the lowest states for alcohol freedom, with a state monopoly over wine and spirits retail and beer wholesaling. It is one of the better non-initiative states for cannabis, with decriminalization and a reasonably broad medical law. However, maximum penalties are rather high, high-level possession is a felony, and *Salvia divinorum* was banned in 2011–12. Vermont took travel freedom with one hand and gave back more with the other in 2013–14, enacting a primary cell phone ban, which research has shown to be useless, but also letting illegal immigrants get driver's licenses and placing some limits on automated license plate readers (though the latter law has sunset as of this writing). Vermont has almost no legal gambling. Physician-assisted suicide was enacted in 2013–14. The state does well on educational freedom because some towns are allowed to "tuition out" students, a century-old practice approximating a voucher law. Homeschool regulations are fairly tough. Tobacco freedom is extremely low, with airtight smoking bans, vending machine and Internet purchase restrictions, and high cigarette taxes. The incarceration rate is about average for its crime rate, but victimless crime arrest rates are very low. Vermont has one of the better asset forfeiture laws, but police frequently evade it. Same-sex marriage was enacted in 2009–10, replacing civil unions.

---

131. "Sunrise Review," Office of Vermont Secretary of State, https://www.sec.state.vt.us/professional-regulation/sunrise-review.aspx.

VIRGINIA

2014 RANK
21st

Population, 2014
8,326,289

Share of total U.S. population
2.6%

Population ranking	Net migration rate
12th	**2.4%**

ECONOMIC   PERSONAL   OVERALL

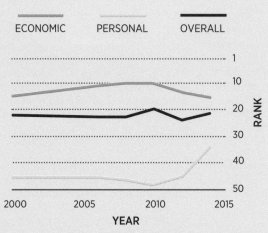

RANK

YEAR

State Taxes, Percent
of Personal Income, FY 2014
4.4%

Local Taxes, Percent
of Personal Income, FY 2012
3.8%

Partisan Lean, 2012
R +0.0

POLICY RECOMMENDATIONS

- **Fiscal:** Trim government employment across the board.

- **Regulatory:** Legalize independent practice with full prescriptive authority for nurse practitioners, adopt a nursing consultation exception for interstate practice, and allow dental hygienists to clean teeth without dentist supervision.

- **Personal:** Reform sentencing for nonviolent offenses with an eye toward reducing the incarceration rate to the national average in the long term.

Real Per Capita Personal
Income, 2013, in 2009 $
$44,233

Real Personal Income
Growth, CAGR, 2000–13
1.53%

ANALYSIS

As a historically conservative southern state, Virginia has usually done much better on economic than personal freedom. However, we record some significant improvements in personal freedom in recent years. Due in part to rising cost of living, the Old Dominion has had one of the worst growth records in the country since 2006, though still better than neighbor Maryland.

Virginia is a somewhat fiscally decentralized state with an average local tax burden (about 3.8 percent of income) and a below-average state tax burden (about 4.4 percent of income, a significant decline from FY 2007). Virginians' choice in local government is subpar, with just half a competing jurisdiction per 100 square miles. Government subsidies and debt are low, and employment is average. These policies show little change over time.

Virginia's land-use freedom is generally good, although local zoning rules have tightened in recent years, especially in the northern part of the state. Eminent domain reform has been effective. Labor law is well above average, with a right-to-work law, no minimum wage, fairly relaxed workers' comp rules, and a federally consistent anti-discrimination law. Health insurance mandates have long been much higher than the national average and amount to more than 50 percent of the cost of an average premium. Cable and telecommunications have been liberalized.

Occupational licensing is more extensive than in the average state. Nurses and dental hygienists enjoy little practice freedom. Insurance freedom is a bit above average, but Virginia has a CON law, price-gouging law, and mover licensing. The civil liability system is about average.

Virginia's criminal justice policies are worsening. It now has one of the highest incarceration rates in the country, even controlling for crime rates. Victimless crime arrest rates are about average. Asset forfeiture is virtually unreformed, and local police frequently circumvent it anyway with equitable sharing. The state's approach to cannabis producers and consumers is draconian. Even low-level cultivation carries a yearlong mandatory minimum sentence, and life imprisonment is possible for a single marijuana offense not involving minors. Virginia is one of the best states for gun rights and has improved over time. Alcohol freedom is subpar but improved in the early 2000s as some regulations were withdrawn. State liquor store markups are still huge. Virginia has little legal gambling. Educational freedom grew substantially in 2011–12 with a new tax credit scholarship law. Tobacco freedom is better than average, with comparatively low cigarette taxes and respect for the property rights of private workplaces. The state was forced to legalize same-sex marriage in 2014, which also overturned the state's oppressive super-DOMA banning all relationship-style contracts between two gay people.

WASHINGTON

32nd

Population, 2014
7,061,530

Share of total U.S. population
2.2%

Population ranking	Net migration rate
13th	**5.5%**

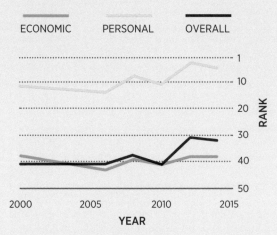

ECONOMIC   PERSONAL   OVERALL

RANK

YEAR

State Taxes, Percent of Personal Income, FY 2014
5.1%

Local Taxes, Percent of Personal Income, FY 2012
3.8%

Partisan Lean, 2012
D +5.1

POLICY RECOMMENDATIONS

- **Fiscal:** Enact strict, *ex post* balanced budget requirements to bring state debt down over time.

- **Regulatory:** Better protect property rights by enacting further-reaching eminent domain reform and reducing centralized land-use planning by repealing or amending the Growth Management Act and the Shoreline Management Act.

- **Personal:** Repeal teacher licensing and mandatory state approval and registration for private schools, ease the annual testing requirement for homeschoolers, and require homeschooling parents to keep only a record of attendance, not teaching materials. As modest as these changes are, they would have been sufficient to raise Washington to first place on personal freedom in 2014.

Real Per Capita Personal Income, 2013, in 2009 $
$43,109

Real Personal Income Growth, CAGR, 2000–13
1.78%

ANALYSIS

Although Washington has had one of the more regulated economies in the United States for a long time, it has benefited from the fact that other West Coast states have had the same. Since 2006, we show decent gains in personal freedom and fiscal policy, along with some losses on regulatory policy.

Washington lacks an income tax; as a result, its fiscal policy is fairly good. Localities raise about the national average in taxes, 3.8 percent of personal income. State government, meanwhile, raises 5.1 percent of income, a little below the national average. Despite recent incorporations, Washingtonians have little choice in local government, just 0.51 per 100 square miles of private land. Government subsidies are, unfortunately, much higher than average, as is government debt. Public employment is also a bit higher than average, but it has fallen since 2010.

Washingtonians do not enjoy much freedom to use their own land. Local and regional zoning and planning rules have become quite strict. Eminent domain abuse is almost unchecked. The state has a modest renewable portfolio standard. Washington is one of the worst states on labor-market freedom. It lacks a right-to-work law, limits choices for workers' comp programs, and has extremely high minimum wages relative to its wage base. Cable and telecommunications have not been liberalized. Occupational licensing has become much more extensive than the national average. Its sunrise commission law has proved useless. However, nurse practitioners and physician assistants enjoy broad scope of practice. Insurance freedom is quite poor. New rating classification prohibitions were passed in 2013–14. The civil liability system is mediocre but may have improved slightly since 2006.

Washington's criminal justice policies are among the best in the nation. Incarceration and victimless crime arrest rates are far below national averages. The state recently legalized recreational cannabis. However, virtually nothing has been done about civil asset forfeiture abuse. Washingtonians have enjoyed same-sex marriage since 2012 and civil unions since 2008. Gun laws are quite good, especially for a left-leaning state, and some Class III weapons have been legalized in recent years. Washington increased its alcohol freedom to average from well below by privatizing state liquor stores and allowing spirits in grocery stores. However, taxes on distilled spirits are the highest in the country. Illegal immigrants have been able to get driver's licenses for a long time. The state is fairly mediocre on gambling freedom and prohibits online gaming. Educational freedom is substandard, with very harsh private school and homeschool regulations. Smoking bans are comprehensive, and tobacco taxes are extremely high.

WEST VIRGINIA

2014 RANK

39th

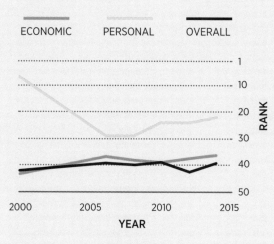

ECONOMIC   PERSONAL   OVERALL

RANK

1
10
20
30
40
50

2000   2005   2010   2015

YEAR

POLICY RECOMMENDATIONS

• **Fiscal:** Reduce state employment, especially in general administration, highways, and public welfare. Further reduce the business income tax.

• **Regulatory:** Cap or abolish punitive damages and abolish joint and several liability.

• **Personal:** Reform sentencing by abolishing mandatory minimums for nonviolent offenses, with an eye toward reducing the incarceration rate to its 2000 level.

Population, 2014
1,850,326

Share of total U.S. population
0.6%

Population ranking
38th

Net migration rate
0.9%

State Taxes, Percent of Personal Income, FY 2014
6.2%

Local Taxes, Percent of Personal Income, FY 2012
2.7%

Partisan Lean, 2012
R +15.3

Real Per Capita Personal Income, 2013, in 2009 $
$37,473

Real Personal Income Growth, CAGR, 2000–13
1.69%

ANALYSIS

West Virginia has usually done better on personal than economic freedom, but we show the two lines converging as the state's public opinion has grown more conservative and Republican. Since 2006, the state has lagged Pennsylvania and Ohio in economic growth.

The Mountaineer State's overall tax burden is about average, but it is centralized at the state level. The state takes about 6.2 percent of income, a significant decline since FY 2007, when it was 7.3 percent, while local governments take 2.7 percent, a figure that has remained steady over time. There are 0.8 effective competing jurisdictions per 100 square miles. State and local subsidies and debt are low and have fallen over time. Government employment is way above average, at 16.5 percent of private employment.

Land-use freedom is broad in West Virginia, although it has come down over time. Labor-market freedom is low despite an effective workers' comp reform in 2007–8. The state enacted a minimum wage in 2013–14 and lacks a right-to-work law (though its labor-market freedom will likely increase in the next edition, given that West Virginia is almost certain to become the 26th right-to-work state following passage of a bill in both the state house and senate in early 2016). Cable

and telecommunications have not been liberalized. Occupational freedom is a bit below average, both in extent of licensure and in scope of practice for second-line health professions. Insurance rate-setting freedom is restricted. West Virginia has a hospital CON law, a price-gouging law, a moving company licensing requirement, and a general "unfair sales" law. The civil liability system is one of the worst, and the state has made no effort to reform it.

West Virginia used to lock up fewer of its residents than most other states, but that is no longer the case. Drug arrests have also increased over time as a share of the user base. Asset forfeiture is essentially unreformed. Cannabis laws are harsh. Even low-level cultivation or sale carries a mandatory minimum of two years in prison. West Virginia is one of the best states for gun rights, and despite state involvement in alcohol distribution, it is also better than average for alcohol freedom. The seat belt law was upgraded to primary in 2013–14, reducing freedom. New legal gambling came online in 2011–12. Mixed martial arts competitions were legalized in that same session. Private schools and homeschools are fairly heavily regulated. Tobacco freedom is better than average. Same-sex marriage was legalized by court order in 2014.

WISCONSIN

2014 RANK
27th

ECONOMIC   PERSONAL   **OVERALL**

RANK

1
10
20
30
40
50

2000   2005   2010   2015

YEAR

POLICY RECOMMENDATIONS

• **Fiscal:** Reduce the income tax burden while continuing to cut spending on employee retirement and government employment.

• **Regulatory:** Abolish price controls.

• **Personal:** Eliminate teacher licensing and mandatory state approval for private schools.

Population, 2014
5,757,564

Share of total U.S. population
1.8%

Population ranking
20th

Net migration rate
−0.9%

State Taxes, Percent of Personal Income, FY 2014
5.8%

Local Taxes, Percent of Personal Income, FY 2012
4.4%

Partisan Lean, 2012
D +1.7

Real Per Capita Personal Income, 2013, in 2009 $
$43,392

Real Personal Income Growth, CAGR, 2000–13
2.07%

ANALYSIS

For all the talk about Scott Walker's "radical reforms," we find that economic freedom has been more or less constant since 2011, relative to other states, whereas personal freedom has grown substantially.

The Badger State has relatively high taxes, which have fallen only marginally since 2012. State taxes are projected to be 5.8 percent of personal income in FY 2015, while local taxes have risen since FY 2000 and now stand at 4.4 percent of income, above the national average. Wisconsinites have ample choice among local governments, with more than two and a half effective competing jurisdictions per 100 square miles. State and local debt has fallen somewhat since FY 2007, and government employment and subsidies are below average. Overall, Wisconsin has seen definite improvement on fiscal policy since 2010, but it hasn't yet reached the national average.

On regulatory policy, we see little change in recent years, although our index does not yet take account of the 2015 right-to-work law. Land-use freedom is a bit better than average; local zoning has not gotten out of hand, though it has grown some. The state has a renewable portfolio standard, but it is not high. Apart from its right-to-work law, Wisconsin was already reasonably good on labor-market policy. Cable and telecommunications have been liberalized. Occupational licensing increased dramatically between 2000 and 2006; still, the state is about average overall on extent of licensure. Nurse practitioners enjoy no independent practice freedom. Insurance freedom is generally good, at least for property and casualty lines. The state has a price-gouging law, as well as controversial, strictly enforced minimum-markup laws for gasoline and general retailers. The civil liability system is above average and improved significantly since 2010, due to a punitive damages cap.

Wisconsin is below average on criminal justice policies, but it has improved substantially since 2010 because of local policing strategies. The incarceration rate has fallen, as have nondrug victimless crime arrest rates. The state's asset forfeiture law is one of the stricter ones in the country, but equitable sharing revenues are a little higher than average, suggesting some evasion of the law. The state was required to legalize same-sex marriage in 2014. Tobacco freedom is extremely low, due to airtight smoking bans and high taxes. Educational freedom grew significantly in 2013–14 with the expansion of vouchers. However, private schools are relatively tightly regulated. There is almost no legal gambling, even for social purposes. Cannabis law is unreformed. Wisconsin is the best state for alcohol freedom, with no state role in distribution, no keg registration, low taxes (especially on beer—imagine that), no blue laws, legal happy hours, legal direct wine shipment, and both wine and spirits in grocery stores. The state is now about average on gun rights after the legislature passed a shall-issue concealed-carry license, one of the last states in the country to legalize concealed carry.

WYOMING

2014 RANK

14th

ECONOMIC   PERSONAL   **OVERALL**

RANK

1
10
20
30
40
50

2000   2005   2010   2015

YEAR

POLICY RECOMMENDATIONS

• **Fiscal:** Privatize hospitals to reduce government employment and allow sales taxes to be cut. Wyoming spends far more on health and hospitals as a share of its economy than any other state.

• **Regulatory:** Let employers buy workers' compensation coverage from any willing seller. Consider privatizing the state fund.

• **Personal:** Abolish "policing for profit" by limiting equitable sharing, directing forfeiture revenues to the general fund, and putting the burden of proof on the government.

Population, 2014
584,153

Share of total U.S. population
0.2%

Population ranking
50th

Net migration rate
5.7%

State Taxes, Percent of Personal Income, FY 2014
4.0%

Local Taxes, Percent of Personal Income, FY 2012
4.5%

Partisan Lean, 2012
R +23.5

Real Per Capita Personal Income, 2013, in 2009 $
$51,410

Real Personal Income Growth, CAGR, 2000–13
3.69%

ANALYSIS

As a highly resource-dependent state, Wyoming's fiscal situation fluctuates greatly from year to year. Improving regulatory policy can be a way to diversify the economy, and the Equality State could also stand to improve on personal freedom, where it is below average.

Wyoming is a relatively fiscally decentralized state, especially for its small population. Excluding mineral severance revenues, state taxes come to a projected 4.0 percent of personal income in FY 2015, well below the national average and a big decline from FY 2009. Local taxes stand at about 4.5 percent of income, slightly above the national average. However, Wyomingites have little choice in local government, with less than 0.10 effective competing jurisdictions per 100 square miles of private land, thus squandering the advantages of fiscal decentralization. The state spends almost nothing on subsidies, and government debt is the lowest in the country (a mere 6.8 percent of income), but state and local employment is enormous (19.4 percent of private employment, a big increase over 2008 when it was 17.8 percent).

Wyoming does well on land-use freedom, although we show that regulation has increased over the 2000s. Labor law is generally good, with no minimum wage and a right-to-work law, but employers must obtain workers' compensation coverage from a monopoly state fund, and anti-discrimination law goes beyond the federal minimum. A telecom deregulation bill was passed in 2013–14. Occupational licensing has grown over time but is still well below the national average. Nurse practitioners and physician assistants also enjoy broad scope of practice. Wyoming is the best state for insurance freedom, lacking price controls on property and casualty lines. Still, life insurance policies require prior approval, even though the state is a member of the IIPRC. Its price-gouging law was repealed many years ago, but it still has a Depression-era "unfair sales act" on the books. Its civil liability system is good, even though the state has not reformed punitive damages at all.

Wyoming's criminal justice policies are similar to those of a Mississippi or Alabama. Incarceration and victimless crime arrest rates are high and have generally risen over time. Asset forfeiture is virtually unreformed (owners must prove their innocence), and so local law enforcement chooses not to participate in equitable sharing much. Cannabis laws are predictably bad, though not among the very harshest. Wyoming is one of the very best states for gun rights, having passed constitutional carry in 2009–10. The only areas where it could improve involve removing location restrictions for carry, allowing nonresident licenses, and specifying no duty to retreat in public. Alcohol freedom is a bit above average despite state liquor stores, because taxes are so low. The state has almost no legal gambling other than social games. Nonsectarian private schools are strictly regulated, and there are no private school choice programs. Tobacco freedom is above average. Same-sex marriage was judicially enacted in 2014.

DIMENSION, CATEGORY, AND VARIABLE WEIGHTS

Key:
Dimension
    Category
        Policy Variable

FISCAL POLICY: 29.5%–32.0%
    State taxation: 13.4%
    Local taxation: 7.6%–10.1%
    Government subsidies: 2.3%

GOVERNMENT DEBT: 2.1%
    Land-use freedom: 10.5%
        Local rent control: 6.0%
        "Land-use" court mentions: 2.2%
        Wharton Residential Land-Use Regulatory Index: 1.1%
        Renewable portfolio standards: 1.0%
        Regulatory taking compensation: 0.2%
        Eminent domain reform index: 0.1%
        Health insurance freedom: 7.4%
        Parking lot gun mandate: 0.01%
        Mandated free speech on private property: <0.01%

    Health insurance freedom: 7.4%
        Community rating: small groups: 2.7%
        Individual health insurance mandate: 2.7%
        Health insurance mandates index: 2.4%
        Individual guaranteed issue: 0.7%
        Small-group rate review: 0.6%
        Community rating: individuals: 0.5%
        Mandated direct access to specialists: 0.4%
        Individual rate review: 0.06%
        Mandated standing referrals: 0.03%
        Individual policies: elimination riders banned: 0.03%

Mandated external grievance review: 0.02%

Financial incentives to providers banned: 0.01%

"Mandate-light" or "mandate-free" policies: <0.01%

Labor-market freedom: 5.7%

General right-to-work law: 2.8%

Short-term disability insurance: 1.0%

Workers' compensation coverage regulations: 0.6%

Workers' compensation funding regulations: 0.6%

Minimum wage: 0.5%

Employer verification of legal status: 0.2%

Employee anti-discrimination law: 0.01%

Paid family leave: <0.01%

Occupational freedom: 4.5%

Employment-weighted licensure (extent): 1.2%

Nurse practitioner independence index: 0.9%

Summed education and experience requirements: 0.6%

Number of licensed occupations: 0.6%

Regulatory keywords in statutes: 0.6%

Summed exam requirements: 0.2%

Dental hygienist scope of practice: 0.1%

Summed fees for licensed occupations: 0.07%

Physician assistant prescribing authority: 0.05%

Sunrise commissions: 0.05%

Nurse Licensure Compact membership: 0.04%

Nursing consultation exception: 0.04%

Sunset review: 0.01%

Lawsuit freedom: 3.7%

Miscellaneous regulatory freedom: 2.9%

Certificate of need for hospitals: 0.9%

Rate filing requirements: personal auto insurance: 0.5%

Rate filing requirements: homeowner's insurance: 0.3%

Anti-price-gouging laws: 0.2%

General sales-below-cost laws: 0.2%

Rate classification prohibitions: 0.2%

Interstate Insurance Product Regulation Compact: 0.2%
State form filing requirements for life insurance: 0.2%
Sales-below-cost law for gasoline: 0.1%
Direct auto sales: 0.1%
State rate filing requirement for workers' compensation: 0.04%
Moving company entry regulation: 0.02%
Mandatory labeling law: 0.2%

Cable and telecommunications: 1.1%
Telecom deregulation: 0.7%
Statewide cable franchising: 0.4%

PERSONAL FREEDOM: 29.4%
Incarceration and arrests: 6.6%
Crime-adjusted incarceration rate: 4.2%
Drug enforcement rate: 1.4%
Arrests for nondrug victimless crimes, % of population: 0.5%
Arrests for nondrug victimless crimes, % of all arrests: 0.5%

Marriage freedom: 4.0%
Same-sex partnerships laws: 2.2%
Super-DOMA: 1.0%
Sodomy laws: 0.4%
Cousin marriage: 0.4%
Covenant marriage: 0.1%
Blood test required: 0.01%
Total waiting period: 0.01%

Education: 3.2%
Tax credit/deduction: 1.2%
Publicly funded voucher law: 0.7%
Private school teacher licensure: 0.6%
Private school approval requirement: 0.2%
Compulsory schooling years: 0.2%
Private school curriculum control: 0.2%
Public school choice: 0.1%
Homeschooling curriculum control: 0.04%
Homeschooling standardized testing: 0.03%

Homeschooling record-keeping requirements: 0.03%
Homeschooling notification requirements: 0.02%
Homeschooling teacher qualifications: 0.01%
Private school registration: <0.01%
Homeschool statute: <0.01%

Gun control: 3.2%
Local gun ban: 1.0%
Concealed-carry index: 0.4%
Initial permit cost: 0.4%
Firearms licensing index: 0.3%
Waiting period for purchases: 0.3%
Initial permit term: 0.2%
Stricter minimum age: 0.2%
Assault weapons ban: 0.1%
Open carry index: 0.05%
No duty to retreat: 0.05%
Any other weapon: 0.04%
Dealer licensing: 0.03%
Built-in locking devices: 0.03%
Nonpowder guns: 0.03%
Restrictions on multiple purchases: 0.03%
Background checks for private sales: 0.02%
Registration of firearms: 0.02%
Design safety standards: 0.01%
Machine guns: 0.01%
Ammo microstamping: 0.01%
Large-capacity magazine bans: 0.01%
Sound suppressor: <0.01%
Short-barreled shotguns: <0.01%
Short-barreled rifles: <0.01%
.50 caliber ban: <0.01%

Alcohol: 2.9%
Alcohol distribution index: 1.1%
Blue law index: 0.4%
Sales and grocery stores: 0.4%
Spirits taxes: 0.3%

Wine taxes: 0.2%

Beer taxes: 0.2%

Direct wine shipment ban: 0.2%

Keg regulations/ban: 0.1%

Happy hour ban: 0.03%

Mandatory server training: <0.01%

Marijuana freedom: 2.1%

Medical marijuana index: 0.9%

Possession decriminalization: 0.6%

Marijuana misdemeanor index: 0.1%

Mandatory minimums: 0.1%

Some sales legal: 0.1%

Salvia ban: 0.1%

Gambling: 1.9%

Gaming revenues: 1.8%

Gambling felony: 0.02%

Social gambling: 0.02%

Internet gaming prohibition: <0.01%

Asset forfeiture: 1.8%

Asset forfeiture law: 0.9%

Equitable sharing: 0.9%

Tobacco: 1.7%

Cigarette tax: 1.3%

Smoking ban, bars: 0.3%

Internet purchase regulations: 0.06%

Smoking ban, private workplaces: 0.03%

Smoking ban, restaurants: 0.03%

Vending machine regulations: 0.03%

Travel freedom: 1.4%

Automated license plate readers: 0.4%

Driver's licenses without Social Security number: 0.3%

Sobriety checkpoints: 0.2%

Seat belt laws: 0.2%

Fingerprint for driver's license: 0.1%
Uninsured/underinsured coverage requirement: 0.1%
Motorcycle helmet law: 0.1%
Open-container law: 0.01%
Cell phone ban: 0.01%

Mala prohibita and civil liberties: 0.5%
Prostitution legal: 0.2%
Trans-fat bans: 0.1%
Raw milk legal: 0.1%
Mixed martial arts legal: 0.1%
Fireworks laws: 0.05%
Physician-assisted suicide legal: 0.03%
Equal rights amendment: 0.02%
DNA database index: 0.01%
Religious Freedom Restoration Act: 0.01%

Campaign finance: 0.1%
Individual contributions to candidates: 0.03%
Individual contributions to parties: 0.02%
Grassroots PAC contributions to candidates: 0.02%
Grassroots PAC contributions to parties: 0.01%
Public financing: <0.01%

Note: Because of rounding, percentages listed do not sum to exactly 100. Because of how we weight the local taxation variable, the weights for the fiscal policy dimension range from 29.5 (New Jersey) to 32.0 (Hawaii). For more on this, see "Local Taxation" under "Fiscal Policy" in the first chapter.

ALTERNATIVE INDICES

This appendix gives alternative freedom indices based on the exclusion of
right-to-work laws and the inclusion of various positions on abortion policy
and of universal same-sex marriage, respectively.

LABOR-MARKET FREEDOM—ALTERNATIVE INDICES

The first set of alternative indices excludes right-to-work laws. Consequently,
new rankings are generated for labor policy, regulatory freedom, economic freedom, and overall freedom.

Rank	State	Labor-Market Freedom without Right-to-Work Laws, 2014	Rank	State	Labor-Market Freedom without Right-to-Work Laws, 2014
1.	Texas	0.030	26.	Louisiana	0.005
2.	Tennessee	0.020	27.	Illinois	0.004
3.	Georgia	0.017	28.	Delaware	0.004
4.	Virginia	0.017	29.	South Carolina	0.003
5.	North Carolina	0.016	30.	South Dakota	0.002
6.	Wisconsin	0.016	31.	Massachusetts	0.000
7.	Arkansas	0.014	32.	Idaho	−0.002
8.	Indiana	0.013	33.	Maryland	−0.003
9.	Iowa	0.013	34.	Colorado	−0.003
10.	Kansas	0.013	35.	Vermont	−0.003
11.	Alabama	0.013	36.	Alaska	−0.006
12.	Mississippi	0.013	37.	Connecticut	−0.007
13.	Oklahoma	0.012	38.	West Virginia	−0.008
14.	Florida	0.011	39.	Montana	−0.010
15.	Maine	0.010	40.	North Dakota	−0.011
16.	Missouri	0.008	41.	Ohio	−0.017
17.	Nevada	0.008	42.	Wyoming	−0.018
18.	Michigan	0.007	43.	Arizona	−0.018
19.	Nebraska	0.006	44.	Oregon	−0.020
20.	New Mexico	0.006	45.	Washington	−0.021
21.	New Hampshire	0.006	46.	New York	−0.034
22.	Minnesota	0.005	47.	New Jersey	−0.036
23.	Pennsylvania	0.005	48.	Hawaii	−0.040
24.	Utah	0.005	49.	Rhode Island	−0.043
25.	Kentucky	0.005	50.	California	−0.050

TABLE B2

Rank	State	Regulatory Policy without Right-to-Work Laws, 2014	Rank	State	
1.	Idaho	0.122	26.	Montana	−0.054
2.	Indiana	0.066	27.	Ohio	−0.055
3.	Wyoming	0.066	28.	Nevada	−0.056
4.	Kansas	0.058	29.	Vermont	−0.058
5.	Iowa	0.047	30.	Delaware	−0.067
6.	North Dakota	0.046	31.	Minnesota	−0.069
7.	South Dakota	0.045	32.	Virginia	−0.073
8.	Nebraska	0.035	33.	North Carolina	−0.084
9.	Utah	0.032	34.	Texas	−0.090
10.	Oklahoma	0.021	35.	Oregon	−0.113
11.	Mississippi	0.020	36.	Pennsylvania	−0.116
12.	Wisconsin	0.015	37.	New Mexico	−0.120
13.	Alaska	0.012	38.	Massachusetts	−0.130
14.	South Carolina	0.001	39.	Louisiana	−0.131
15.	Tennessee	−0.014	40.	Illinois	−0.133
16.	Georgia	−0.020	41.	Hawaii	−0.157
17.	Missouri	−0.021	42.	West Virginia	−0.163
18.	Michigan	−0.026	43.	Washington	−0.187
19.	Colorado	−0.026	44.	Maine	−0.191
20.	Alabama	−0.038	45.	Rhode Island	−0.200
21.	Kentucky	−0.041	46.	Connecticut	−0.211
22.	Florida	−0.044	47.	New Jersey	−0.387
23.	Arizona	−0.050	48.	California	−0.414
24.	New Hampshire	−0.050	49.	Maryland	−0.423
25.	Arkansas	−0.053	50.	New York	−0.442

Rank	State	Economic Freedom without Right-to-Work Laws, 2014		Rank	State	Economic Freedom without Right-to-Work Laws, 2014
1.	South Dakota	0.317		26.	North Carolina	0.006
2.	Idaho	0.279		27.	Pennsylvania	0.004
3.	Tennessee	0.265		28.	Kentucky	−0.015
4.	New Hampshire	0.243		29.	Ohio	−0.020
5.	Oklahoma	0.224		30.	Arkansas	−0.024
6.	Florida	0.185		31.	Nevada	−0.025
7.	Alaska	0.164		32.	Delaware	−0.041
8.	North Dakota	0.143		33.	Mississippi	−0.042
9.	Alabama	0.142		34.	Louisiana	−0.064
10.	Missouri	0.133		35.	Massachusetts	−0.136
11.	Wyoming	0.124		36.	West Virginia	−0.148
12.	Montana	0.108		37.	Oregon	−0.148
13.	Indiana	0.097		38.	Washington	−0.188
14.	Georgia	0.093		39.	New Mexico	−0.193
15.	Utah	0.093		40.	Minnesota	−0.207
16.	Virginia	0.071		41.	Vermont	−0.209
17.	Iowa	0.069		42.	Rhode Island	−0.223
18.	Arizona	0.065		43.	Maine	−0.286
19.	Kansas	0.064		44.	Illinois	−0.290
20.	Texas	0.063		45.	Connecticut	−0.323
21.	South Carolina	0.053		46.	Maryland	−0.423
22.	Michigan	0.049		47.	New Jersey	−0.444
23.	Nebraska	0.044		48.	Hawaii	−0.457
24.	Colorado	0.030		49.	California	−0.562
25.	Wisconsin	0.006		50.	New York	−0.978

TABLE B4

Rank	State	Overall Freedom without Right-to-Work Laws, 2014	Rank	State	Overall Freedom without Right-to-Work Laws, 2014
1.	New Hampshire	0.357	26.	Michigan	0.034
2.	Alaska	0.296	27.	Nebraska	0.019
3.	Oklahoma	0.249	28.	New Mexico	−0.009
4.	Indiana	0.247	29.	Delaware	−0.023
5.	South Dakota	0.245	30.	Washington	−0.027
6.	Tennessee	0.234	31.	Massachusetts	−0.030
7.	Idaho	0.230	32.	Texas	−0.033
8.	Colorado	0.207	33.	Arkansas	−0.054
9.	Florida	0.183	34.	Ohio	−0.055
10.	Iowa	0.174	35.	Oregon	−0.076
11.	Montana	0.168	36.	Minnesota	−0.084
12.	Missouri	0.166	37.	Louisiana	−0.089
13.	Arizona	0.153	38.	West Virginia	−0.091
14.	Nevada	0.146	39.	Vermont	−0.100
15.	North Dakota	0.145	40.	Kentucky	−0.121
16.	Wyoming	0.139	41.	Maine	−0.125
17.	South Carolina	0.117	42.	Mississippi	−0.129
18.	Kansas	0.117	43.	Rhode Island	−0.148
19.	North Carolina	0.107	44.	Illinois	−0.230
20.	Utah	0.106	45.	Connecticut	−0.236
21.	Virginia	0.074	46.	Maryland	−0.379
22.	Pennsylvania	0.060	47.	New Jersey	−0.403
23.	Georgia	0.059	48.	Hawaii	−0.465
24.	Alabama	0.055	49.	California	−0.477
25.	Wisconsin	0.052	50.	New York	−0.951

ABORTION POLICY—ALTERNATIVE INDICES

In this edition of the freedom index, abortion remains excluded from the main scores and rankings, given our discussion at the beginning of the book. However, we have for the first time developed alternative abortion policy indices here, which feed into personal and overall freedom, should the readers wish to personalize their results according to their view of the relation between abortion policy and freedom. The first alternative index is a pro-life abortion policy ("freedom from abortion") index. For this alternative index, more state restrictions on abortion are always pro-freedom, as is the lack of state subsidies for abortion through Medicaid.

The second alternative index is a moderately pro-choice abortion policy index. For this index, restrictions on late-term abortions and lack of subsidies for abortion are pro-freedom, though for a different reason from pro-lifers in the latter case (respect for conscience), whereas restrictions on early-term abortions are anti-freedom. For the moderately pro-choice index, restrictions on abortion that apply mostly but not entirely to late-term abortions and parental involvement laws for minors' abortions do not count at all.

Finally, there is a strong pro-choice abortion policy index. For this alternative index, all limits on abortion are anti-freedom, and subsidies for abortion are pro-freedom.

We devised weights for policies on the assumption that for a pro-lifer, the estimated, measurable value of an aborted fetus's life is $5 million (caveat: this is an actuarial-type estimate, but we consider the moral value of life—whenever life begins—to be truly unmeasurable and view policies relating to unjust killings to be an insoluble problem for any index, including those of human rights and civil liberties internationally). For pro-choicers, the value of the freedom to abort depends on the "consumer surplus" (in economic jargon, this term means the difference between what consumers would have paid and what they actually paid) derived from the observed price elasticity of demand for abortion, multiplied by the "constitutional weight" of 10 consistent with our methodology for the rest of the index. We derive the estimate of $5 million from a high-end estimate of the statistical value of an average human life ($7.5 million), multiplied by two-thirds because young fetuses of the age when abortion typically occurs are naturally aborted by the mother's body roughly one-third of the time.[132] This is, obviously, merely a ballpark figure based on actuarial-type estimates. Moreover, we admit that this type of economic language and reasoning can be difficult, sterile, limiting, and perhaps even less accurate than we'd like (though it is hard to calculate in other ways consistent with the overarching methodology of the index).

132. Binyamin Appelbaum, "As U.S. Agencies Put More Value on a Life, Businesses Fret," *New York Times*, February 16, 2011, http://www.nytimes.com/2011/02/17/business/economy/17regulation.html; Mayo Clinic, "Diseases and Conditions: Miscarriage," http://www.mayoclinic.org/diseases-conditions/pregnancy-loss-miscarriage/basics/definition/con-20033827; WebMD, "Pregnancy and Miscarriage," http://www.webmd.com/baby/guide/pregnancy-miscarriage.

The policies included in these alternative indices are as follows: abortions must be performed by a licensed physician (2.2 percent of overall pro-life freedom, 0.01 percent of overall moderate freedom, 0.01 percent of strong pro-choice freedom); some abortions must be performed in hospitals (0.02 percent pro-life, 0 percent moderate, 0.01 percent strong pro-choice); and some abortions require the involvement of a second physician (0.02 percent pro-life, 0 percent moderate, 0.01 percent strong pro-choice). Policies also include gestational limit on abortions (0.4 percent pro-life, 0.7 percent moderate, 0.03 percent strong pro-choice); partial-birth abortion ban (0.04 percent pro-life, 0.07 percent moderate, <0.01 percent strong pro-choice); public funding of abortion (6.9 percent pro-life, 0.1 percent moderate, 0.3 percent strong pro-choice); restrictions on private insurance coverage of abortion (20.3 percent pro-life, 0.1 percent moderate, 0.1 percent strong pro-choice); state-mandated waiting periods (7.3 percent pro-life, 0.1 percent moderate, 0.1 percent strong pro-choice); and parental notification and consent laws (3.2 percent pro-life, 0 percent moderate, 0.02 percent strong pro-choice).

Interestingly, for a pro-lifer, abortion policy is worth a full 40.4 percent of overall freedom. If you believe that the life of the marginal (in the economic sense) aborted fetus is worth (again, statistically, not morally) about the same as that of any other human being, then you must think of abortion as by far the most important policy that states can control. You should be close to a single-issue voter. By contrast, moderate and strong pro-choicers should be far less interested in abortion policy. For moderates, abortion policy is worth 1.2 percent of overall freedom, while for strong pro-choicers, abortion policy should be worth only about 0.6 percent of overall freedom. Why is the freedom to abort worth so little? The evidence suggests that abortion demand in economic terms may be quite price-elastic, implying that the consumer surplus is low. Since this is our first attempt at handling this very difficult moral, political, and methodological issue, we offer these alternative indices as a start rather than the definitive word on this issue and hope they will be treated in that light.

Rank	State	Freedom from Abortion (Pro-Life Index), 2014
1.	Oklahoma	0.759
2.	Kansas	0.759
3.	North Dakota	0.759
4.	Idaho	0.758
5.	Missouri	0.758
6.	Kentucky	0.758
7.	Nebraska	0.757
8.	Michigan	0.684
9.	Indiana	0.104
10.	Ohio	0.104
11.	South Carolina	0.104
12.	Virginia	0.104
13.	Arkansas	0.104
14.	Louisiana	0.104
15.	Utah	0.104
16.	Mississippi	0.103
17.	Alabama	0.103
18.	Pennsylvania	0.103
19.	North Carolina	0.103
20.	Texas	0.102
21.	South Dakota	0.067
22.	Georgia	0.066
23.	Wisconsin	0.028
24.	Arizona	−0.041
25.	Tennessee	−0.042
26.	Wyoming	−0.043
27.	Florida	−0.080
28.	Minnesota	−0.080
29.	Iowa	−0.081
30.	Colorado	−0.092
31.	Rhode Island	−0.098
32.	Nevada	−0.117
33.	Delaware	−0.118
34.	Maine	−0.118
35.	New Hampshire	−0.145
36.	West Virginia	−0.183
37.	Massachusetts	−0.188
38.	Maryland	−0.226
39.	Alaska	−0.237
40.	Hawaii	−0.263
41.	New Mexico	−0.273
42.	Montana	−0.279
43.	Illinois	−0.280
44.	New York	−0.318
45.	Connecticut	−0.318
46.	California	−0.318
47.	Washington	−0.318
48.	New Jersey	−0.329
49.	Oregon	−0.329
50.	Vermont	−0.329

| | | Moderate Pro-Choice Abortion Policy |
Rank	State	Index, 2014

Rank	State	Index	Rank	State	Index
1.	Tennessee	0.008	26.	North Carolina	0.003
2.	Rhode Island	0.006	27.	Pennsylvania	0.003
3.	Delaware	0.006	28.	Texas	0.003
4.	Florida	0.006	29.	Wisconsin	0.003
5.	Iowa	0.006	30.	Hawaii	0.003
6.	Maine	0.006	31.	Maryland	0.003
7.	Nevada	0.006	32.	Massachusetts	0.003
8.	Wyoming	0.006	33.	Arizona	0.002
9.	Montana	0.005	34.	Kansas	0.002
10.	Arkansas	0.005	35.	Michigan	0.002
11.	Georgia	0.005	36.	North Dakota	0.002
12.	Indiana	0.005	37.	Oklahoma	0.002
13.	Louisiana	0.005	38.	Minnesota	0.000
14.	Mississippi	0.005	39.	Idaho	0.000
15.	Ohio	0.005	40.	Kentucky	0.000
16.	South Carolina	0.005	41.	Missouri	0.000
17.	South Dakota	0.005	42.	Nebraska	0.000
18.	Utah	0.005	43.	New Hampshire	−0.010
19.	Virginia	0.005	44.	Colorado	−0.012
20.	California	0.003	45.	New Mexico	−0.013
21.	Connecticut	0.003	46.	New Jersey	−0.015
22.	Illinois	0.003	47.	Oregon	−0.015
23.	New York	0.003	48.	Vermont	−0.015
24.	Washington	0.003	49.	Alaska	−0.015
25.	Alabama	0.003	50.	West Virginia	−0.017

Rank	State	Strong Pro-Choice Abortion Policy Index, 2014	Rank	State	Strong Pro-Choice Abortion Policy Index, 2014
1.	Oregon	0.006	26.	Wyoming	−0.001
2.	Vermont	0.006	27.	Tennessee	−0.001
3.	New Jersey	0.006	28.	Wisconsin	−0.003
4.	New Mexico	0.006	29.	Georgia	−0.003
5.	Alaska	0.006	30.	South Dakota	−0.003
6.	California	0.006	31.	Texas	−0.003
7.	Washington	0.006	32.	North Carolina	−0.003
8.	Connecticut	0.006	33.	Alabama	−0.003
9.	New York	0.006	34.	Pennsylvania	−0.003
10.	Hawaii	0.005	35.	Mississippi	−0.003
11.	Illinois	0.005	36.	Utah	−0.003
12.	Montana	0.005	37.	Arkansas	−0.003
13.	Maryland	0.005	38.	Louisiana	−0.003
14.	Massachusetts	0.005	39.	Indiana	−0.003
15.	West Virginia	0.004	40.	Ohio	−0.003
16.	Minnesota	0.003	41.	South Carolina	−0.003
17.	Arizona	0.002	42.	Virginia	−0.003
18.	New Hampshire	0.000	43.	Michigan	−0.006
19.	Colorado	0.000	44.	Nebraska	−0.006
20.	Delaware	0.000	45.	Kentucky	−0.006
21.	Maine	0.000	46.	Idaho	−0.006
22.	Nevada	0.000	47.	Missouri	−0.006
23.	Iowa	−0.001	48.	North Dakota	−0.007
24.	Florida	−0.001	49.	Kansas	−0.007
25.	Rhode Island	−0.001	50.	Oklahoma	−0.007

Rank	State	Pro-Life Personal Freedom, 2014		Rank	State	Pro-Life Personal Freedom, 2014
1.	Kansas	0.812		26.	Mississippi	0.017
2.	Missouri	0.792		27.	Alabama	0.016
3.	Oklahoma	0.784		28.	Texas	0.007
4.	North Dakota	0.760		29.	South Dakota	−0.006
5.	Nebraska	0.732		30.	Rhode Island	−0.023
6.	Idaho	0.709		31.	Wyoming	−0.029
7.	Michigan	0.669		32.	New Hampshire	−0.031
8.	Kentucky	0.652		33.	Tennessee	−0.073
9.	Indiana	0.255		34.	Florida	−0.082
10.	North Carolina	0.204		35.	Massachusetts	−0.083
11.	South Carolina	0.169		36.	New Mexico	−0.090
12.	Pennsylvania	0.159		37.	Delaware	−0.100
13.	Utah	0.117		38.	Alaska	−0.105
14.	Virginia	0.107		39.	West Virginia	−0.127
15.	Colorado	0.085		40.	Washington	−0.158
16.	Louisiana	0.079		41.	Maryland	−0.182
17.	Arkansas	0.074		42.	Vermont	−0.219
18.	Wisconsin	0.074		43.	Montana	−0.220
19.	Ohio	0.069		44.	Illinois	−0.220
20.	Nevada	0.054		45.	Connecticut	−0.230
21.	Arizona	0.046		46.	California	−0.233
22.	Maine	0.044		47.	Oregon	−0.257
23.	Minnesota	0.043		48.	Hawaii	−0.271
24.	Georgia	0.032		49.	New Jersey	−0.288
25.	Iowa	0.024		50.	New York	−0.291

		Moderate Pro-Choice Personal Freedom,
Rank	State	2014
1.	Nevada	0.177
2.	New Mexico	0.170
3.	Maine	0.168
4.	Colorado	0.165
5.	Washington	0.164
6.	Indiana	0.156
7.	Minnesota	0.123
8.	Alaska	0.117
9.	Iowa	0.111
10.	Massachusetts	0.109
11.	North Carolina	0.105
12.	New Hampshire	0.104
13.	Vermont	0.095
14.	Connecticut	0.090
15.	Arizona	0.090
16.	California	0.089
17.	Rhode Island	0.081
18.	South Carolina	0.070
19.	Montana	0.064
20.	Illinois	0.063
21.	Pennsylvania	0.059
22.	Oregon	0.057
23.	Kansas	0.055
24.	Wisconsin	0.049
25.	Maryland	0.048
26.	West Virginia	0.039
27.	Missouri	0.034
28.	New York	0.030
29.	Oklahoma	0.027
30.	New Jersey	0.026
31.	Delaware	0.024
32.	Wyoming	0.020
33.	Utah	0.019
34.	Virginia	0.008
35.	North Dakota	0.003
36.	Florida	0.003
37.	Hawaii	−0.005
38.	Michigan	−0.013
39.	Louisiana	−0.020
40.	Tennessee	−0.024
41.	Arkansas	−0.025
42.	Nebraska	−0.025
43.	Georgia	−0.029
44.	Ohio	−0.030
45.	Idaho	−0.049
46.	South Dakota	−0.067
47.	Mississippi	−0.082
48.	Alabama	−0.084
49.	Texas	−0.092
50.	Kentucky	−0.106

Rank	State	Strong Pro-Choice Personal Freedom, 2014
1.	New Mexico	0.189
2.	Colorado	0.177
3.	Nevada	0.171
4.	Washington	0.166
5.	Maine	0.162
6.	Indiana	0.147
7.	Alaska	0.138
8.	Minnesota	0.125
9.	Vermont	0.116
10.	New Hampshire	0.114
11.	Massachusetts	0.111
12.	Iowa	0.105
13.	North Carolina	0.098
14.	Connecticut	0.093
15.	California	0.091
16.	Arizona	0.090
17.	Oregon	0.078
18.	Rhode Island	0.075
19.	Illinois	0.065
20.	Montana	0.064
21.	South Carolina	0.061
22.	West Virginia	0.060
23.	Pennsylvania	0.052
24.	Maryland	0.050
25.	Kansas	0.047
26.	New Jersey	0.047
27.	Wisconsin	0.042
28.	New York	0.032
29.	Missouri	0.027
30.	Oklahoma	0.018
31.	Delaware	0.017
32.	Wyoming	0.014
33.	Utah	0.010
34.	Virginia	−0.001
35.	Hawaii	−0.003
36.	Florida	−0.003
37.	North Dakota	−0.005
38.	Michigan	−0.021
39.	Louisiana	−0.028
40.	Nebraska	−0.032
41.	Tennessee	−0.032
42.	Arkansas	−0.033
43.	Georgia	−0.037
44.	Ohio	−0.038
45.	Idaho	−0.055
46.	South Dakota	−0.076
47.	Mississippi	−0.090
48.	Alabama	−0.090
49.	Texas	−0.099
50.	Kentucky	−0.112

Rank	State	Pro-Life Overall Freedom, 2014		Rank	State	Pro-Life Overall Freedom, 2014
1.	Oklahoma	1.039		26.	Alaska	0.089
2.	Idaho	1.019		27.	Arkansas	0.080
3.	North Dakota	0.934		28.	Nevada	0.060
4.	Kansas	0.907		29.	Wisconsin	0.054
5.	Missouri	0.899		30.	Louisiana	0.045
6.	Nebraska	0.807		31.	Ohio	0.024
7.	Michigan	0.749		32.	Mississippi	0.005
8.	Kentucky	0.612		33.	Montana	−0.137
9.	Indiana	0.382		34.	Delaware	−0.166
10.	South Dakota	0.342		35.	Minnesota	−0.189
11.	South Carolina	0.252		36.	Massachusetts	−0.244
12.	Utah	0.241		37.	Maine	−0.268
13.	North Carolina	0.240		38.	Rhode Island	−0.271
14.	Tennessee	0.222		39.	West Virginia	−0.300
15.	Virginia	0.208		40.	New Mexico	−0.308
16.	Alabama	0.189		41.	Washington	−0.371
17.	New Hampshire	0.187		42.	Oregon	−0.430
18.	Georgia	0.156		43.	Vermont	−0.454
19.	Arizona	0.142		44.	Illinois	−0.536
20.	Pennsylvania	0.137		45.	Connecticut	−0.579
21.	Florida	0.134		46.	Maryland	−0.630
22.	Wyoming	0.126		47.	Hawaii	−0.754
23.	Iowa	0.124		48.	New Jersey	−0.757
24.	Texas	0.100		49.	California	−0.821
25.	Colorado	0.090		50.	New York	−1.294

Rank	State	Pro-Life Overall Freedom, No Right-to-Work Laws, 2014	Rank	State	Pro-Life Overall Freedom, No Right-to-Work Laws, 2014
1.	Oklahoma	1.008	26.	Texas	0.070
2.	Idaho	0.989	27.	Alaska	0.059
3.	Missouri	0.925	28.	Arkansas	0.050
4.	North Dakota	0.903	29.	Ohio	0.049
5.	Kansas	0.876	30.	Nevada	0.029
6.	Nebraska	0.776	31.	Louisiana	0.015
7.	Michigan	0.718	32.	Mississippi	-0.026
8.	Kentucky	0.637	33.	Montana	-0.112
9.	Indiana	0.351	34.	Delaware	-0.141
10.	South Dakota	0.311	35.	Minnesota	-0.164
11.	South Carolina	0.222	36.	Massachusetts	-0.219
12.	New Hampshire	0.212	37.	Maine	-0.243
13.	Utah	0.210	38.	Rhode Island	-0.246
14.	North Carolina	0.210	39.	West Virginia	-0.274
15.	Tennessee	0.192	40.	New Mexico	-0.283
16.	Virginia	0.178	41.	Washington	-0.346
17.	Pennsylvania	0.163	42.	Oregon	-0.405
18.	Alabama	0.158	43.	Vermont	-0.429
19.	Georgia	0.125	44.	Illinois	-0.510
20.	Colorado	0.116	45.	Connecticut	-0.553
21.	Arizona	0.111	46.	Maryland	-0.605
22.	Florida	0.103	47.	Hawaii	-0.729
23.	Wyoming	0.096	48.	New Jersey	-0.732
24.	Iowa	0.094	49.	California	-0.795
25.	Wisconsin	0.080	50.	New York	-1.269

Rank	State	Moderate Pro-Choice Overall Freedom, 2014
1.	New Hampshire	0.322
2.	Alaska	0.311
3.	Indiana	0.283
4.	Oklahoma	0.281
5.	South Dakota	0.280
6.	Tennessee	0.272
7.	Idaho	0.261
8.	Florida	0.219
9.	Iowa	0.211
10.	Arizona	0.186
11.	Nevada	0.183
12.	North Dakota	0.177
13.	Wyoming	0.175
14.	Colorado	0.169
15.	South Carolina	0.153
16.	Kansas	0.150
17.	Montana	0.147
18.	Utah	0.142
19.	Missouri	0.141
20.	North Carolina	0.141
21.	Virginia	0.109
22.	Georgia	0.094
23.	Alabama	0.089
24.	Michigan	0.067
25.	Nebraska	0.050
26.	Pennsylvania	0.037
27.	Wisconsin	0.029
28.	Texas	0.001
29.	Arkansas	-0.018
30.	Delaware	-0.043
31.	New Mexico	-0.048
32.	Washington	-0.049
33.	Massachusetts	-0.052
34.	Louisiana	-0.053
35.	Ohio	-0.075
36.	Mississippi	-0.093
37.	Minnesota	-0.109
38.	Oregon	-0.116
39.	West Virginia	-0.134
40.	Vermont	-0.140
41.	Maine	-0.144
42.	Kentucky	-0.146
43.	Rhode Island	-0.167
44.	Illinois	-0.252
45.	Connecticut	-0.258
46.	Maryland	-0.401
47.	New Jersey	-0.443
48.	Hawaii	-0.487
49.	California	-0.499
50.	New York	-0.973

TABLE B14

Moderate Pro-Choice Overall Freedom, No Right-to-Work Laws, 2014

Rank	State		Rank	State	
1.	New Hampshire	0.347	26.	Michigan	0.036
2.	Alaska	0.281	27.	Nebraska	0.019
3.	Indiana	0.252	28.	Delaware	−0.017
4.	Oklahoma	0.250	29.	New Mexico	−0.023
5.	South Dakota	0.250	30.	Washington	−0.024
6.	Tennessee	0.242	31.	Massachusetts	−0.027
7.	Idaho	0.230	32.	Texas	−0.029
8.	Colorado	0.195	33.	Arkansas	−0.049
9.	Florida	0.188	34.	Ohio	−0.050
10.	Iowa	0.180	35.	Minnesota	−0.084
11.	Montana	0.173	36.	Louisiana	−0.084
12.	Missouri	0.166	37.	Oregon	−0.091
13.	Arizona	0.155	38.	West Virginia	−0.108
14.	Nevada	0.152	39.	Vermont	−0.114
15.	North Dakota	0.147	40.	Maine	−0.119
16.	Wyoming	0.145	41.	Kentucky	−0.120
17.	South Carolina	0.122	42.	Mississippi	−0.124
18.	Kansas	0.119	43.	Rhode Island	−0.142
19.	Utah	0.111	44.	Illinois	−0.227
20.	North Carolina	0.110	45.	Connecticut	−0.232
21.	Virginia	0.079	46.	Maryland	−0.375
22.	Georgia	0.064	47.	New Jersey	−0.418
23.	Pennsylvania	0.063	48.	Hawaii	−0.462
24.	Alabama	0.058	49.	California	−0.474
25.	Wisconsin	0.055	50.	New York	−0.948

Rank	State	Strong Pro-Choice Overall Freedom, 2014		Rank	State	Strong Pro-Choice Overall Freedom, 2014
1.	Alaska	0.332		26.	Pennsylvania	0.031
2.	New Hampshire	0.332		27.	Wisconsin	0.023
3.	Indiana	0.274		28.	Texas	-0.005
4.	Oklahoma	0.273		29.	Arkansas	-0.027
5.	South Dakota	0.272		30.	New Mexico	-0.029
6.	Tennessee	0.264		31.	Washington	-0.047
7.	Idaho	0.254		32.	Delaware	-0.049
8.	Florida	0.213		33.	Massachusetts	-0.051
9.	Iowa	0.204		34.	Louisiana	-0.062
10.	Arizona	0.186		35.	Ohio	-0.084
11.	Colorado	0.182		36.	Oregon	-0.095
12.	Nevada	0.177		37.	Mississippi	-0.102
13.	North Dakota	0.169		38.	Minnesota	-0.107
14.	Wyoming	0.169		39.	West Virginia	-0.113
15.	Montana	0.147		40.	Vermont	-0.119
16.	South Carolina	0.145		41.	Maine	-0.150
17.	Kansas	0.141		42.	Kentucky	-0.152
18.	Missouri	0.135		43.	Rhode Island	-0.174
19.	North Carolina	0.134		44.	Illinois	-0.250
20.	Utah	0.134		45.	Connecticut	-0.256
21.	Virginia	0.101		46.	Maryland	-0.399
22.	Georgia	0.086		47.	New Jersey	-0.422
23.	Alabama	0.083		48.	Hawaii	-0.485
24.	Michigan	0.059		49.	California	-0.497
25.	Nebraska	0.043		50.	New York	-0.971

TABLE B16

Strong Pro-Choice Overall Freedom, No Right-to-Work Laws, 2014

Rank	State		Rank	State	
1.	New Hampshire	0.358	26.	Michigan	0.028
2.	Alaska	0.302	27.	Nebraska	0.013
3.	Indiana	0.244	28.	New Mexico	-0.003
4.	Oklahoma	0.242	29.	Washington	-0.022
5.	South Dakota	0.242	30.	Delaware	-0.024
6.	Tennessee	0.233	31.	Massachusetts	-0.025
7.	Idaho	0.224	32.	Texas	-0.036
8.	Colorado	0.207	33.	Arkansas	-0.057
9.	Florida	0.182	34.	Ohio	-0.058
10.	Iowa	0.174	35.	Oregon	-0.070
11.	Montana	0.173	36.	Minnesota	-0.082
12.	Missouri	0.160	37.	West Virginia	-0.087
13.	Arizona	0.155	38.	Louisiana	-0.092
14.	Nevada	0.146	39.	Vermont	-0.093
15.	North Dakota	0.138	40.	Maine	-0.125
16.	Wyoming	0.138	41.	Kentucky	-0.127
17.	South Carolina	0.114	42.	Mississippi	-0.132
18.	Kansas	0.111	43.	Rhode Island	-0.149
19.	North Carolina	0.104	44.	Illinois	-0.225
20.	Utah	0.103	45.	Connecticut	-0.230
21.	Virginia	0.070	46.	Maryland	-0.373
22.	Pennsylvania	0.056	47.	New Jersey	-0.397
23.	Georgia	0.056	48.	Hawaii	-0.460
24.	Alabama	0.052	49.	California	-0.472
25.	Wisconsin	0.049	50.	New York	-0.945

Rank	State	Personal Freedom Ranking, Universal Same-Sex Marriage		Rank	State	Personal Freedom Ranking, Universal Same-Sex Marriage
1.	New Mexico	0.180		26.	West Virginia	0.053
2.	Colorado	0.173		27.	Pennsylvania	0.052
3.	Nevada	0.168		28.	Kansas	0.050
4.	Maine	0.158		29.	Louisiana	0.049
5.	Washington	0.156		30.	Nebraska	0.048
6.	Indiana	0.147		31.	Arkansas	0.043
7.	Alaska	0.129		32.	Wisconsin	0.042
8.	Minnesota	0.119		33.	Maryland	0.041
9.	New Hampshire	0.110		34.	Georgia	0.039
10.	Vermont	0.106		35.	Ohio	0.038
11.	Massachusetts	0.102		36.	New Jersey	0.037
12.	Iowa	0.101		37.	New York	0.023
13.	North Carolina	0.098		38.	Oklahoma	0.021
14.	Missouri	0.085		39.	Tennessee	0.020
15.	Arizona	0.084		40.	Delaware	0.014
16.	Connecticut	0.083		41.	Wyoming	0.011
17.	California	0.081		42.	Utah	0.010
18.	North Dakota	0.075		43.	South Dakota	0.001
19.	Rhode Island	0.071		44.	Virginia	−0.001
20.	Florida	0.071		45.	Hawaii	−0.012
21.	Oregon	0.068		46.	Alabama	−0.014
22.	South Carolina	0.061		47.	Texas	−0.022
23.	Michigan	0.058		48.	Kentucky	−0.033
24.	Illinois	0.056		49.	Mississippi	−0.035
25.	Montana	0.055		50.	Idaho	−0.053

FURTHER READING

FEDERALISM AND DECENTRALIZATION

Buchanan, James M. "Federalism as an Ideal Political Order and an Objective for Constitutional Reform." *Publius* 25 (Spring 1995): 19–27. Reprinted in *The Collected Works of James M. Buchanan.* Vol. 18, pp. 67–78. Indianapolis: Liberty Fund, 2001.

Fischel, William A. *The Homevoter Hypothesis: How Home Values Influence Local Government Taxation, School Finance, and Land-Use Policies.* Cambridge, MA: Harvard University Press, 2001.

Nozick, Robert. "Utopia." Part III of *Anarchy, State, and Utopia.* New York: Basic Books, 1974.

Somin, Ilya. "Foot Voting, Federalism, and Political Freedom." In *NOMOS LV: Federalism and Subsidiarity,* edited by James E. Fleming and Jacob T. Levy. New York: New York University Press, 2014.

Storing, Herbert J., and Murray Dry, eds. *The Anti-Federalist: Writings by the Opponents of the Constitution.* Chicago: University of Chicago Press, 1985.

Tabarrok, Alexander. "Arguments for Federalism." Speech given at the Hastings Law School, University of California, San Francisco. September 20, 2001. http://www.independent .org/issues/article.asp?id=485.

Tiebout, Charles. "A Pure Theory of Local Expenditures." *Journal of Political Economy* 64 (1956): 416–24.

Weingast, Barry R. "The Economic Role of Political Institutions: Market-Preserving Federalism and Economic Development." *Journal of Law, Economics, and Organization* 11, no. 1 (Spring 1995): 1–31.

STATE POLITICS AND POLICY

Enns, Peter K., and Julianna Koch. "Public Opinion in the U.S. States: 1956–2010." *State Politics and Policy Quarterly* 13, no. 3 (2013): 349–72.

Erikson, Robert S., Gerald C. Wright, and John P. McIver. *Statehouse Democracy: Public Opinion and Policy in the American States.* Cambridge: Cambridge University Press, 1993.

Gelman, Andrew. *Red State, Blue State, Rich State, Poor State: Why Americans Vote the Way They Do.* Princeton, NJ: Princeton University Press, 2008.

Sorens, Jason, Fait Muedini, and William Ruger. "U.S. State and Local Public Policies in 2006: A New Database." *State Politics and Policy Quarterly* 8, no. 3 (2008): 309–26.

Tausanovitch, Chris, and Christopher Warshaw. "Measuring Constituent Policy Preferences in Congress, State Legislatures, and Cities." *Journal of Politics* 75, no. 2 (2013): 330–42.

THE RELATIONSHIP BETWEEN LIBERTY AND VIRTUE

Block, Walter. "Libertarianism and Libertinism." *Journal of Libertarian Studies* 11, no. 1 (Fall 1994): 117–28.

Meyer, Frank S. "The Locus of Virtue." In *In Defense of Freedom and Related Essays.* Indianapolis: Liberty Fund, 1996, pp. 128–48.

Nock, Albert Jay. "On Doing the Right Thing." *American Mercury,* November 1924. Reprinted in *The State of the Union: Essays in Social Criticism*, edited by Charles H. Hamilton. Indianapolis: Liberty Press, 1991.

Ruger, William, and Jason Sorens. "Virtue Libertarianism." Forthcoming, *Reason*.

Smith, Adam. *The Theory of Moral Sentiments*. 1759.

RENT SEEKING

Krueger, Anne O. "The Political Economy of the Rent-Seeking Society." *American Economic Review* 64, no. 3 (June 1974): 291–303.

Olson, Mancur. *The Rise and Decline of Nations: Economic Growth, Stagflation, and Social Rigidities*. New Haven, CT: Yale University Press, 1982.

Tullock, Gordon. "The Welfare Costs of Tariffs, Monopolies and Theft." *Western Economic Journal* 5, no. 3 (June 1967): 224–32.

PERSONAL FREEDOM

Locke, John. "A Letter Concerning Toleration." 1689. http://oll.libertyfund.org/?option=com_staticxt&staticfile=show.php%3Ftitle=764&chapter=80887&layout=html&Itemid=27.

Mill, John Stuart. "Of the Liberty of Thought and Discussion." Chapter 2 in *On Liberty*. 1859.

Ruger, William. "Why Tolerance Is Different than Acceptance: Let Ideas, Debate, and Freedom Bloom." *The Federalist*, August 18, 2015. http://thefederalist.com/2015/08/18/why-tolerance-is-different-than-acceptance/.

FREEDOM AND JUSTICE

Boaz, David. *The Libertarian Mind: A Manifesto for Freedom*. New York: Simon & Schuster, 2015.

Buchanan. James M. "Classical Liberalism and the Perfectability of Man." In *Why I, Too, Am Not a Conservative: The Normative Vision of Classical Liberalism*, pp. 11–21. Cheltenham, UK: Elgar, 2005.

Friedman, Milton. *Capitalism and Freedom*. Chicago: University of Chicago Press, 1962.

Kant, Immanuel. "On the Common Saying: 'This May Be True in Theory, but It Does Not Apply in Practice.'" 1793.

Locke, John. *Second Treatise of Civil Government*. 1690.

Madison, James. "Property." *National Gazette,* March 29, 1792. http://teachingamericanhistory.org/library/index.asp?document=600.

Nozick, Robert. "State-of-Nature Theory, or How to Back into a State without Really Trying" and "Beyond the Minimal State?" Parts I and II of *Anarchy, State, and Utopia*. New York: Basic Books, 1974.

Spencer, Herbert. *Social Statics, or the Conditions Essential to Happiness Specified, and the First of Them Developed*. London: John Chapman, 1851.

ACKNOWLEDGMENTS

We wish to acknowledge our sincere gratitude to all those who have read, commented on, and helped improve our study in past years. A partial list of those to whom we owe a particular debt of thanks includes David Boaz, Alison Fraser, Jacob Levy, Dylan McLean, Claire Morgan, Fait Muedini, John Samples, Ilya Somin, Dean Stansel, Varrin Swearingen, Ken Zuver, everyone at the Mercatus Center at George Mason University who did such an excellent job producing and promoting the first three editions of this index, and everyone at the Cato Institute who is helping us put out this edition, along with countless, unnamable readers and listeners who have approached us at events or e-mailed us their questions and comments.

ABOUT THE AUTHORS

William P. Ruger is Vice President of Policy and Research at the Charles Koch Institute and Charles Koch Foundation. Ruger is the author of the biography *Milton Friedman* and a coauthor of *The State of Texas: Government, Politics, and Policy*. His work has been published in *International Studies Quarterly, State Politics and Policy Quarterly, Armed Forces and Society,* and other outlets. Ruger earned an AB from the College of William and Mary and a PhD in politics from Brandeis University. He is a veteran of the war in Afghanistan.

Jason Sorens is Lecturer in the Department of Government at Dartmouth College. His primary research interests include fiscal federalism, public policy in federal systems, secessionism, and ethnic politics. His work has been published in *International Studies Quarterly, Comparative Political Studies, Journal of Peace Research, State Politics and Policy Quarterly,* and other academic journals, and his book *Secessionism: Identity, Interest, and Strategy* was published by McGill-Queen's University Press in 2012. Sorens received his BA in economics and philosophy, with honors, from Washington and Lee University and his PhD in political science from Yale University.

Disclaimer: The views and opinions expressed in this book are solely those of the authors and do not necessarily reflect the position of the Charles Koch Institute, the Charles Koch Foundation, the U.S. Navy, Dartmouth College, or any other organization associated with them.

INSTITUTE

The Cato Institute is a public policy research organization—a think tank—
dedicated to the principles of individual liberty, limited government, free
markets, and peace. Its scholars and analysts conduct independent, non-
partisan research on a wide range of policy issues.

Founded in 1977, Cato owes its name to *Cato's Letters*, a series of essays
published in 18th-century England that presented a vision of society free
from excessive government power. Those essays inspired the architects
of the American Revolution. And the simple, timeless principles of that
revolution—individual liberty, limited government, and free markets—
turn out to be even more powerful in today's world of global markets and
unprecedented access to information than Jefferson or Madison could
have imagined. Social and economic freedom is not just the best policy
for a free people, it is the indispensable framework for the future.

STAFF FOR THIS BOOK

David Lampo, director of publications
Jon Meyers, art director
Melina Yingling, book designer
Joanna Andreasson, cover illustration
Joanne Platt, Publications Professionals LLC, copyeditor

To reach the authors of this publication or ask questions about state
and local policy, please contact John Samples at the Cato Institute at
jsamples@cato.org or (202) 789-5248.